International acclaim for Peter Stanford's *Heaven:*

"This book represents a deeply felt attempt to understand private grief in terms of universal longings."
—*The Independent on Sunday*

"This look at notions of afterlife in assorted religions is bold, accessible and diverting."
—*The Church Times*

"A fascinating book about something just about everyone has thought about one way or another."
—*Sunday Tribune* (Dublin)

"*Heaven* is Peter Stanford's best book to date: chatty, opinionated, and learned."
—*Mail on Sunday*

"Amid images of the cherubim and seraphim, of crystal heavenly walls and golden thrones, this book contains much to enjoy . . . it may be as close to Paradise as we get."
—*Sunday Telegraph*

"A revelation . . . Stanford regards myths of paradise as our emotional and imaginative responses to death . . . there is a great deal to admire about this attitude and the book as a whole . . . crammed full of curious information, stimulating reflections and fascinating anecdotes . . . thoroughly entertaining."
—Thomas Wright, *Daily Telegraph*

ALSO BY PETER STANFORD

Catholics and Sex

*Cardinal Hume and the Changing Face
of English Catholicism*

Catholics and their Houses

Lord Longford

The Devil: A Biography

The She-Pope

The Legend of Pope Joan

Bronwen Astor: Her Life and Times

HEAVEN

A GUIDE TO THE UNDISCOVERED COUNTRY

PETER STANFORD

To my mother, Mary Catherine Stanford (1921 – 1998), in the hope that the very best of what follows may now be true for her

and

To my mother-in-law, Emily Celine Cross (1934 – 2001), who inspired me with her trust in God to believe that it could be.

HEAVEN

First published 2004 by PALGRAVE MACMILLAN™
175 Fifth Avenue, New York, N.Y. 10010 and
Houndmills, Basingstoke, Hampshire, England RG21 6XS.
Companies and representatives throughout the world.

PALGRAVE MACMILLAN is the global academic imprint of the Palgrave Macmillan division of St. Martin's Press, LLC and of Palgrave Macmillan Ltd. Macmillan® is a registered trademark in the United States, United Kingdom and other countries. Palgrave is a registered trademark in the European Union and other countries.

ISBN 1-4039-6360-6

Library of Congress Cataloguing-in-Publication Data available from
the Library of Congress.

First published in 2002 by HarperCollins Publishers.

First PALGRAVE MACMILLAN edition: January 2004.

10 9 8 7 6 5 4 3 2 1

Printed in the United States of America.

CONTENTS

'The undiscovered country, from whose bourn
No traveller returns ...'
SHAKESPEARE: *Hamlet* (Act III, Scene 1)

LIST OF ILLUSTRATIONS

ACKNOWLEDGEMENTS

W e all wonder, at some point, what happens to us after we die. Even if we conclude there is nothing beyond this life, it is a topic that concerns us all. I hope this book will be read in a spirit of universal interest; not as a specifically religious tome, but as an insight into the human psyche. It is not, nor is it intended to be, an exercise in preaching or polemics; rather it is an opportunity to think about mortality, a deeply unfashionable subject in our Western, consumerist world, in the context of history, theology, science and the thoughts and experiences of others.

This has not, then, of necessity, been a solitary journey and I am grateful to those who have offered advice, knowledge and personal testament along the way: Bronwen Astor, Roger Bolton, Edward Chesser, Serafina Clarke, Lucinda Coxon, Rosie Dawson, Emer Gillespie, Professor Susan Greenfield, Bishop David Jenkins, Professor Tony Johns of the Australian National University, Elleke van Kraalingen, Father Oliver McTernan and Caroline Willson all gave freely of their time to try and keep me on the right road. My son, Kit,

accompanied me to Stanley Spencer's own little bit of heaven.

The London Library, the British Library and that wonderful but neglected gem, the Catholic Central Library, next to London's Euston Station, have all been favoured stopping-off points. In my knapsack as reading material three contrasting sorties to heaven have been omnipresent – the American academic Jeffrey Burton Russell's fine and scholarly *History of Heaven* (1997), Colleen McDannell's and Bernhard Lang's broad, historical survey, *Heaven: A History* (1988), and Carol and Philip Zaleski's delightful and eclectic anthology, *The Book of Heaven* (2000). Everyone will have their favourite painting, book or poem about heaven, and I make no claim at the outset to be comprehensive. The examples I quote are simply my own personal favourites and the ones that speak most to me.

I have been fortunate to have been joined en route at different stages by wise and engaging counsellors, none more so than the outstanding religious historian of our age, Karen Armstrong, who has challenged me directly and by her own example to think more deeply whenever I have been tempted to take the path of least resistance.

Finally, back at base camp, I have been ably supported as ever by my agent, Derek Johns, my publisher at HarperCollins, Richard Johnson, his colleague, Marian Reid, and most of all by my wife, soul-mate and sternest but most constructive critic, Siobhan.

INTRODUCTION

It is five in the morning and my five-month-old baby daughter, already settled into a pattern as an inveterate dawn riser, is shifting around in my arms, her eyes wide open, her back arching, and looking every inch a miniature version of my own mother. It is not so much the composition and arrangement of her features that bridges the generations, as a particular grimace of steely resolution that she makes, and the look she sometimes gives, with eyes guarded and slightly nervous, as she weighs you up before volunteering a broad but bashful smile. In these moments, the coincidence of her birth and my mother's death within twelve months of each other makes me believe, without a shadow of a doubt, in reincarnation.

Bleary-eyed through lack of sleep, I see such a familiar expression that unthinkingly I latch on to it. For an instant I am as true a believer in reincarnation as if I were kneeling in saffron-coloured robes in a temple in the East: for, despite however many rules of science it violates, it seems so obvious that some essence of the life that is now over has been reborn in the new life in front

of me. I even convince myself that it's more than just the looks: they seem to share the same spirit – determined, unswerving, but cautious. As I slip back into a half-slumber, my daughter is distracted by an old watch strap, which she sucks and stretches. I add a few Christian ingredients to my Buddhist brew and fondly conjure up a scene in that mythical white tunnel which, in the standard church imagery of heaven, links this world to the next. There is, I imagine, a halfway point where those going back to the pavilion pass those going out to the crease. My mother and my daughter are both there, frozen in time, suddenly alone and utterly absorbed in each other. In my dream both can walk, though for the last twenty-five years of her life my mother was a wheelchair user. They embrace, and, as they take their leave to go in opposite directions, my mother kisses my daughter gently and hands over a parcel of her own characteristics, her legacy to the grand-daughter whom she will never know in straightforward earthly terms.

At this point in the dream my wife wakens me, and suddenly our daughter, who is still doggedly playing with the watch strap, appears in an entirely different light – her own mother's double. As swiftly as I signed up to my own hybrid version of afterlife, I now see its absurdity. My certainty dispels so quickly that I cannot even get a grip on what it was that had, only seconds before, seemed so cosy and real. Any assurance I had is gone.

Of course, when my mind is more alert and my thoughts more earthbound, I realise that the popularly understood concept of reincarnation is the ultimate comfort-blanket with which our age soothes away all the traumas and difficult questions of life. Reincarnation focuses on this life, which we know, rather than on some other life which

we can only dream of. Thus it works in the short-term to assuage any anxiety about mortality, and can even take the edge off grieving. As a long-term prospect, though, it has its drawbacks. In the sixth century BC Buddha developed the already existing idea of samsara, constant rebirth, and regarded reincarnation as something negative. He wanted to liberate his followers from the cycle of dying and being born since, far from welcoming the prospect of having another go at life, many of them were terrified by the prospect of death after death. If they had had hospices and morphine perhaps they would have thought differently, but at that time it was considered bad enough to have to go through all those final agonies once, without having to do it ad infinitum. Buddha taught of nirvana, not as a physical place akin to heaven where one might get off the treadmill, but as a psychological state of release, separate from death, that could be achieved in this life.

There is an enormous contrast, then, between the reality of Buddha's teachings and my half-awake efforts at toying with reincarnation as something to keep grief and loss at bay when cold reason offers no relief. As a simple answer to the eternal dilemma of suffering, Buddha realised, reincarnation only works in parts. It introduces a tangible degree of justice into each individual death to replace the injustices of each individual life by teaching that sinners will return humbled and the righteous will enjoy greater favour in their next incarnation, but fundamentally it embraces earthly suffering as each individual goes on and on and on trying to achieve enlightenment.

There is another drawback, even to the caricature of reincarnation that is now embraced by many in the West as a way of avoiding their own mortality. Such a scheme

of things can only reassure those who have a high opinion of their own merits. My mother, who suffered the ravages of multiple sclerosis for forty years with exemplary steadfastness, once admitted to me, devout Catholic though she was, that she had tried to imagine reincarnation, albeit distorted through the filter of Catholic guilt, but had decided that rather than get an upgrade she would come back as a cow and have to endure what for her was unendurable – flies constantly landing on her face and her having no way of shooing them away.

Flirting with reincarnation appeals only to that arrogant, selfish, self-absorbed part of us all that cannot quite believe that our own death will be the end. This is the eternal attraction of every other form of belief in an afterlife. We may act every day as though we disbelieve the inevitability of death – driving too fast along a rain-soaked motorway, hanging on to the tail lights of the car in front, popping pills which will give us a high but which may also kill us – but in the midst of our oddly ambiguous relationship with mortality, there is always the abiding thought that, even if the inevitable happens, our unique being, shaped so laboriously, must live on in some form. Surely we cannot just vanish in a split second.

Sometimes I sit at traffic lights, my foot twitching on the accelerator of the car, and try to contemplate what would happen if I shot out into the line of oncoming traffic. More specifically, what would happen if I killed myself doing it? Would it all go blank at once, as doctors tell grieving relatives, reassuring them that their loved one wouldn't have felt a thing at the moment of death? Or would I, in best Hollywood tradition, float up out of my body and look down on the crumpled tangle of cars

I had left in my wake? And, if there is an afterlife, at what stage does it kick in? Straight away, after the funeral when I have the Church's blessing, or after a sojourn in purgatory when I have waited in a queue for a few months (or years) and people on earth have prayed for the repose of my soul? I've never been good at queuing, and even if I managed to stick it out, what would I get to at the end? Would I even recognise it as having any connection with what went before? Would it be a physical landscape, or an illusory one? Would it exist outside my imagination, or would it even exist at all? Would others be there too? Would they recognise me? Suddenly oblivion seems so much more straightforward. As the lights turn to green and I cautiously set off on my way, I realise that these seemingly overwhelming questions are so earthbound as to be trivial compared with what I am contemplating.

Yet what is absolutely true is that we fear death because we fear the unknown: the rich build monuments to earn immortality, the wordy write books which will sit in library catalogues forever after, and the competitive strain to get their names engraved on cups and shields and prizes. All offer a kind of life after death. For the majority, however, the choice is simpler: children and/ or a belief in the afterlife are our antidotes to death, the best way of cheating what scientists in a secular age tell us is the unavoidable fact of oblivion. Children can, of course, let us down as they grow up – run away from home, never darken our doorstep, and, God forbid, even predecease us – but afterlife never will. Potentially, it is the ultimate happy ending. As, it would seem, we cannot try it out and report back any feelings of disappointment, it remains nothing more than a glorious but untried promise, utterly open to the wiles of our imagination.

Yet it is a promise that is so finely attuned to our own needs and desires that it has been with humankind from the start, predating written language and philosophy and organised religion. From the time when the first Neanderthal sat next to the lump of dead protein that had been his or her mate and realised that something had to be done about the smell, we have wondered what, if anything, comes next. People have generally assumed that there should be something. When that body was put in a cave or a ditch or on to a fire or pushed over a ledge into a ravine, the one left behind looked into the void that was left and felt an emptiness and abandonment. So arose the myths, traditions and literature, the shamans and soothsayers, the priests and popes, and the poets, writers and dramatists who would attempt to provide the answer.

And so arose, too, that intimate connection between belief in a God and the hope of reward with Him or Her in life everlasting. In many faiths – particularly Western – the two are synonymous, and the link therefore goes unquestioned, but not all the world's great religions have signed up for the two-for-the-price-of-one package deal. Buddhism has its deity, but though highly ambiguous and elusive it is basically indifferent to the notion of afterlife, which it regards as a red herring, and as something that makes religion other-worldly, irrelevant and even pessimistic. To treat nirvana as heaven would distract one from the pursuit of enlightenment in this life. Buddhism advocates the reaching of a higher state in this life rather than letting one's dreams of a better time to come after death take hold. So Buddhism challenges its adherents to do the right thing now, for its own sake, rather than have half an eye on what might happen after death, thereby preventing any possibility of opting out

of this world, standing aloof from it as certain religious groups have done down the ages, or even, as in the case of the various gnostic sects, rejecting this world as irredeemably evil. When there is nothing to work with other than the now, you have to get on with it, engage at every level. Buddhists believe one's fate in both the present life and forever is bound up in this engagement. Most importantly, Buddhists must work to make the earth a place of justice rather than rely on inequalities being sorted out posthumously by the deity. There is no excuse for accepting the status quo.

Put briefly and in such terms, it sounds so attractive that it suddenly becomes hard to understand why the notion of heaven ever put down such deep roots. And this conviction strengthens when Buddhism's rejection of a theology which places a greater premium on the afterlife than it does on this life is seen in the context of similar creeds which arose in the same period, roughly from 700 BC to 200 BC, known to historians as the Axial Age. Hinduism in India and Confucianism and Taoism in the Far East all stress the importance of practical compassion and concentrate on the here and now.

Yet not all faiths at this transition point in the history of religions took the particular route that excluded any great concentration on heaven. Judaism, and thereafter by association its younger sister, Christianity, was the main exception to the Axial Age trend. Infected by Zoroastrianism during the Babylonian exile (586–536 BC), Judaism has lived ever after with a highly developed eschatology (the doctrine of the last things which revolves around death, judgement and afterlife). This eschatology came as part of a parcel of beliefs. Judaism, which had hitherto flirted with other deities, also adopted a strictly monotheistic approach from Zoroastrianism. Unusually for its time, it taught of a single, good god – Ahura Mazda, the god of light – rather than a pantheon of gods and ancestor or nature spirits. Christianity and then Islam were later to join the ranks of the monotheistic faiths and also have a strong concept of heaven.

There is then a link between extolling the virtue of a single God, responsible for everything on this earth, and belief in an afterlife. If you centre your hopes, prayers and expectations on just one God, you inevitably concentrate on the 'personality' of that God, so much more than you would if you have tens or hundreds of gods to choose from, and, as a consequence, you nurture a hope of making contact with that God face-to-face.

This narrow focus takes its tolls on imaginations, or at least channels them in a particular direction, and often makes for a palpable sense that God must be near at hand. This in its turn leads to an exaggerated interest in the place where God lives and to where the faithful might one day travel. But the chain of connections between monotheism and heaven goes deeper. The omnipotent God upheld by monotheistic faiths embodies good and evil in a single source, as opposed to parcelling both out across a whole range of spirits, some of them two-faced. Christianity may itself have diluted this by invoking the devil in practice at least, if not in theory, as an equal and opposing force to God, but that should not distract from the fact that the creation of such a powerful, unified divine principle inevitably brings with it a sense of human-kind's smallness and impotence before their God, and also, therefore, a turning away from each person's indi-vidual resources (as preached in Eastern faiths) towards a greater public search for oneness with the divine which necessitates a public arena – i.e. heaven – for fulfilment.

The tension between the two radically different emphases – on this life and on the next life – is, in effect, both the argument for and against heaven. Both have their strengths. The first places great and potentially empowering emphasis on each person to cultivate an internalising spirituality. For some this burden is too much of a challenge. Putting it all off until after death with the promise of a heaven – especially one where, as in the Christian New Testament, God will roll out the red carpet for the workers who only spend the last hour of the day in His vineyard as readily as He will for those who have toiled since sun-up – is much more palatable. Death-bed repentance, in theory at least, allows for brink-manship – a life of wonderful hedonism followed by a last minute change of heart, half an hour of piety and remorse and then a heavenly hereafter.

For some, the 'jam tomorrow' approach of mono-theism belongs in the nursery, but to its adherents, in more mature vein, it offers consolation in the face of the inevitability and finality of death. It also requires a moral framework which can be carefully calibrated (often by clerical hierarchies) as a step-by-step guide to achieving a good afterlife. Immanuel Kant, the eigh-teenth-century German philosopher and religious scep-tic, once remarked that without heaven no system that sought to teach, preach or impart morality could survive.

How to decide between the Eastern and the Western approach? Conventional wisdom – shared for once by scientists and clerics – is that there can be no verifiable communication with the other side as a way of assessing which has most merit. Central to Eastern ideas of rebirth is forgetting all that has gone before. There have always been, however, unconventional individuals able to service those who are too restless to wait and see. The Victorians went to spiritualists and mediums; we, in our turn, devour the literature of near-death experiences to satisfy our hankering to know if there is anything more to come. The American bestseller, *Hello from Heaven* (edited by Bill and Judy Guggenheim), was a collection of 353 accounts of communications from beyond the grave.

To accept absolute oblivion after death, a brain that stops functioning and a body that rots, would be to accept the polar opposite of heaven. It is increasingly popular as an option. There is even some scriptural foundation for such a stance: in the Old Testament, Job suffers endless adversity as part of a debate between Yahweh and Satan on the nature of human goodness. When he survives the ordeal, his reward is to have 'twice as much as he had before' in this life. There is no suggestion that there is any other.

Most of us, however, find the idea that death is the end unappealing, unthinkable or untenable – or a combination of all three. We cling fearfully and in hope to the notion, common in monotheistic religions, of the soul, that invisible but integral part of us that is above the messy business of physical death. Yet despite its enduring popularity, a heavenly hereafter for the souls of the faithful departed has been officially declared by the mainstream churches as being beyond our imagination.

The fact that it is unimaginable but nonetheless officially there is, however, just another aspect of heaven's appeal. We can sign up for it without having to think too hard about what that means. It's like taking out an insurance policy without ever having to study the small print.

When in 1999 Pope John Paul II pronounced that heaven was a 'blessed community' which was 'neither abstraction nor physical place', he was following the recent tendency to underplay what could be regarded as the Churches' trump card. Clerics are curiously nervous of mentioning heaven, despite its potential as a crowd puller, especially with the elderly. When a senior English archbishop gave an address at a Roman synod the same year, in which he blandly mentioned heaven in passing, I wrote to him to ask if we might meet so he could develop what seemed an intriguing theme. He wrote back by return saying that he was busy for the foreseeable future and couldn't really add to the words he had offered already. Yet he had said nothing.

One might almost conclude that the Western churches are, behind the scenes, realising that their Buddhist and Hindu confrères in the East have hit upon something in their lack of interest in the afterlife and so are gently repositioning their doctrines as a result. But that would be to ignore the lesson of history. For the Pope's almost embarrassed talk of heaven is part of a long Christian tradition. There are mentions of heaven aplenty in the New Testament. Some Christian fundamentalists believe that the Book of Revelation goes so far as to provide a street plan. Saint Augustine, arguably the most influential writer and thinker in Christian history, would, however, be pleased to hear the modern-day Vatican trying to quell speculation on the hereafter. In the fifth century he insisted that heaven was 'ineffable' – beyond words. It was indeed Augustine who established the term *ineffabilis* in theology as a way of summing up one of his favourite maxims – that it is easier to say what God is not than to say what He is.

Augustine's word, rather like John Paul II's, has not

always been law in this, nor in other matters. Sketching out their own imaginary topography of Christian heaven has been a long line of theologians, mystics, artists, writers and the builders of the great Gothic cathedrals, whose spires reached to the skies. Usually starting with Revelation, which pictured paradise as a cleaned-up version of Jerusalem without its Temple, these seers have constructed the pearly gates and enlisted harps (first heard in the New Testament Apocrypha – the early Church texts considered too unorthodox to make it into the Holy Bible).

Outside the cloister, Dante mapped out his Paradiso of the skies in the fourteenth century with Renaissance precision and with every bit the same authority as he had invested in his Inferno in the bowels of the earth, though by a quirk of human nature it is the latter that has continued to fascinate us more. The same, incidentally, is true of John Milton in the seventeenth century. His *Paradise Lost* has been vastly influential in shaping modern thinking on the Devil and his hellish lair, but those sections of the text which describe heaven are overlooked. Perhaps it is a desire amongst readers not to appear presumptuous as to their final destination that has traditionally allowed hell to eclipse heaven in terms of the popular imagination. Or perhaps it is just the dominance of fear in our emotional range. More practically, it may be art for once imitating the attitudes of those in power. The post-Reformation churches of Milton's time were much keener on frightening people in to the pews with talk of hell than in enticing them with pictures of heaven.

Despite its unfathomable promise, heaven has eternally been the poor relation of hell; the quieter, paler sibling, the bland-looking friend that some attractive men and women take round with them so as to make themselves shine ever more brightly in comparison. George Bernard Shaw waspishly remarked in *Man and Superman* (1903): 'Heaven, as conventionally conceived, is a place so inane, so dull, so useless, so miserable, that nobody has ever ventured to describe a whole day in heaven, though plenty of people have described a day at the seaside.' Shaw may have correctly identified early the relative silence on heaven that took hold in the twentieth century, but he was, of course, exaggerating for effect. Down the ages, when heaven has occasionally managed to raise its subtly attractive head above the flames of the hell fires, it has gripped imaginations and produced some memorable and influential images. This is the world of Fra Angelico's *Last Judgement*, Luca Signorelli's *Coronation of the Elect*, William Blake's *The Meeting of a Family in Heaven* and Stanley Spencer's *Resurrection: Cookham*, a place of music, dancing, good health, sex, self-congratulation and plenty. It is the Elysian Fields, an image shamelessly borrowed from Virgil by the early Christians and entered symbolically through a gate, where, according to the *Aeneid*, those amongst the dead chosen for their heroic virtues 'train on grassy rings, others compete in field games, others grapple on the sand; feet moving to a rhythmic beat, the dancers move in formation as they sing'. Heaven is where, according to Dante, the 'Great Light shines in three circles', where, the Revd Charles Kingsley wrote to his beloved wife, Fanny, 'marital love will be without oscillation, even at the same glorious full tide of delight', and where, in Steven Spielberg's *Always*, Audrey Hepburn presides in a green glade.

Despite official urgings to the contrary, theologians, artists and writers have kept up a lively debate about the nature of heaven. There are three basic views. The first has appealed most to theologians and mystics – somewhere we spend eternal solitude with God alone. Here the traveller is in an unknown territory without landmarks, somewhere imaginable only in moments of intense prayer or spiritual introspection. All earthly relationships – spouses, parents, children – are as nothing in this place, and the body and bodily pleasures are exchanged for a vaguely defined inner peace. The imagination, a key component in any approach to heaven, is directed solely to God Himself and the backdrop is irrelevant. For the medieval mystics, God was so much the centre of their reveries that heaven was sexual fulfilment with Christ the Bridegroom.

The second view is much more tangible, familiar and easy to plot. It allows for some overlap between heaven and earth, and hence relationships outside the central bond with God. The necessary inspiration is all at hand. In the one and only conversation I ever had with my mother about death, on the occasion of my grandmother's death, she told me that her own image of heaven was of a welcoming committee of my great aunts greeting their sister with, 'Well, Annie, what took you so long?' This is the flip side of Jean-Paul Sartre's remark in *Huis Clos* that 'hell is other people'. The same may be said, in more upbeat mood, of heaven.

The hopes of being reunited in death were never more poetically expressed than in the seventeenth century by Henry King, Bishop of Chichester, in his celebrated *An Exequy*, written in 1657 after the death of his wife, Anne:

Sleep on (my Love!) in thy cold bed
Never to be disquieted.
My last Good-night! Thou wilt not wake
Till I thy fate shall overtake;
Till age, or grief, or sickness must
Marry my body to that dust
It so much loves; and fill the room
My heart keeps empty in thy tomb.

But hark! My pulse, like a soft drum
Beats my approach, tells thee I come;
And, slow howe'er my marches be,
I shall at last sit down by thee.
The thought of this bids me go on,
And wait my dissolution
With hope and comfort.

The third and commonest approach historically is a hybrid of the first two – somewhere to be with God alone, yet also a place where the imagination inevitably wanders into providing some shape and form, usually a garden, and to other relationships which may continue from earth.

All three approaches have their appeal depending on whether it is comfort, freedom from fear, or the search for another dimension beyond the banalities of earthly life that is prompting the seeker. Opinion has vacillated between this trinity – one theocentric (or based on God), another anthropocentric (focused on the human) and the third without a grand tag, but fundamentally a cocktail of the other two. Often all three have been promoted by different groups at the same time and the Churches, for their part, have never quite made up their minds.

The New Testament, for example, talks of heavenly

liturgies, bodies that are but spirit and an angelic, celibate lifestyle in the hereafter. In the same theocentric vein, St Augustine spoke of death as the 'flight in solitude of the Solitary'. The Protestant reformers, the Puritans and the Jansenists embraced the God-centred view of heaven. Yet alongside this trend, there has been a parallel one which insists on creating heaven in the image of a spruced-up earth. In the second century, Irenaeus of Lyons, taking his lead from Revelation, held that the chosen would, for a thousand years after their death, inhabit what was in effect a renewed earth. In this plan whatever you had been denied the first time round, you received in abundance in the rerun.

Heaven as a compensation for all you have missed on earth has always been an attractive gospel. In Renaissance times, theologians joined with humanists and artists in humanising heaven. Borrowing from the Golden Age and the Isles of the Blest (an alternative form for the Elysian Fields) of classical mythology, they fashioned a 'forever environment' where men and women met, played, kissed and caressed against a pastoral backdrop. Often God would be removed from direct participation in this pleasure garden and heaven would be given two or even three tiers, the furthest away being the domain of the exclusively spiritual, characterised solely in terms of intensity of light.

More recently in the eighteenth century, the influential, though much-neglected writings of the Swedish scientist-turned-religious-guru Emanuel Swedenborg gave the earth-linked heaven a romantic edge. He is one of the architects of the modern heaven. His *Heaven and Hell*, part of a body of works known as *Arcana Coelestia*, which were much-read and remarked upon by the remarkable William Blake among others, describes the author's encounter with angels as he moves between the spirit world and the material world. It was an image to inspire both popular nineteenth-century authors and twentieth-century film-makers who turned heaven into a cosy, twee copy of the earth, where love and good will conquer all.

There has always, it should be noted, been traffic between the different positions on heaven. Usually it has ended up in the fudge of the third way. Some of those who once preached of a God-centred heaven changed their mind in later life when it seemed they were about to test the validity of their theories. Augustine, in old age, began describing an afterlife where God was very important but where there was time too for long lunches with old friends and enjoyment of physical beauty, but without, of course, his *bête noire*, sex.

The rise of Christian fundamentalism has added a new twist to the eternal three-way split. For many born-again Christians have embraced a concept known as rapture, which represents a new departure in thinking about heaven. It has grown out of a very particular reading of St Paul's prediction that when God descends in judgement 'those who have died in Christ will be the first to rise and then those of us who are still alive will be taken up in the clouds, together with them, to meet the Lord in the air' (I Thess 4:14–17). This meeting will, the new breed of fundamentalists believe, be shortlived; a refuge in the time of trial predicted by Revelation before Christ instigates a millennium of direct rule on earth and the visitors to heaven return to take their rightful place at his side. The concept that heaven can be a temporary haven, almost a holiday destination, goes against every other Christian tenet. Yet it is disarmingly popular. A key exponent of rapture, the former Mississippi tug-boat captain turned Christian fundamentalist, Hal Lindsey, has seen his book, *The Late Great Planet Earth*, sell thirty-five million copies worldwide.

Such a reappraisal illustrates, in one sense, how flexible the idea of heaven (and indeed the New Testament) can be in the hands of believers. Something that can only live in the imagination is, by its very nature, almost impossible to control. Yet for many of us who have some kind of faith, it can be, for much of our lives, almost an irrelevancy. Until very recently, on the rare occasions that I plucked up the courage to look my post-mortem fate straight in the eye, my instinct had always been to postpone thinking about heaven. Focusing on the next world, it seemed to me, was a cop-out.

Heaven, I therefore know from experience, can very easily be left to one side as one of those tricky parts of the total religious package, accepted implicitly but without thought, something to think about on a rainy day. It largely depends on what stage of life you're at. If the subject did come up in my teenage years at my Catholic school, it was as the flip side of hell, an altogether more worrying entity in those angst-ridden years. Heaven was certainly too much to contemplate in my fallen adolescent state. In my twenties, I lacked the romantic spirit of Keats who, at the age of twenty-five, when passion for life is at its peak (and also just a year before his death), wrote in *Ode to a Nightingale*:

> *Darkling I listen; and, for many a time*
> *I have been half in love with easeful Death,*
> *Called him soft names in many a mused rhyme,*
> *To take into the air my quiet breath;*
> *Now more than ever seems it rich to die,*
> *To cease upon the midnight with no pain.*

But in my late thirties, the recent experience of losing one of my parents and then a much-loved mother-in-law has led me, if not to welcome death as a form of release like Keats, then to consider both it and heaven as never before. As I drove behind the hearse carrying my mother's coffin to the church for her funeral, I thought of all the hundreds of times I had seen other sombre processions pass and scarcely paused in the business of living, let alone said a prayer. Belief, A. A. Gill once wrote, is like holding on to the end of a piece of string that disappears into the sky. Sometimes that string is yanked and it forces you to think.

Having had my string pulled, this book is, at least in part, my own traveller's tale of searching for some sort of answer via a journey, real and imaginative, to the place where the Catholic Church of my upbringing tells me my mother has gone. The notion of a metaphorical or spiritual journey to heaven is a tried, tested and often fruitful one. In both the apocryphal writings of the first centuries AD and in the visionary ecstasies of the medieval age those who told of heaven spoke in terms of having travelled there. Most of the lasting accounts of paradise have effectively been travel books. It is in this spirit that I have included in this account of my own journey brief extracts from the tales told by contemporary travellers who have attempted to go one step beyond, and also, at various key moments in the history of heaven, excerpts from the travel journal I kept when I visited particular places which seemed to offer the possibility of a glimpse of the transcendent.

In the interests of completeness I have tried to keep an open mind and see beyond the more standard tenets of my Christian start in life. Most faiths have some sort of belief in another life but some schedule the route as a domestic departure – i.e. as all about transcending this life. This then remains a book written primarily for a Western audience with a Judeo-Christian heritage, but written in the knowledge that such a heritage cannot be understood or evaluated with looking carefully at the alternatives.

Such a broad scope has the advantage of carrying with it the potential to quell my own greatest anxiety at the start of this journey, namely that there may be nothing at its end, that I may be going nowhere (now or ever), and that heaven is religion's biggest con-trick, its way of ensuring that churches, synagogues and mosques will remain full and flourishing. If I reach such a conclusion, I comfort myself now, at least I can then fall back on the Buddhist position of seeking enlightenment in this life by way of consolation.

A Gallup Poll in the early 1980s suggested that in the West, at least, the majority of voters still place their trust in heaven, even if its manifesto is no longer very precise. The 71 per cent who signed up for it were only one point down on the number in a similar survey in 1952. As long as there are men and women afraid of death and anxious to believe that it is not the end, there is a ready audience, happy to take the anaesthetic to life's worries that heaven provides. But perhaps oblivion shouldn't be an anxiety for any of us. Nothing may be better than the torment which the old-style Catholicism of the *Penny Catechism* promised in purgatory, limbo or, worst of all, hell. If you put your faith in heaven, then you had to be prepared for the dreadful consequences of not getting your grades.

Today, of course, it is arguably easier. There is no mention of hell from the pulpits of the mainstream churches. Purgatory and limbo have been put to grass, and the assumption in most religious circles is that we are all bound for some sort of heaven, even if that isn't stated categorically too often. When set against the secular alternative, this pared-down, consumer-driven religion should be more enticing. Yet the pews are emptying at a ferocious rate in the developed world. Why isn't heaven still working its magic?

Perhaps it has something to do with the fact that we live in an age when the whole thrust of contemporary attitudes is not to think about death. If it comes knocking at our door – if a close friend or relative dies – then we are encouraged to forget it as quickly as possible. The secular answer to the mystery of death is effectively to deny death an airing. We freely admit our inability even to contemplate the scale or the individual significance of the global deaths we cause and have the potential to cause with our nuclear weapons, our environmental destruction and our indifference to the north–south divide. And when we face death in our own backyard, as it were, amongst our family and friends, we sweep it under the carpet and instead grow ever more obsessed with our living bodies – new diets, health regimes and endless work-outs – in the hope that somehow we can arrest the march of time. Death has become a kind of failure – a failure to eat the right food, or exercise, or avoid the sun. Death has become each individual's responsibility, not humanity's destiny.

For those who are left behind by the death of a loved one, the message is clear: you've got to put it behind you, as I was told, countless times, by well-meaning souls in the weeks and months after my mother's death. The subtext, I see now, was 'for God's sake don't make us think about death'. Any suggestion that I didn't want to rush to forget was taken as a sign of morbidity of Queen

Victoria-like proportions and eventually prompted a referral to an analyst. Mourning is now considered perverse if it lasts more than a week. Twenty years ago we would not, for instance, go out to the cinema or the theatre or dinner if a close relative had just died. Today we are cajoled into outings on the grounds that they will be a comfort. Some comfort.

A hundred years ago we had great public funerals and private sex – one to do with the cult of death, the other with, *inter alia*, the hope of life. Now we have the opposite. And so with death, even among the rituals of a Christian funeral, we refrain from pressing our noses against the smell of our own physical corruption, from seeing, touching or holding a dead body. We rely on undertakers and hospices to maintain a cordon around the unpalatable reality and save our most flamboyant grieving for those we know only through the media and therefore can't touch: for the British it was the Princess of Wales, for the Americans, John Kennedy Junior, when he dropped out of the sky.

Yet I sense a welcome reaction against this sanitisation of death, another Gothic revival. The literature of AIDS, as the historian Jonathan Dollimore has noted in his study *Death, Desire and Loss in Western Culture*, has brought us back into touch with the trauma of death, questioning what happens next for so many promising lives which have ended prematurely. In Jim Crace's Booker-shortlisted novel *Being Dead*, the intimate link between the physical horror of violence, sexuality and death dominates the narrative.

I hope that this very personal quest for some sort of heaven, wherever it may be, marrying the religious and the secular, the real and imaginary, will in its own way add some small momentum to this movement to reconnect us with death. If we ignore the pain and gloss over death, then we will spend correspondingly little time on heaven. To live fully we have to think about death when we are fully alive.

My atheist and scientist friends tell me that the notion of an immortal soul is absurd. What I'm really talking about, they say, is the mind and the personality, which are located in the brain. When the brain dies, they perish; nothing is left. When I tell them about the thoughts that cross my mind as I sit, cradling my daughter, the most they will concede is that a predisposition can be passed down from one generation to another. Mozart was good at music because it ran in the family. He might have been good even if it hadn't, but they will accept that his genius might be down to more than nurture or chance.

When I try out this theory, as I lie half awake in the morning with my baby daughter and my dreams of reincarnation, I see it as a starting point, somewhere science and religion, psychology and faith, all touch. So though I make no promise at the outset of reaching my destination, there is, I venture, a glimmer of hope.

PART ONE

Knowledge of Angels

CHAPTER ONE

Dust to Dust

Christianity, the arch-promoter of heaven, is the second-hand rose of world religions. Nearly every item in its bulging wardrobe has been begged, borrowed or stolen from a previous owner, be it from the Jews, the Greeks, the Romans or various Near Eastern belief systems. What enabled Christianity to flourish in the West was a combination of inspired leadership, the tremendous passion it managed to generate, and, most of all, its unique synthesis of time-honoured ideas into a code that had both a universal resonance and a simplicity. In its early days, Christianity was happy to acknowledge its debts. Newness and originality were not regarded as a plus in religious terms at the time. Continuity was more important. Radical departures were regarded as impious, while the cloak of antiquity conferred many advantages. It was only much later, when at the height of its powers, that Christianity began to rewrite its past and edit out those who had influenced it.

This wider pattern is clearly seen in the development of the idea of heaven. The Christians were by no means the first travellers to hit on paradise as a destination where all the stresses and strains of this world would waft gently away amid clouds, soothing music and the omnipresence of the ultimate guide. Nevertheless, they realised to the full the potential appeal of such a place as an antidote to what for most was a miserable life on earth, and so promoted it with a vigour hitherto unseen. It proved an effective way of wooing waverers into their fold and, when heaven was twinned with hell as a carrot and stick, keeping them there. However, the origins of this paradise in the sky predate the birth of Jesus by many centuries.

From earliest times, there had been an interest in the concept of a destination to which the dead travelled. For many, this was a collective experience and involved no system of judgement. The Dieri of southeastern Australia are an aboriginal people whose customs have not changed since the Neolithic age. They envisage the dead as going to what they call the River of the Sky, located in the stars of the Milky Way. Although they have a fine time there, they do continue to communicate with those left behind and occasionally return as spirits to haunt their relatives' sleep.

Others, however, evolved more complex and judgemental systems. In Egypt, the civilisation that thrived along the Nile and its delta from the fourth millennium BC until the time of classical Greece and Rome, had unusually well-refined notions of an afterlife, even if religion was not organised in any institutional form. They were an integral part of Egyptian life, as much taken for granted as the ebb and flow of the Nile. The Egyptians searched in their religion for something collective beyond the cycles of everyday existence, for a timeless, unchanging cosmos. The afterlife was part of that search, as the mummies and artefacts in the death chambers of the pyramids make abundantly clear.

They believed that a part of the body, thought to be either the heart or the stomach, and roughly equivalent to what we now call the soul, left the body at death and remained active on earth. It was often depicted as a human-headed bird, the ba, and was acknowledged to have physical needs, occasionally returning to the corpse. Hence the advanced art of mummification, so that the body would not rot, and the supplies of food that were left in the grave, along with a route out of the burial chamber or pyramid. The Egyptians also believed in the ka – the intellect and spirit of the person. This in turn had two parts – one which was effectively the body's double and which stayed with the corpse in the tomb, and another which was the part that soared to a new world.

The Egyptians labelled this place the kingdom of the god Osiris, the lord of the dead and the judge of souls in afterlife. Osiris was based on a historical figure, the first pharaoh, who, after his own death, became ruler of the world beyond. The ka would be ushered into Osiris's court by Anubis, a jackal-headed god. The candidate would then be put on one side of a set of scales. On the other was an ostrich feather. Since goodness was deemed to be very light, if he or she had been good they would not tip the balance and would be welcomed in to an eternal pleasure dome of banquets, contests, dancing and fun, where there was no illness, hunger, sorrow or pain. If they tipped the scales, they were consigned to an ill-defined underworld of monsters. The verdict was recorded in a court record by Thoth, Osiris's son.

Thoth was credited with producing the illustrated *Book of the Dead* (c. 1580–1090 BC). As well as frightening

depictions of the ghouls of the underworld and rec-
reations of the court-room weigh-ins, it also contained
hints on how you could ensure that the verdict went your
way once you came before Osiris. At different stages of
the pharaohs' rule, the qualities necessary to achieve that
ultimate lightness were different. In one age it would be
courage in battle, in another loyal service to the ruler, in
another great wisdom or moral strength. The admission
criteria for the Egyptian heaven were set according to
the needs of the present. As the practice became more
popular, the scroll would also include a map of the land
beyond this life – with its seven gates, rivers and valleys
of the sky and potential traps – and was routinely placed
alongside the bodies of kings when they were buried.

The influence of such ideas on the heaven that Christianity promoted so assiduously is, however, remote. A
much more immediate embarkation point is Judaism, in
effect Christianity's elder sibling. Unlike the Egyptians,
it initially had little interest in an afterlife. This is the
view that dominates the opening sections of the Old
Testament or Hebrew scriptures and which prevailed
while the Israelites established themselves in the Holy
Land from around 1200 BC onwards. In addition to the
here and now, these Jews believed there were two other
worlds – one above and unobtainable, heaven, the abode
of the gods which was ruled over by Yahweh (who was
not yet regarded as the only God), and one below and
inevitable, subterranean sheol – a word borrowed from
Semite faiths in the region – to which were consigned
all the dead, regardless of the merits or faults of their
earthly lives. There was no suggestion that virtuous mortals might aspire to take the 'up-lift' to the heavens when
they died. Entry was strictly restricted to a named and

heroic handful – for example, the prophet Elijah. His journey to the skies – after his historic victory over the pagan monarchs Ahab and Jezebel and their deity Baal – is the only such voyage detailed in the Old Testament: 'Now as they [Elijah and his pupil Elisha] walked on, talking as they went, a chariot of fire appeared and horses of fire, coming between the two of them; and Elijah went up to heaven in the whirlwind.' (2 Kings: 2:11–12) Another similarly honoured was Enoch, a devoted servant of Yahweh, who is described in the Book of Genesis as 'walking with God' during his lifetime (365 years, according to Genesis, a figure dwarfed by his son Methuselah's 969 years) and then rather vaguely as 'vanishing because God took him' (5:24).

Since almost no-one went there, Judaism wasted no time trying to map out the realm of the gods. There was also little interest in sheol. Tradition taught that it was a dark, silent mausoleum, separated from this life, but the sort of questions we now ask about personal immortality would have been met with blank stares by Jews of the period. The lines of communication between sheol, heaven and earth as the three sides of a triangle were, however, well-established. In the First Book of Samuel (Chapter 28), King Saul prepares for a battle by donning a disguise and consulting a necromancer at Endor. The ghost that she conjures up 'rises from the earth'. It is Samuel himself, and Saul wants his dead ancestor, called reluctantly from slumber in sheol, to intervene in heaven with Yahweh, who he believes has abandoned the Israelites. Samuel accurately predicts that Saul will die. But Saul's interest was not in his own personal immortality, his own fate after death; rather, he had a broader political concern. This is the key theme in the great prophets. Their teachings were bound up with

this world and the problems affecting Israel, principally
its survival.

Lack of interest in heaven continued unchallenged
until the eighth century BC, when the Jews found themselves increasingly under threat from their mighty
Assyrian neighbours to the north and east. In extremis,
the people were encouraged to change tack and focus
their faith on Yahweh, cutting down on intermediaries
or other spirits and gods. Practices of ancestor worship,
it was said, distracted from Yahweh, disappointed Him,
and therefore had brought about military defeats. So, the
souls of the faithful and unfaithful departed were, at a
stroke, cast into outer darkness. King Josiah (640–609 BC),
for instance, introduced new legal taboos on the disposal
of corpses in an effort to stamp out remaining tendencies
towards veneration of the dead. They were to be buried
swiftly and then forgotten, he decreed, while necroman-
cers and wizards were outlawed. As with all such official
sanctions in matters of faith and morals, the Jews did
not wipe out the practice of ancestor worship altogether,
but they certainly marginalised it.

The living and the dead henceforth were eternally separated. The dead had no knowledge of the living and
therefore could not distract from events on earth. The
Book of Ecclesiasticus describes the dead, in the Lord's
eyes, as 'those who do not exist' (17:28) and, a few verses
further on, drives home the point when it says of
Yahweh: 'He surveys the armies of the lofty sky, while
all men are no more than dust and ashes.' (17:32) Historical and archaeological records show that here was a
religion which did not attempt to buttress its position
on earth by the promise of an eternal reward. Rather,
and bravely by our own standards, it stood or fell on
its earthly merits. Yahweh was understood in terms of

what He could do for the Israelites in this life. So any suggestion of a bonus for good service to their God was couched in terms either of national victory over Israel's oppressors, or, as in the case of Job once he had suffered endless adversity as part of a debate on the nature of human goodness between Yahweh and Satan, in purely material terms.

Heaven, or any effort to describe or plot the afterlife, remained of almost no concern until 586 BC, when Nebuchadnezzar captured Jerusalem and destroyed its holiest of holies, the Temple. The Jews began the trauma of fifty years of exile in Babylon. One consequence of adjusting to the enormity of this defeat was the birth of a school of thought that dreamed and planned of a new Israel that would rise from the ashes. This was in part simply a nationalistic movement, inspired by the image of a free homeland, a restored Temple and a liberated Jerusalem. But it was also about something more, because it had a strong religious and spiritual dimension. 'About Zion I will not be silent,' it was written in Isaiah at this time, 'about Jerusalem, I will not grow weary, until her integrity shines out like the dawn and her salvation flames like a torch.' (Is 62:1–2). These words refer to more than the building blocks of a city, though that extra something could simply be attributed to the exuberant imagery of the prophet. However, four chapters further on, there can be no mistake: 'For as the new heavens and the new earth I shall make will endure before me – it is Yahweh who speaks – so will your race and name endure.' (Is 66:22–23).

The new Israel with the new Jerusalem was not simply an independent earthly kingdom, but a quasi-mystical place, halfway between heaven and earth, where the living and their dead ancestors would mix and co-exist under the benign gaze of Yahweh. It is one of the most powerful and enduring images of afterlife in the Bible. In wanting to cloak themselves with both the protection of Yahweh *and* the aura of their illustrious ancestors, the exiled Israelites had introduced two vital ingredients into the story of heaven. The first was the notion that there could be some higher sphere here on earth, a renewed and perfected place where death no longer separated those who had loyally followed Yahweh from the living. Rather than the old horizontal division with a remote heaven at the top, earth in between and a catch-all sheol at the bottom, this new scheme preferred vertical lines that linked both living and dead with the Lord on the basis of their faith.

The second idea, closely associated with the first, was that of bodily resurrection – that the dead could literally rise from their graves to be with their descendants and their Lord. It seems likely that the Jews borrowed this concept from their captors in Babylon, many of whom embraced Zoroastrianism, the major belief system in the Middle East before Islam. Details of Zoroaster are few and far between, but he is believed to have lived around 1200 BC in Bactria, the area known today as Iran. He broke with the tradition, near-universal at the time, of invoking a pantheon of gods, and taught instead that there were only two gods, one good and one bad, who were locked in a cosmic battle with earthlings their cannon fodder. When Ahura Mazda, the good god, finally triumphed over his opponent, the fiendish Ahriman or Angro Mainyush, the dead would be summoned for a Last Judgement. The righteous would be restored in body *and* spirit and returned to a cleansed earthly paradise – the word comes from *pairidaeza* in old Persian, meaning the enclosed garden of the Persian king – the true and eternal kingdom of Ahura Mazda where everyone would live for ever.

Though the Babylonian exile occurred during the key period of the Axial Age, Zoroastrianism was not essentially an Axial religion, but, rather, a transitional faith between ancient pantheistic creeds and modern monotheism. One of the things that distinguished it from other Axial religions, such as Buddhism or Hinduism, was its emphasis on eschatology – and in the battle between Ahura Mazda and Ahriman this was a very violent eschatology. By contrast to such bloody fights at the end of time, Buddhism and Hinduism promoted a more compassionate ethic. Yet it was Zoroastrianism that the Jewish exiles imbibed, and so the post-exile prophets of the Old Testament began, for the first time, to talk of a new heaven and a new earth. Moreover, these post-exile prophecies were later inserted into the oracles associated with earlier prophets to give the semblance of continuity. History was being rewritten.

Zoroastra's influence on Jewish thinking about afterlife is seen most clearly in the Book of Ezekiel. Ezekiel was a priest and visionary who was active among the exiles in Babylon between 593 and 571 BC. He writes of seeing a valley full of dried bones. Yahweh breathes new life into them and raises them from the dead. 'I mean to raise you from your graves, my people,' is the message He gives to Ezekiel, 'and lead you back to the soil of Israel.' (Ez: 37:1–14) Leaving dead bodies to rot above the ground – as in Ezekiel's vision – was a religious practice of the Zoroastrians, but not of the Jews who preferred to bury them. The concept of bodily resurrection after death – in this case as a way of participating in a magnificent new era for Israel – had entered the mainstream of Judaism.

As a result of the Babylonian exile, the psychology of this shift in attitudes ran deep. For the Israelites, it had been all very well leaving heaven a remote place, accessed only by a chosen few, when Yahweh had been helping them slug it out with the various other tribes of the Near East. However, as their horizons broadened and they faced other opponents, the Israelites had begun to move towards monotheism, belief in a single God, focusing on Yahweh as more than simply a national mascot. When they were defeated and carted off into exile in Babylon, this process accelerated. Yahweh had to acquire bigger dimensions. He had to be Lord not just of their tribe, but of a wider universe if He was to help the Jews to be free once more. This is a theme developed in the second and third sections of the Book of Isaiah, written during the exile, where monotheism is embraced clearly and unequivocally, and Yahweh is painted as not just the God of Israel, but the God of all, even if the others don't yet recognise Him as such.

With such a conclusion, then, Yahweh couldn't be restricted to one part of the earth, or carried around in the Ark of the Covenant. Equally, when the Israelites' oppressors were so awful – in this case destroying the Temple – that no earthly punishment would be good enough for them, and no earthly restoration sufficient to avenge the insult to Yahweh, the notion of heaven as a court of final and absolute justice over and above the whole earth had great appeal. Monotheism almost inevitably brought heaven in its wake.

This link between heaven and judgement was strengthened when Jewish thought shifted decisively again, some three hundred years later. An echo of Ezekiel's vision is found in the Book of Daniel, one of the last additions to the Old Testament, thought to have been written between 167 and 164 BC. Here Daniel writes 'of those who lie sleeping in the dust of the earth', i.e. on its surface. Yet he goes further: they will awake, he writes, 'some to everlasting life, some to shame and everlasting disgrace' (Dn 12:2). He was describing what later became a standard feature of the Christian heaven – the process by which each and every aspirant for entry is judged on the basis of how they have lived their earthly lives.

The Book of Daniel is illustrative of an emerging trend in Judaism that placed emphasis on individual vice or virtue rather than on the national fate, as the Babylonian exiles had. Personal immortality was now an issue. Sheol as a catch-all for the dead was becoming discredited. It was being remodelled into two alternatives – heaven for the blessed and hell for the damned, though not quite so explicitly as yet. The basic justice in the construct had been emerging for some time and is seen in documents older than Daniel. Psalm 73, for instance, questions the traditional Jewish view that the wicked do well in this world and suffer no eternal punishment for their sins on earth. The psalmist claims that he or she has 'pierced the mystery' by invoking God's judgement in death. The righteous who lead good lives will go to God – 'I look to no-one else in heaven, I delight in nothing else on earth' – while the evil-doers are punished: 'Those who abandon you are doomed, you destroy the adulterous deserter.' (v. 27). The emphasis is on personal, not collective, wrong-doing. The message is also found in Psalm 49. Those who embrace worldly goods and power without a thought for God will end up in sheol, while the upright will enjoy God's favour:

Like sheep to be penned in sheol,
death will herd them to pasture
and the upright will have the better of them.

Dawn will come and then the show they made will
* disappear,*
sheol the home for them!
But God will redeem my life
from the grasp of sheol, and will receive me.

If hitherto Judaism had portrayed a place at God's right hand as beyond the reach and indeed desire of all but a tiny number of prophets, here now was a suggestion that everyone could go there as well, albeit departing only after a final day of judgement. In theory, people would be taken up from the Mount of Olives in Jerusalem, where Jews had long been taught to expect the coming of the Messiah, and so this became – and remains in Judaism even for such sinners as the late Robert Maxwell – the favoured place for burial. Key doctrinal pronouncements, however, such as that endorsing the concept of bodily resurrection made at the Council of Jamnia as late as AD 90, emphasised that the metaphorical meaning of the Mount could embrace Jews buried anywhere.

If Judaism took its notions of bodily resurrection from Zoroastrianism, then it subsequently borrowed the parallel concept of an immortal soul from the Greco-Roman tradition. In the end it was Christianity that effectively fused the two hitherto mutually exclusive ideas into one. Greco-Roman writers in this period were revising the standard definitions of afterlife as the dim and undifferentiated nether world favoured by Greek epic poets such as Homer. The shadowy and insubstantial Hades he wrote about around the ninth century BC was akin to the traditional Jewish sheol, but the Roman writer Virgil (70–19 BC) described instead a paradise of Elysian Fields and Isles of the Blest (an image that appeared in Homer) in his *Aeneid*. If Hades was comprehensive in its intake, Virgil's paradise was avowedly selective. Entered symbolically through a gate (again later an essential part of the heavenly hardware), the dead who sought admission had to pass an examination in heroic virtue.

Virgil's paradise is recognisable geographically as an idealisation of the Italian countryside which he knew and loved; the plains covered with wheat, the vineyards heavy with grapes, and nature's rich crop everywhere in evidence. This romantic, pastoral vision was a powerful one that has always retained an appeal for Western civilisation, as evident in examples such as the Champs Elysées in Paris, or the Elysian Fields that were part of such classic and celebrated eighteenth-century English gardens as that built at Painshill Park in Surrey by Charles Hamilton.

The point of all this agrarian and horticultural imagery for the Greco-Romans of the first century BC was that paradise recaptured a mythical golden age of simplicity and comfort, when people were unsullied by war, untroubled by famine and oblivious to political machinations. The same thought process in Christianity was later to cast heaven in the likeness of the Garden of Eden. Heaven was both a recreation of a past perfect life and the antithesis of what people were actually enduring on earth.

Virgil's was not a lone voice. Cicero (106–43 BC) and Plato (428–348 BC) had both already described a place above the stars where the souls of the righteous could thrive, though civic achievement was the cardinal virtue for Cicero in *Scipio's Dream*, written in 52 BC. These souls would be freed of the shackles of an earthly body. The Greeks, unlike the Jews after the exile, had little time for the idea of a bodily resurrection. For Plato in his dialogue *Phaedo* the *psyche* or life force was immortal along with the *nous* or mind. The body was by contrast dispensable:

> It has been proved to us by experience that if we would have true knowledge of anything, we must be quit of the body – the soul in herself must behold things in themselves: and then we shall attain the wisdom which we desire, and of which we say we are lovers; not while we live, but after death; for if while in company with the body the soul cannot have pure knowledge, knowledge must be attained after death, if at all. And thus having got rid of the foolishness of the body we shall be pure and have converse with the pure, and know of ourselves the clear light everywhere, which is no other than the light of truth. For the impure are not permitted to approach the pure . . . and what is purification but the separation of the soul from the body?

From this position, Plato then argued that since knowledge was all, we have ideas that cannot be derived from experience. Thus the soul must have existed before birth as well as after it. Of the domain beyond earth where the soul begins and ends its journey, Plato wrote that it was:

> a region of purity, and eternity, and immortality, and unchangeableness, which are her [the soul's] kindred and with them she ever lives, when she is by herself, and is not let or hindered; then she ceases from her erring ways, and being in communion with the unchanging is unchanging.

Plato's heaven encompassed the gods, but he paid them scant regard. Its most important qualities were mental and intellectual, not physical. It was the place of philosophers, somewhere they could continue arguing pure principle for ever.

An exact interchange of ideas between the Jews and the Greeks before the time of St Paul is difficult to pin down, but there is sufficient evidence of overlap in the writings of Philo of Alexandria (20 BC–45 AD), the Jewish philosopher who made an extensive study of Greek ideas at the same time as upholding the spirit of the Hebrew scriptures. He wrote, borrowing from the Greek heroic tradition (but also with echoes of Elijah), of souls being transported up to heaven in chariots to join the angels. He even imagined specific and distinct destinations within heaven for philosophers, for angels, and for the gods, but stressed that all shared an existence that was blessed, eternal, incorporeal and asexual.

The final noteworthy shift in Jewish thinking on heaven came between 250 BC and AD 200, sometimes called the 'inter-testamental period' because it falls roughly between the youngest book of the Old Testament and the oldest of the New. It is also known as the apocalyptic period (from the word *apokalypsis*, meaning revelation) – a reference to its chosen literary style, seen in a plethora of texts which claimed to be accounts of visions from some of the great figures of the Old Testament. These apocalyptic documents fall into two main categories – the Old Testament Apocrypha, books that were at one time accepted as holy scripture but which later were denied admission to the authorised version, and the Pseudepigrapha, those which were never accepted by either Jewish or Christian authorities and which relied most heavily on the revelatory dreams featuring dead prophets. Almost all assumed that the end of the world was imminent – spurred on by the continued political subjugation of Israel first by the Syrians, ended by a revolt of the Maccabees in 161 BC, and then by the Romans, who in AD 70 destroyed the Second Temple. These reverses prompted a spirit of despair and bitter internal divisions amongst the Jews. The texts responded by projecting themselves forward into the next world, returning to the theme of a new Israel and a new Jerusalem, where Yahweh would come to defeat Israel's enemies and reign for ever in peace and harmony. Some writers endorsed the existing idea of a bodily resurrection, but others suggested the risen body would be transformed into something as perfect and celestial as an angel.

The Book of Enoch is one of the best preserved of these texts. It was composed by several different authors, writing between 250 BC and 50 BC, and claimed to convey what Enoch – who, as we have seen, was one of the few in early Judaism to have his name on the electoral roll of heaven – had witnessed on high. Enoch's paradise was a two-tier one – another new and subsequently important development. The righteous lived in what was a transformed earth, a literal heaven, while God, the saints and assorted luminaries inhabited a higher, less recognisable and hence largely inaccessible plain – the spiritual heaven:

> In the vision the winds were causing me to fly and rushing me high up into heaven. And I kept coming until I approached a wall which was built of white marble and surrounded by tongues of fire ... And I came into the tongues of fire and drew near to a great house which

was built of white marble, and the inner wall were [sic] like mosaics of white marble, the floor of crystal, the ceiling like the path of the stars and lightnings between which [were] fiery cherubim, and their heaven of water, and flaming fire surrounded the wall, and its gates were burning with fire. And I entered into the house, which was hot like fire and cold like ice, and there was nothing inside it; fear covered me and trembling seized me. And as I shook and trembled, I fell upon my face and saw a vision. And behold there was an opening before me [and] a second house, which is greater than the former, and everything was built with tongues of fire . . . It is imposs-ible for me to recount to you concerning its glory and greatness. As for its floor, it was of fire and above it was lightning and the path of the stars; and as for the ceiling, it was flaming fire. And I observed and saw inside it a lofty throne – its appearance was like crystal and its wheels like the shining sun; and I [heard] the voice of the cherubim; and from beneath the throne were issuing streams of flaming fire. It was difficult to look at it. And the Great Glory was sitting upon it – as for His gown, which was shining more brightly than the sun, it was whiter than any snow . . . The flaming fire was round about him, and a great fire stood before Him.

(Book of Enoch 1:20–21, 49–50)

The authors of Enoch provide further details: there is an alabaster mountain, topped by sapphire, which is the throne of God and a sweet-smelling tree-of-life (like the Hesperides Tree of Greek mythology), which will be enjoyed in the north-east of heaven by the meek and the just for eternity. Moreover, they echo the Book of Daniel (it is unclear which text came first) in employing one of the most enduring descriptions of heavenly figures. In his dream about heaven, Daniel sees the 'Ancient of Days'. 'His robe was white as snow, the hair on his head as pure as wool.' (Dn 7:9–10) Enoch speaks of the same figure, protected by the wings of the Lord of the Spirits, with hair as white as wool.

These first detailed descriptions of the shadowy domain of heaven reflected a substantial body of disillusioned opinion within Judaism in the first century AD which was turning its gaze skywards in despair at what was happening on earth. As such, it had a direct influence on the new Jesus cult that arose at this time and was to become Christianity. The ruling group of Sadducees, a priestly caste based on the Temple, may have had little time for talk of resurrection and so dismissed texts such as Enoch as a distraction from the central need to police ritual purity in the here and now, but their rivals, the Pharisees, and the rebel group of Essenes, best known now through the Dead Sea Scrolls, embraced the apocalyptic thinking behind such books. The Pharisees for their part dreamed of a renewed Judaism that would rise, in the terms of the Book of Daniel, from the dry bones of a conquered Israel. The Essenes were more otherworldly, removing themselves to the desert at Qumran near the Dead Sea, rejecting politics and national concerns, and anticipating the imminent dawn of a new, mystical Jewish state under the leadership of a messiah. Their fervent belief in the End of Days focused their attention ever more closely on what was to come in the new life. Their one aim was to get as close to Yahweh as possible in this life in preparation for the next. They wanted to blur the boundaries. So, as well as their taste for apocryphal literature, they tried to prepare themselves physically by leading an austere existence. They were mainly celibate, their food was frugal and monotonous and they always bathed in cold water. Only in the white garments that they wore at communal gatherings was there a hint that the heaven they were trying to anticipate in their lifestyle would, in its detail, be in any way celebratory.

Traveller's Tales: 1

Just a year before his death in 1989, at the age of seventy-eight, the celebrated British philosopher A. J. 'Freddie' Ayer choked on a piece of smoked salmon while in hospital being treated for pneumonia. He passed out and then, technically, he died. His heart stopped for four minutes before medical staff were able to revive him. A convinced atheist and rationalist, Ayer subsequently spoke to friends of his vivid experience on the other side. His biographer, Ben Rogers, writes:

> He had been confronted by a bright red light, painful even when he turned away from it, which he understood was responsible for the government of the universe. 'Among its ministers were two creatures who had been put in charge of space. These ministers periodically inspected space and had recently carried out such an inspection. They had, however, failed to do their work properly, with the result that space, like a badly fitting jigsaw, was slightly out of joint.' Ayer could not find any of the 'ministers' responsible for space, but he realised that ministers who had been given charge of time were in his neighbourhood and remembering that, according to Einstein, space and time were one, he tried but failed to signal to them by walking up and down and waving the watch and chain he had inherited from his grandfather. Ayer became 'more and more desperate' as his efforts elicited no response. At this point his memory of the experience stopped, although when he regained consciousness, he woke talking about a river –

presumably the River Styx – which he claimed to have crossed.

(from *A. J. Ayer: A Life*, Ben Rogers)

In subsequent interviews, Ayer admitted that the experi-ence had made him 'wobbly' about the possibility of an afterlife, but soon reverted to type and labelled himself a 'born-again atheist'. His mind and brain had continued work-ing when his heart had stopped, he explained, and he had had a bad dream. His wife Dee told friends that 'Freddie had got so much nicer since he died.'

CHAPTER TWO

Come Back and Finish What You Started

Judaism moved forward from the Axial Age by developing the idea of a personal God whose ways soared above those of humanity as the heavens tower above the earth. Other contemporaries, though, travelled in the opposite direction. They rejected the single, personal God as too limiting, prone to become a projection of our own fears, needs and desires. They opted instead for an impersonal and opaque deity which was less constrained, less clearly defined, less of an encouragement to complacency within a system of rewards and punishments, and more of a challenge to individuals to journey beyond language, dogma and earth-bound imagery in order to explore the transcendent within.

On the Indian subcontinent, there is some surviving evidence that the reincarnation-based belief system later encapsulated in Hinduism had in fact existed since prehistoric times. On the basis of archaeological findings, for instance, scholars believe that faith in reincarnation existed in the Dravidian people of southern India and northern Sri Lanka. However, in the Vedas – the first sacred texts of Indian civilisation, composed in the second millennium BC – there is the conviction of a life after death but no details about how it is achieved. It is merely a land of shadows akin to the oldest Jewish beliefs.

The Axial Age saw the emergence of both Hinduism and Buddhism. The stance they took on afterlife was radically different from that taken first by Judaism, under the influence of Zoroastrianism, and later by Christianity and Islam. Between 600 and 300 BC, some of the key documents of Hinduism, the Upanishads, were written down by scholars and philosophers of the highly developed civilisation which was based on the River Indus. The Upanishads, while paying homage to the Vedas, substantially developed their ideas on what happened after death by teaching something called samsara – literally a chain of embodiments – whereby individuals died and were reborn according to how they had lived their previous life, i.e. by what 'karma' they had achieved.

In places the Upanishads were very specific. If you had stolen grain in one life, you would become a rat in the next. If you killed a priest, you would be reborn as a pig. By twinning reincarnation and karma, the principle that you reap what you sow was set in stone. The Upanishads made it plain that there was not one, single journey upwards. Rather, there would be many twists and turns in an individual's spiritual journey, because that was how the principle of karma operated. It was a gradual process of education, seeking after moksha – the liberation of the soul from the oppression of the body. Part of the learning curve was to see the self in the wider context. The atman – or 'individual soul part' – of the Brahman-Atman – or 'world soul' – gave people a seed of the divine which had to be cultivated and, ultimately, liberated.

The process of death and rebirth, therefore, was not envisaged as an endless one. The goal was to continue learning and growing until you had reached such a high level of karma that you could relinquish any sense of yourself and be absorbed into the divine, for at the end of the line stood the gods. It was all about self-learning, self-improvement and self-control. When you reached the highest point, the Upanishads said, you were realising your own destiny. Instead of heaven then, one attained a state of mind or of being, described in one passage in the Upanishads as self-abandonment. The way you lived your life could block your ascent: self-centredness, for instance, was deemed to hinder your absorption into what was called the 'Great Self'. 'Little Self' was egotism; 'Great Self' was understanding your place in the divine plan.

In the *Kausitaki Upanishad* there is a description, using familiar imagery of place and landscape, to convey the idea of union with the infinite spirit or brahman, but there is little sense of the reader being invited to take what he or she reads literally. It seems instead an effort to put into words what is in fact beyond words. When people depart this world, it states, they go to the moon, which is both the doorway to new life – rebirth on earth – and to the final destination. When they get to the moon, most become rain and are rained down on to the earth, where they are reborn. (Later Hindu belief allowed for a place of temporary respite, called Priti Loka, where one could recharge one's batteries before returning to earth.) A small number of people, however, are allowed to pass into the inner sanctum where a long, winding path, lined by solicitous angel-like nymphs, leads to the world of brahman:

He first arrives at the lake Ara. He crosses it with his mind, but those who go into it without complete knowledge drown in it. Then he arrives near the watchmen, Muhurta, but they flee from him. Then he arrives at the river Vijara, which he crosses with just his mind. There he shakes off his good and bad deeds, which fall upon his relatives – the good deeds upon the ones he likes and the bad deeds upon the ones he dislikes. It is like this – as a man driving a chariot would look down and observe the two wheels of his chariot, so he looks down and observes the days and nights, the good and bad deeds, and all the pairs of opposites. Freed from his good and bad deeds, this man, who has knowledge of brahman, goes on to brahman.

(*Upanishads*, translated by Patrick Olivelle)

Brahman, the divine soul anthropomorphised and sitting on a couch that is described as 'life breath', with one leg each for past, present, prosperity and nourishment, asks the new arrival to identify him or herself:

I am the season. I am the offspring of the season. I was born from the womb of space as the semen for the wife, as the radiance of the year, as the self [atman] of every being. You are the self of every being. I am who you are . . . the real.

The system of reincarnation and karma was closely linked in the Upanishads with earthly developments, notably the institutionalisation of the caste system in around 500 BC. Your karma was measurable by what class you belonged to on earth. It was difficult, therefore, within any one life-time to rise through the ranks. Hence the Brahmins (or priestly caste) were acknowledged as enjoying good karma accumulated in previous lives, while the Shudras (or servant caste) were suffering as a result of past bad karma. Ultimately, it made for an enclosed and hopeless world-view, effectively shutting off the possibility of developing and growing within a life and rising above your circumstances.

In so far as they were seen to buttress the existing political order by giving it a divine stamp of approval, the Upanishads came under attack. Moreover, because they taught that reaching the point of absorption into the Great Self was extremely rare, and that, even when achieved, it was a divine status that could easily be lost, with the consequent return to death and rebirth, their core message became, for many, a depressing and pessimistic one. Samara was part of an eternal grind of Sisyphean proportions.

Two movements arose simultaneously to challenge this bleak prospect. Mahavira (c. 540–468 BC), the most revered figure among the Jains, and Siddhartha Gautama Buddha (c. 563–c. 483) both suggested that karma should be seen as an exclusively spiritual quality which could not be directed to the practical end of propping up the caste system: no matter what level of society you were born into, you could still be a good spirit and grow and develop towards the ultimate within yourself inside that one lifetime. Mahavira advocated an asceticism, which included veganism, nudity and celibacy, and non-violence towards all living creatures as the key to salvation from the cycles of reincarnation. His was a rigorous self-help credo, placing as a realisable goal liberation from the flesh and the world into a realm of mental and spiritual bliss called Isatpragbhara or Kevala at the top of the universe.

Jainism was a fundamentalist version of mainstream

Hinduism and continues to thrive today with around two million adherents. Much more widespread, however, are the 350 million Buddhists worldwide (though very few are now in India itself). Buddhism took a gentler, less extreme course. Siddhartha Gautama was born in the sixth century BC, the son of a king in the foothills of the Himalayas in the north of India. His legend tells that when he was a young man he married, but he was afflicted by a strange malaise. He abandoned his prosperous family and his life of pleasure and indulgence, embarking instead on fasting, asceticism and meditation on sacred texts, finally achieving release from earthly desires and suffering under a Bodhi tree in his Great Enlightenment. Life on earth could be miserable, he taught, and each must seek liberation in this life, not by the self-denial of the Jains, or the resignation of the Upanishads, but rather by searching after knowledge of spiritual truths. There were, he said, Four Noble Truths which demonstrated that misery was caused by craving which in its turn could be cured by means of the Noble Eightfold Path. This led to the breaking of samsara and, ultimately, to nirvana – a mental state of blessedness. The eight steps on the path concerned growing in understanding and spiritual wisdom, living a moral life, and cultivating the mental discipline to prepare for nirvana. In Sanskrit, the word nirvana means 'extinguished' and for Buddha – the 'enlightened one' – it was a place for the extinguishing of human misery and cravings by self-knowledge.

While Buddha accepted the cycle of reincarnation and karma taught by the Upanishads, he offered as a release from samsara an achievable nirvana. Part of that nirvana was the knowledge of a deity, but, unlike Judaism, Buddha focused not on a personal god but on individual and internal enlightenment. This could, Buddha warned, be a long time coming. One of the most popular books in Buddhism is the Jatakas – birth-stories – which contains some 550 accounts of previous births of the Buddha in various human and animal forms.

Nirvana was not supernatural. 'He did not rely,' writes his biographer, the distinguished religious historian, Karen Armstrong, 'on divine aid from another world, but was convinced that nirvana was a state that was entirely natural to human beings and could be experienced by any genuine seeker. Gautama believed that he could find the freedom he sought right in the midst of this imperfect world. Instead of waiting for a message from the gods, he would search within himself for the answer, explore the furthest reaches of his mind and exploit all his physical resources.'

From the third century BC, Buddhism began to spread, notably to China. Legend tells that in the first century BC a Han emperor sent envoys along the Silk Route to India. They returned with written versions of Siddhartha Gautama's teachings which so impressed their readers that Buddhism immediately took root in China. The truth is more complex. Whereas in other parts of southeast Asia Buddhism had quickly and easily assimilated with existing beliefs, in China it stood in stark contrast to the two dominant ideologies, Confucianism and Taoism, both much more perfunctory in their attitude to the afterlife and transcendence. There was, therefore, a clear choice and a long period of conflict and competition.

Confucianism was a decidedly worldly creed which discouraged any great emphasis on either the hereafter or the mystical, and promoted instead practical imperatives on social responsibility, collective action, family values and hard work. Confucius (551–479 BC) was the codifier of an existing but ill-defined system of natural justice, someone who took received wisdom and moulded it in a robust package of beliefs. He was notably inhospitable to any supernatural concepts, but he did appeal to the individual to develop their intellectual powers and to act fairly in terms of following 'the way of heaven'. This led all, whether high-born or low-born, ultimately to the reward of Tian, a paradise for virtuous souls governed by a 'supreme spiritual presence'. This supreme being was later to be confused by Confucians with the person of the Emperor of China, in an effort to shore up political authority, but it was an understandable mistake for Confucius had great respect for the instruments of government (though he did not regard rulers as divine per se). The supreme spiritual being was ill-defined and vague, certainly not a Western-style god of judgement, and a force seldom active on earth.

Tian was not, characteristically, an original idea of Confucius's. Meaning 'sky' it had been a part of Chinese thought for several thousand years before the philosopher annexed it to his code of ethics as a reward for good behaviour. Traditionally, Tian was ruled over by the god Tianshen and those who joined him there after death would be nobles or kings. Some Chinese tombs discovered by archaeologists, thought to belong to rulers dating back to before 1000 BC, include the remains of dogs, horses and servants, all apparently sacrificed so as to assist their master on his passage to Tian.

For the lowly-born, the only chance of entry was as a vassal or a scribe, keeping records by which Tianshen could judge the lives of those who came before him.

Confucius, however, rejected such a system and attempted instead to make Tian a more democratic place, open to all on the basis of their earthly virtue and industry rather than rank and the arbitrary judgement of a deity. He was also less enthusiastic about the ancient Chinese practice of ancestor worship, believing it a distraction from current needs, but, again, his teachings have evolved down the years and have been interpreted as making a clear connection between heaven and earth. Hence sacrifices were offered in his name to dead emperors, various nature gods and even to Confucius himself.

Taoism, founded by Lao-tzu in the fifth century BC, was more open than Confucianism to supernatural ideas, but was still fundamentally wary of them. It was a much less worldly credo, rejecting institutions and politics and advocating instead a return to simplicity and harmony with nature in line with Tao – the hidden principle of the universe. The ideal was 'wu wei', non-doing or non-action, and in this passive belief system the notion of working to earn some sort of reward in an afterlife was anathema. With such an essentially blank canvas, as the historian Geddes Macgregor writes in *Images of Afterlife*, Taoism was 'as much directed towards the this-worldly as has been the philosophy of Confucius. True, as Taoism grew into a popular religion that accommodated all sorts of emotional influences, it became capable of hospitality to almost any sort of practice, including magical techniques for the attainment of immortality, but such developments have tended to be peripheral to the mainstream from the Chinese outlook.'

Taoism is, by its very passivity, something of a jumble of ideas which has been imposed on the vague and amorphous founding principle over the centuries, and therefore at different stages has embraced both a deity – a holy trinity of Three Pure Ones, including Lao-tzu – and an approach to paradise, Mount K'unlun. This nine-level hill leads up through various disciplines to the gateway to eternal bliss which stands at the summit. Those who enter come under the protection of Hsi Wang Mu, a queen with power over the mortality and destiny not only of the dead but also of the living. Her powers are so great that one Tao legend teaches she can dispense a magic potion to her favourites which allows them to experience eternal bliss without having to die first – similar to the dream-like journeys of apocalyptic literature. The focus in the Taoist legend, though, is not so much on what is seen but on plots to steal the potion. Immortality, and the key to it, is more important than the actual nature of life after death.

Set against such worldly belief systems, Buddhism had a strong mystical appeal when it first came to China. Its doctrines of individual liberation stood in contradiction to the more corporatist leanings of Confucianism and Taoism. There has never been one, single form of Chinese Buddhism, but a whole variety of alternatives, some developing highly disciplined monastic schools – for example in Tibet – others straying into magic and sorcery.

Two of these are of particular interest because they developed more explicit ideas of paradise than those of Buddha himself: Ching-tu or 'Pure Land' Buddhism was formulated in China by T'an-luan (AD 476–542). Devotees believe that they reach an equivalent to nirvana not only through their own powers and their own interior journey towards transcendence but also through devotion to and dependence upon a later incarnation of the Buddha, Amida Buddha, 'the Lord of Light' who presides over a pure land or land of bliss. The modification to encompass a more defined and judgemental deity means that paradise, as that deity's court, also is necessarily more precise, as set out in the *Sukhavativyuha Sutra*:

> Breezes blow spontaneously, gently moving these bells [that hang from trees in the four corners of the land], which swing gracefully. The breezes blow in perfect harmony. They are neither hot nor cold. They are at the same time calm and fresh, sweet and soft. They are neither fast nor slow. When they blow on the nets and the many kinds of jewels, the trees emit the innumerable sounds of the subtle and sublime Dharma [the principles behind the law] and spread myriad sweet and fine perfumes. Those who hear these sounds spontaneously cease to raise the dust of tribulation and impurity. When the breezes touch their bodies, they all attain a bliss comparable to that accompanying a monk's attainment of the samadhi of extinction.
>
> Moreover, when they blow, these breezes scatter flowers all over, filling this buddha-field. These flowers fall into patterns, according to their colours, without ever being mixed up. They have delicate hues and strong fragrance. When one steps on these petals, the feet sink four inches. When one lifts the foot, the petals return to their original shape and position.
>
> (from *Land of Bliss*, Luis Gomez)

This Pure Land is thought to exist in a particular place – beyond the sunset in the West – but it still remains, for all the detail, at heart a state of mind, the end point in the cycle of reincarnation achieved by those who raise themselves mentally and spiritually above day-to-day existence. There may be more of a focus on Ching-tu than on other forms of Buddhism, but still there is none of the resurrection hope that fuels monotheistic heavenly visions.

Tibet was slower than China to develop an interest in Buddhism. Its ancient creed, Bon, was an earthbound spirituality, with deities who were attuned to the landscape. The god Za, for instance, produced hailstones and lightning to damage the crops. This magical link between land and the gods was a practical support for a farming people, and they saw no need to replace it. Buddhism, when it came, had to be imposed on them by their rulers. In the eighth century King Trisongdetsen hoped that Buddhism would be a way of encouraging a higher, more sophisticated and more philosophical culture among his people. When it eventually took root, Tibetan Buddhism held fast to the essential beliefs of Buddha, though it modified them, resorting, for instance, to Vajrayana, a form of meditation undertaken by students and teachers which has the power to bring the enlightened state into everyday life.

Tibetan Buddhism, more so than its near relatives, has traditionally had a strong sense of the closeness of death. The Indian master Padmasambhava, 'the Lotus-Born', is credited as the founder of Tibetan Buddhism (though some doubt he ever existed), and he is said to have abandoned palaces to live on the charnel ground, a cemetery where dead bodies were traditionally left to rot as a reminder to the faithful of the unimportance of the human form and also because of a lack of fuel with which to burn corpses. Padmasambhava

found the charnel ground an excellent place for meditation on the importance of letting go of your ego and
your attachment to this life. It provided, he believed,
the impetus to see beyond life and death to ultimate
enlightenment.

Tibetan Buddhism followed his emphasis on death. In
the Tibetan *Book of the Dead*, much is made of bardo, or
the often frightening gap that opens up when you lose
touch with life. It is a transitional state, but covers both
the approach of physical death and the preface to enlightenment which can happen while you are alive. The two
are seen as one. Bardo is dominated by a brilliant light
which allows the true nature of the mind to be seen in
all its glory. For those who can take this vision, liberation
from the cycle of death and rebirth is at that moment
possible, but the *Book of the Dead* teaches that most people
in this transitory state are too confused and so are swept
along, via a path of sometimes terrifying, sometimes
peaceful, visions to new birth.

> Even they offer you a chance to gain understanding, as
> long as you remain vigilant and alert. A few days after
> death, there suddenly emerges a subtle illusory dream-
> body also known as the 'mental body'. It is impregnated
> with the after-effects of your past desires, endowed with
> all sense-faculties, and has the power of unimpeded
> motion. It can go through rocks, hills, boulders and walls,
> and in an instant it can traverse any distance. Even after
> the physical sense-organs are dissolved, sights, sounds,
> smells, tastes and touches will be perceived, and ideas
> will be formed. These are the result of energy still resid-
> ing in the six kinds of consciousness, the after-effects of
> what you did with your body and mind in the past. But
> you must know that all you perceive is a mere vision, a

mere illusion, and does not reflect any really existing objects.

(*Buddhist Scriptures*, translated by Edward Conze)

This is followed by visions, by being confronted by a deity with the 'shining mirror' of karma, and by the dawning of 'the six places of rebirth'. Setting out, dazed and desirous on a walk across deserts of burning sands, tormented by beasts who are half human, half animal and by hurricanes, you head for a place of refuge.

Everywhere around you, you will see animals and humans in the act of sexual intercourse. You envy them, and the sight attracts you. If your karmic coefficients destine you to become a male, you feel attracted to females and you hate the males you see. If you are destined to become a female, you will feel love for the males and hatred for the females you see. Do not go near the couples you see, do not try to interpose yourself between them, do not try to take the place of one of them. The feeling which you would then experience would make you faint away, just at the moment when egg and sperm are about to unite. And afterwards you will find that you have been conceived as a human being or as an animal.

The *Tibetan Book of the Dead* symbolises the penultimate one of the five alternative explanations of what happens after death. Complete oblivion was to be posited later, with the advance of science and reason, and so, long before the birth of Christianity, a choice of four beliefs existed with a shadowy afterlife in the earliest civilisations; immortality of the soul as preached by the Greeks; resurrection of body and soul, increasingly popular within Judaism; and reincarnation, the evolution to a higher form of life in this life and the constant cycle of death and rebirth found in most Eastern traditions.

CHAPTER THREE

⸻ ⧢ ⸻

But Not Life as We Know it

There is a school of thought which claims Jesus was an Essene, and that he is the 'righteous teacher' referred to in the Dead Sea Scrolls. However, the case remains unproven and is scorned by many eminent religious historians. What is true is that in Jesus' pronouncements on heaven and afterlife recorded in the Gospels, he shows more than a touch of Essene influence. Generally, early Christian ideas about heaven broadly mirror the contemplative Essenes in that they are little concerned with the fate of Israel, or indeed with anything to do with this world, being almost exclusively focused on a personal experience of the divine be it compensation for whatever ills have befallen individuals in their earthly lives, or, more simply, anticipation of the promised all-consuming experience in death which will wipe out all that has gone before.

Christianity distanced itself from its Jewish inheritance, in that heaven was seen as being exclusively with God in the hereafter, with no ongoing ties to this world. Gradually, over the centuries, the new religion moved to rejecting the idea of a heaven on earth. God's kingdom, as far as Christianity was concerned, was elsewhere. The Gospels and epistles offer little by way of brochure details for those contemplating travel to this faraway heaven. In this they mirror their Jewish roots. What they do say is confused, woolly and sometimes downright contradictory. No iconic picture emerges. You take your pick of the options on offer – as indeed Christians have done ever after.

The New Testament gives the overall impression of regarding this particular aspect of eternal life as of little more than academic importance. Certainly there are few echoes of the detail-encrusted dreams of Enoch. Yet at the same time, Jesus and his followers operated within a society where the popularity of inter-testamental litera- ture demonstrates a healthy appetite for speculation about what life after death would be like. The Gospels report that Jesus was occasionally drawn into debates about the nature of heaven. Even in these, though, there is a vagueness, especially around the use of the phrases 'the kingdom of God' and 'the kingdom of heaven'. While the former carries with it the sense of an alterna- tive to secular and prevailing attitudes, and hence could exist on earth, it is also often used interchangeably with 'the kingdom of heaven' as a description of a better and separate place ruled over by God.

The confusion seems to revolve around two issues – first fudging the Jewish idea of a renewed earth under direct rule by God so as to embrace it in an all-inclusive picture of heaven; and second the fervent expectation of the second coming and how the early Christians dealt with the disappointment of those hopes. In Mark's Gos- pel, written supposedly by St Peter's interpreter and dated around AD 64, Jesus refers continually to the king- dom of God rather than of heaven. Yet fifteen years later, in Matthew's writing, when there still had been no second coming and the leaders of the fledgling Christian community were starting to scratch around for ways of explaining this away, there is a higher incidence of the expression 'the kingdom of heaven'. It postponed the day when Christianity's claims would be put to a public test.

In both Matthew and Mark there is an account of a discussion Jesus had with a group of Sadducees about the potential fate of a much-married widow in heaven. However, Luke's later account, said to be written around the same time as Matthew, is the fullest and most intriguing:

Some Sadducees – those who say that there is no resurrection – approached him [Jesus] and they put this question to him, 'Master, we have it from Moses in writing that if a man's married brother dies childless, the man must marry the widow to raise up children for his brother. Well then, there were seven brothers; the first, having married a wife, died childless. The second and then the third married the widow. And the same with all seven, they died leaving no children. Finally the woman herself died. Now, at the resurrection, to which of them will she be wife since she had been married to all seven?'

Jesus replied, 'The children of this world take wives and husbands, but those who are judged worthy of a place in the other world and in the resurrection from the dead do not marry because they can no longer die, for they are the same as angels, and being children of the resurrection they are sons of God. And Moses himself implies that the dead rise again, in the passage about the bush where he calls the Lord the God of Abraham, the

God of Isaac and the God of Jacob. Now he is God, not
of the dead, but of the living; for to him all men are in
fact alive.' (Luke 20:27–38)

By rejecting the Sadducees' question – which was
clearly a carefully baited trap – Jesus directly questioned
a whole barrowload of Jewish notions about the afterlife.
If the hereafter has no place for the recreation of earthly
relationships, then the time-honoured link with ancestors
(implicit in the command to raise your dead brother's
children and much treasured by the Sadducees) is of no
importance. Moreover, the breaking of that bond only
serves to emphasise Jesus' description of heaven as somewhere entirely other – not of this world, not concerned
with this world, and certainly not a recreation, however
cleaned up and diamond-clad; the standard view of the
apocalyptic writers. In effect he was saying, yes, there
was life after death, but not life as we know it.

By including that striking final sentence about the God
of the living, Jesus was moreover making an intriguing
proposal. Jewish theology assumed that, save for a tiny
number of favoured individuals, all others would have
to wait until the day of final judgement to get their exam
results and find out if they had gained their place with
God in heaven. Yet Jesus seemed to be saying that no
such delay was necessary. The three patriarchs he quoted
were not kicking their heels in sheol but were already
with God in heaven. If God is the God of the living, not
the dead, then the righteous dead will have already risen
to be fully alive with him. However, it would be dangerous to push this too far – for, given the confusion over
the kingdom of God and the kingdom of heaven, it may
simply be that Jesus was talking about those who followed God's commands while on earth being with him

already in spirit. In this hint of separating heaven from the day of judgement, and allowing for a fast track for entrants, rather than admission at one fell swoop come the last day, Jesus was creating a picture of heaven coexisting with earthly life that had hitherto been little known in Judaism.

Jesus' questioning of conventional wisdom on the afterlife was taken a step further by another passage in Luke's Gospel which contrasted the fate of a rich man and Lazarus, the beggar at his gates. Lazarus, covered with sores that dogs licked, was taken up to heaven by the Old Testament figure of Abraham. The rich man by contrast went to hell from where he looked up, saw Lazarus, and begged him to dip his finger in water to cool his tongue:

> 'My son,' Abraham replied, 'remember that during your life good things came your way, just as bad things came the way of Lazarus. Now he is being comforted here while you are in agony. But that is not all: between us and you a great gulf has been fixed, to stop anyone, if he wanted to, crossing from our side to yours, and to stop any crossing from your side to ours.'
>
> The rich man replied, 'Father, I beg you then to send Lazarus to my father's house since I have five brothers, to give them warning so that they do not come to this place of torment too.'
>
> 'They have Moses and the prophets,' said Abraham, 'let them listen to them.' (Luke 16:19–31)

This was another unambiguous rejection of any notion that the dead could communicate with the living, but in this story the reports of Jesus added more detail about heaven. Once you're in, you're in for ever, Abraham says.

By the same token, once you're consigned to hell, there's no way back into God's favour. It's all very final: there are two tracks for immortality and you can't switch midstream. Though the idea of judgement on the basis of what you have done in life was already well-established in Judaism, here Jesus was refining the criteria by which those judgements would be made. The poor, it seems, would enjoy positive discrimination while the rich would have to work doubly hard to earn their passage. Heaven's standards would not be, he was saying, the same as earth's.

Taken together, the two passages debunked another long-standing concept – that only a select few could attain heaven. Lazarus was there, along with the oft-married widow and her various spouses. At his crucifixion, Jesus also promised the thief who died next to him: 'Today you will be with me in paradise.' (Luke 23:43) Clearly this would be no exclusive club for the great and good with lesser mortals blackballed – quite the opposite, in fact. Whether it would take a literal, physical shape, however, Jesus didn't specify. In these accounts, he demonstrated almost no interest in the question of bodily resurrection – though his comments about heaven being entirely separate from this world would seem to show a coolness on the subject. Heaven for Jesus was only one thing – oneness with God. That oneness might be spiritual, mental, physical, or all three. He offered few clues, save in the vaguest of terms. According to John's Gospel, at the Last Supper Jesus promised his apostles life everlasting with the words 'there are many rooms in my father's house'. (John 14:2)

In reading the Gospels, it is tempting to see Jesus self-consciously setting out to influence and recast the Jewish canon on the afterlife. This may indeed have been the case, for he was certainly an iconoclast, but these accounts cannot be taken too literally. Jesus certainly did not write them. As documentation on his words and actions, they are at best second-hand. They may reflect the kernel of a central argument Jesus made, but more likely than not they give more of an insight into the particular preoccupations of individuals who were offering their own interpretation of what he reportedly said. The Gospels are, crudely put, not to be taken as gospel, but rather as evidence of a heated, ongoing debate within the leadership of the early church as it separated from Judaism. With regard to the afterlife, the last judgement, the immortal soul and the question of bodily resurrection, there were many conflicting threads to this debate – all of them owing something to Judaism and all of them presenting the next generation of Christians with a hazy, confused picture of heaven.

Alongside the words ascribed to Jesus must be considered those of St Paul. In his biography of Paul (*Paul: The Mind of the Apostle*), the historian and polemicist A. N. Wilson holds that it is impossible to underestimate the importance of this saint in shaping Christian thought. Jesus was, Wilson states bluntly, a minor 'Galilean exorcist' interested in Jewish matters and one of many messiahs who two thousand years ago attracted the attention of a people desperate for divine assistance in overthrowing their Roman overlords. The tiny cult that surrounded him after his death would, he says, have petered out like all the rest had it not attracted the attention of Paul of Tarsus who is, for Wilson, 'a richly imaginative but confused religious genius who was able to draw out a mythological and archetypical significance from the death of a Jewish hero'.

Wilson is certainly right to note how little Paul's writings owe to any recorded words or deeds of Jesus, save for the overriding inspiration of the image of the crucified Christ. Paul, a Greek-speaker, borrowed as liberally from Greco-Roman culture as from Judaism and as a missionary was always alert in fashioning his teachings to the need to create something that would have resonance in the Gentile world rather than simply satisfy an already fragmented Israel. In this sense, today's Christians are not Christians at all, but Paulians.

Another important factor in weighing Paul's writings is that most of them predate the Gospel accounts. His are the earliest records of the Jesus cult. Rather than see Paul as refining Jesus' message and words, as set out in the Gospels, it is more accurate to see the Gospel accounts as offering another take on stories that may have been in the oral tradition, and that may have been adopted as a counterpoint to Paul within the disharmonious and scattered early Church.

Paul differed from Jesus on several points about afterlife. Certainly there was nothing in Paul's writings that suggested that the dead would rise again with God before the last judgement, though Paul fervently believed that this event was near at hand. His view on resurrection came, as with all else in his writing, from the symbol of the risen Christ.

> We believe that Jesus died and rose again, and that it will be the same for those who have died in Jesus: God will bring them with him. We can tell you this from the Lord's own teaching, that any of us who are left alive until the Lord's coming will not have any advantage over those who have died. At the trumpet of God, the voice of the archangel will call out the command and the Lord

himself will come down from heaven; those who have died in Christ will be the first to rise, and then those of us who are still alive will be taken up in the clouds, together with them, to meet the Lord in the air. So we shall stay with the Lord for ever. (I Thess 4:14–17)

With no precise location of this heaven 'in the air' and 'in the clouds' mentioned elsewhere, Paul might well have been speaking metaphorically, but both the apostle and Jesus were utterly at one in emphasising the central importance of being with God in heaven and in dismissing Jewish hopes for an earthly messianic kingdom. From the perspective of earth, Paul wrote in one of his best-known phrases that we can only imagine meeting God as 'we see through a glass, darkly'. However, he gave the theocentric line an imaginative new gloss: God's kingdom, he argued, was already here in one form because Christ was everywhere where people worshipped him and praised him. (This interpretation may indeed be what the author of Luke is driving at when he has Jesus speak of the 'God of the living'.) Heaven, by contrast, would bear little resemblance to this life because, according to Paul, our resurrected bodies would not be our earthly ones.

For we know that when the tent that we live in on earth is folded up, there is a house built by God for us, an everlasting home not made by human hands, in the heavens. In this present state, it is true, we groan as we wait with longing to put on our heavenly home over the other; we should like to be found wearing clothes and not be without them. Yes, we groan and find it a burden being still in this tent, not that we want to strip it off, but to put on the second garment over it and to have

what must die taken up into life . . . we remember that
to live in the body means to be exiled from the Lord.
(2 Cor 5:1–7)

The Acts of the Apostles tells us that Paul was a tent-maker by trade, so the metaphor he uses is apt. The separation of body and soul was, as we have already seen, a distinctly Greek idea, especially in the hands of Plato, and Paul knew Greek as well as any of the early Christian leaders. His talk, of a 'spiritual body', however, was never precise or well-defined. And his insistence that 'flesh and blood cannot inherit the kingdom' (1 Cor 15:50) was strangely at odds with his focus on the image of the risen Christ – who ascended to heaven body and soul.

Indeed there is a good deal of confusion in Paul's writings, for two verses further on, he states that the dead would be raised 'imperishable . . . because our present perishable nature must put on imperishability'. This sounds suspiciously like bodily resurrection. Paul may have spoken Greek, have read Plato, and been influenced by him on the separation of body and soul, but he was also a Jew and Jews did not split up humanity in this fashion. Some argue that the distinction he was making was between 'flesh' (*sarx*), by which he meant the whole human being, body and soul, turned away from God, and 'spirit' (*pneuma*) the whole human being, body and soul, turned towards God.

'Conceivably, had Paul known about atoms and molecules,' writes E. P. Sanders, the American religious historian and admirer of Paul, 'he would have put all this in different terms. What he is affirming and denying is clear: resurrection means transformed body, not walking corpse or disembodied spirit. We can hardly criticise him for not being able to define "spiritual body" more clearly. His information on the topic was almost certainly derived entirely from his experience of encountering the risen Lord.'

In spiritual man, then, Paul could have been suggesting an entirely new kind of human being, for whom there were no adequate words, essentially a transcendent being. Such a radical thought could then be placed alongside Paul's habit of invoking other notions similarly revolutionary (for his time) – namely that there were no divisions between men and women, slave or freeman, Jew or Gentile.

The same might be said about the passage in his Second Letter to the Corinthians which links in closely with this line of thought. Here Paul wrote of a man (taken by many to be a thinly veiled reference to Paul himself) who 'was caught up into paradise' where he 'heard things which must not and cannot be put into human language' and therefore about which he refused to speak when he returned to earth. One approach would be to deduce that here Paul was offering an early hint of what came to be called 'Jewish Throne Mysticism'. This entailed an inward trip, rather like the Buddhist search for nirvana, but done in the form of a symbolic ascent to a place of greater knowledge undertaken within this life. Paul was then encountering heaven, or salvation, but doing so within himself in a mystical form, a theory not wholly inconsistent with the ideas found in the Paulian writing we have already looked at.

Mysticism has traditionally been a difficult concept for the monotheistic creeds to cope with because it cuts against their practical, naturalistic, action-reward philosophies and their taste for the literal. Yet it is ever-present in the history of heaven down the ages. Derived from the Greek verb *musteion*, meaning to close the eyes or mouth, mysticism generally refers to an experience of darkness or silence. It has been one of the main ways in which various religious traditions have attempted to explain the inner world of the psyche and the imagination in relation to a deity, and it has obvious parallels with modern-day psychoanalysis.

In the second and third centuries Judaism developed a strong and well-recorded mystical bent as a way of turning away from external realities of political persecution towards a more powerful internalised divine realm. This may already have been around in Paul's time. The throne of God in this strand of theology was approached via an often terrifying but explicitly imaginary, inward journey through seven heavens. Throne Mysticism thrived within Judaism and even inside the great rabbinic academies until it was overtaken by a new form of mysticism, Kabbalah, in the twelfth century. Karen Armstrong places it in a wider context which links Judaism with other belief systems.

> The visions are not ends in themselves, but means to an ineffable religious experience that exceeds normal concepts. They will be conditioned by the particular religious tradition of the mystic. A Jewish visionary will see visions of the seven heavens because his religious imagination is stocked with these particular symbols. Buddhists see various images of Buddhas ... Christians visualise the Virgin Mary. It is a mistake for the visionary to see these mental apparitions as objective or as anything more than a symbol of transcendence. Since hallucination is often a pathological state, considerable skill and mental balance is required to handle and interpret the symbols that

emerge during the course of concentrated meditation and inner reflection.

(from *A History of God*)

Hence, arguably, St Paul's reticence and refusal to go into detail. His experience had frightened him. However, the episode potentially offers a bridge between Judeo-Christian images of heaven and Eastern concepts of nirvana. Moreover, it brings monotheism and pantheism closer together. Islam too, as we shall see, had a similar tradition with Muhammad ascending symbolically to heaven where he saw and yet did not see the divine presence. That final lack of precision is key to identifying Throne Mysticism. The author must struggle but fail to find the right words, whether it be because they are unsure about what exactly they are seeing, or whether, like St Paul, they simply refuse to go into detail.

On another level, Jewish Throne Mysticism links the outward search for a blueprint of heaven with an acknowledgement that afterlife can only ever, for the living, be an imaginary thing, a type of contemplative experience. This is an important thought to keep in mind when examining the final book of the Bible, Revelation. The traditional view is that Revelation was written by the apostle John in the closing years of the first century, when he had been exiled to the Greek island of Patmos. As a source of inspiration to a Christian church then being persecuted by the Romans, he sent out a vision of the final victory of God to the seven churches of Asia. The basis of this judgement is not obvious from the text, religious scholars point out, and the only consensus is that the author was a person called John who considered himself called to be a prophet. Arguably the Bible's only thorough-going apocalyptic text, Revelation postdated both Paul and the Gospels, and its picture of heaven is clearly governed more by political realities of the time than by any pure or philosophical vision of paradise. Heaven is described in such a way as to cast a poor light on the fate of the late first-century Israel and to mark a stark contrast with the Roman world. If it was composed, as has been suggested, during the persecution of Domitian (AD 51–96), then the terrible fate of the damned towards the end of the book could be read as a quite unholy fantasy about what Christians would like to do to their persecutors if they ever got the chance.

The author of The Revelation to John recounts in classic apocalyptic style how a door was opened in heaven and an angel took him up to watch a heavenly liturgy. The spectacle is something of a cross between a tacky musical extravaganza, a freak show and a zoo, but it remains the most detailed – and the most quoted – of the Bible's very few descriptions of the place of eternal rest for the faithful. God presides at the centre of events in human form, seated on a throne:

> Round the throne in a circle were twenty four thrones, and on them I saw twenty-four elders sitting, dressed in white robes with golden crowns on their heads. Flashes of lightning were coming from the throne and the sound of peals of thunder, and in front of the throne were seven flaming lamps burning, the seven spirits of God. Between the throne and myself was a sea that seemed to be made of glass, like crystal. In the centre, grouped around the throne itself, were four animals with many eyes in front and behind. The first animal was like a lion, the second like a bull, the third animal had a human face and the fourth animal was like a flying eagle. Each of the four animals had six wings and had eyes all the way round

as well as inside; and day and night they never stopped singing. (Rev 4:1–8)

As part of the liturgy, the four horsemen of the apocalypse appeared and were sent to earth to wreak God's vengeance and dispense His judgement. There were, the author reported, a huge number of people in front of the throne who had been persecuted for faith. 'The one who sits on the throne will spread His tent over them,' the author writes, in what must be a direct reference to Paul. They would never go hungry or thirsty again. There would be no sun or wind to plague them because the Lamb who was at the throne would be their shepherd and lead them to the springs of living water where God would wipe away their tears.

The combination of the rituals of a secular court and a Christian liturgy is emphasised later in Revelation when the exact lay-out of heaven is given, based on a Jewish synagogue and the Temple itself. This new Jerusalem would be surrounded by high walls, with twelve gates, each watched over by a designated angel. It would be square in shape – 12,000 furlongs (1500 miles) long and 12,000 furlongs wide. The walls would be of diamonds (echoes of Enoch), and the city itself of pure gold that would have the appearance of polished glass. There would be no day or night – God would provide the light.

Any ambiguity about the new Jerusalem being real and concrete is abandoned by Revelation. It is self-consciously a work of imagination and dazzling imagery. Though it appears superficially to be endorsing the hopes of the Babylonian exiles in the Book of Isaiah, it is reinterpreting them, detaching heaven from this world and relocating it in the cosmos, albeit maintaining a symbolic link. So when the author writes of Jesus returning to

earth, banishing Satan and initiating one thousand years
of messianic rule (the biblical millennium which got fundamentalist Christians over-excited in 2000), he should
not be taken too literally. After this one thousand years
Satan's power would be much reduced but he would
still harry and mislead humankind. Finally, he would
begin a final futile attack by besieging 'the camp of the
saints which is the city that God loves. But fire will come
down on them from heaven and consume them'. In the
moment of God's ultimate triumph, the Book of Life
would be opened. Those named in it would be saved
and ascend to heaven, those not would be consigned to
the depths with Satan.

Frustratingly, once again this heaven of the clouds is
only partly described:

> Then the angel showed me the river of life, rising from
> the throne of God and of the Lamb and flowing crystal
> clear down the middle of the city street. On either side
> of the river were the trees of life, which bear twelve crops
> of fruit in a year, one in each month and the leaves of
> which are the cure for all nations. (Rev 22:1–3)

The references to the throne at the centre of events
suggests another possible reading – in line with Jewish
Throne Mysticism – that would make Revelation a very
dramatic vision of transcendence which exists behind
outwardly recognisable phenomena and which may
break out at the end of time. The author, in this scenario,
was trying to envisage poetically, with equal measures
of ecstasy and awfulness, the Second Coming and the
presence of God on earth.

Despite its drama, end-of-time flavour and position as
the eye-catching final act of the Bible cycle, Revelation

can in no way be counted as resolving all remaining unanswered questions, least of all those about a mental, imaginary or physical heaven. Despite the lack of a clear vision for Christianity on the subject throughout the New Testament, at least the parameters of the debate had been established. By taking bodily resurrection from Judaism and the immortal soul from the Greco-Roman tradition, Christianity had the makings of a distinctive position. As yet that paradise was overshadowed by the anticipation of an actual Second Coming. When this failed to materialise, and as the early Christians suffered persecution and death for their new-found faith at the hands of the Roman Empire and its pagan citizenry, the issue of eternal fate gradually came more and more to the fore in the debate and divisions of the early Church Fathers.

CHAPTER FOUR

The Compensation Culture

I n its first half-millennium, Christianity grew from
being a fringe cult in Galilee to multinational status
as the official religion of the Roman Empire. If its rise
was meteoric, it certainly wasn't smooth. There were
periods of intense persecution by the authorities, and
even after the Church had seemingly reached a safe har-
bour by joining forces with the Roman establishment in
AD 381, its problems were not all solved, for by AD 410
Rome itself was sacked by the Goths and the empire
crumbled in the West, posing the challenge of a period
of instability, decline and lawlessness.

Within the burgeoning Church community were many
rows and splits. Once the hope of an imminent Second
Coming, so tangible in the New Testament, had passed,
the leadership began to adjust to working with, and
explaining God's role in, an imperfect world. They had
to build a comprehensive theology to unite and bring
order to their Church, based on ideas, which were often
confused, passed down by the first generations of Christians. What ultimately emerged was certainly more
systematic, more enforceable, though often no more

coherent. In the case of heaven, this was the period in which the three distinct positions – theocentric, anthropocentric and a combination of both – emerged.

The names of three 'early Church Fathers' in particular dominate this era of consolidation, and they can mark for us the boundaries of the debate on the nature of heaven. These Church Fathers were not, as their designation suggests, a static group of theologians stooped endlessly over their Bibles. Indeed, there was as yet no Bible as we now know it (this was completed by Jerome, in *c.* AD 404). They were not only theologians, but administrators, builders, guides, preachers and proselytisers. The first of these remarkable men is Irenaeus of Lyons (*c.* AD 130–*c.* 202), who, as a youth in Smyrna in Asia Minor, trained under Bishop Polycarp. Irenaeus later claimed that his mentor had 'known John and others who had seen the Lord'. Details of Polycarp's martyrdom are amongst the earliest recorded to have survived, and they give an insight into the persecution that the early Church routinely endured. Challenged by the Roman pro-consul in Smyrna to disown Christ, he refused and was burnt alive in 155. 'The flames made a sort of arch, like a ship's sail filled with wind, and they were like a wall around the martyr's body; and he looked, not like burning flesh, but like bread in the oven or gold and silver being refined in the furnace.' (*Ancient Christian Writers Series*, Vol. 6)

Martyrdom was a recurring theme of Irenaeus's life. After escaping the persecution in Smyrna by travelling to Rome, he later pitched up in Lyons, then a major trading station, second in size in the West only to the imperial capital itself. Its mixed community had sporadic bursts of intolerance, and in a series of flare-ups between 175 and 177 local Christians were targeted and killed by the mob, with the connivance of the local Roman governor. Irenaeus survived, succeeding the murdered Bishop Pothinus as Christian leader in the city. Pothinus's sufferings are recorded in Eusebius's early fourth-century *History of the Church* and clearly illustrate the trials the early Christians faced and the pressing need Irenaeus consequently felt to console his congregation with the hope of eternal life with God.

> Blessed Pothinus was over ninety years of age and physically very weak. He could scarcely breathe because of his chronic physical weakness, but was strengthened by spiritual enthusiasm because of his pressing desire for martyrdom. Even when he was dragged before the tribunal . . . and the whole populace shouted and jeered at him . . . he bore the noble witness. When the governor asked him 'Who is the Christians' God?', he replied: 'If you were a fit person, you shall know.' Thereupon he was mercilessly dragged along beneath a rain of blows, those close by assailing him viciously with hands and feet, and those at a distance hurling at him whatever came to hand, and all thinking it a shocking neglect of their duty to be behind-hand in savagery towards him, for they imagined that in this way they would avenge their gods. Scarcely breathing, he was flung into prison, and two days later he passed away.
>
> (*Eusebius: History of the Church*, edited by
> Andrew Louth)

Pothinus was one of the earliest saints of the church. His feast day, 2 June, marks the day not of his birth but of his death – for that, it was believed, was the time of his birth in heaven. This gives us an insight into how the first Christians regarded death at the hands of their tormentors, and the particular appeal it must have had for some as a sure-fire ticket to eternal life with God. Martyrdom was seen as a magnificent catapult to a heavenly place. Moreover, it was believed that the sacrifice of the martyrs would hasten the Second Coming, for their enemies were seen in these apocalyptic times not just as lions and gladiators, but as embodiments of the Devil. The corollary of doing battle with Satan was safe passage to heaven, as can be seen in *The Passion of Perpetua*, reputedly the autobiography of a young mother torn limb from limb by wild beasts in Carthage in 203 on account of her faith. While still in prison awaiting her fate, Perpetua dreamt of fighting Satan – in the form of 'an evil-looking Egyptian'. She also ascended in her imagination to heaven on a golden ladder.

> I saw a garden of immense extent in the midst of which was sitting a white-haired man dressed as a shepherd; he was tall, and he was milking sheep. And he raised his head and looked at me and said 'Welcome, child.' And he called me and gave me a mouthful of cheese from the sheep he was milking; and I took it with my hands and ate of it, and all those who were standing about said 'Amen.' And then I woke up.
>
> (translated by J. Armitage Robinson)

This is classic vision-literature and the symbolism of the eternal reward should outweigh any temptation to draw a literal interpretation, but Perpetua's account, as well as highlighting the attraction of martyrdom, also demonstrates the ongoing and widening (in terms of the details summoned up) tendency to imaginatively explore the landscape of heaven.

Back in Lyons, there were more practical problems

Fly me to the moon: a sixteenth-century Islamic image of the prophet Muhammad, his countenance veiled, and the angel, Jibril, Allah's messenger, as they travel through the night to paradise on a mystical white beast, with other angels in attendance.

Holy Trinity: three of the most influential figures in the Christian canon on heaven: Saint Augustine (354–430) *right*, pictured with his mother, Saint Monica, in a garden in Ostia as together they make a mystical ascent to heaven; Hildegard of Bingen (1098–1179) *below*, a medieval mystic whose vision of heaven was to be consumed by God; and Thomas Aquinas (1225–74) *below right*, the leading Scholastic thinker, who plotted paradise with great precision.

HILDEGARDIS a Virgin Prophetess, Abbess of S.t Ruperts Nunnerye. She died at Bingen A.° Do.i 1190 Aged 82 yeares.

Reach for the sky: the building of Chartres Cathedral, the masterpiece of twelfth-century early Gothic style, with its elaborately carved exterior and huge, dark, high interior, pierced by rays of light from stained glass windows, was the equivalent to the medieval mind of constructing a heaven on earth, somewhere so far removed from everyday existence and squalor that it literally transported you to paradise.

Party food: one type of heaven, to the medieval mind, was a place where you could make good the deficiencies of everyday life. Since food was short, you would dream of the land of Cockaigne, somewhere you could eat until you burst, as depicted by Pieter Bruegel the Elder in 1567.

Body beautiful: Luca Signorelli's early sixteenth-century frescoes in the Cappella di San Brizio in Orvieto Cathedral are based on the writings of Dante, a portrait of whom Signorelli included in his design (*right*). The Coronation of the Elect, the first level of a three-tier heaven, shows a very human, uninhibited environment where men and women are equal and where some, seen holding hands, appear to recreate their earthly links.

The tunnel: the idea of a tunnel leading from the earth to heaven has been part of the geography of paradise from medieval times up to the present day, where it features in descriptions of Near Death Experiences. Here Hieronymus Bosch (1450–1516) in *Ascent into the Empyrean*, in the Dogue's Palace in Venice, shows the newly departed floating upwards to meet their maker.

confronting Irenaeus. Christians there had been burnt alive by their persecutors who then threw their ashes into the Rhone in a calculated riposte to what they clearly saw as the foolish and even dangerous idea of bodily resurrection. As a gesture, it had great impact. The destruction of the body by flames and the scattering of mortal remains prompted fears amongst the survivors that such treatment left their loved ones with no hope of heaven come judgement day. (Catholicism for this very reason remained opposed to cremation until the late twentieth century.) Irenaeus's response was to calm such fears and, in the process, fashion a theology of heaven which presented it explicitly as the reward for indignities suffered in God's name on this earth. A decent reward, if it was to have the desired effect, needed to be specific, so Irenaeus spoke not in vague, imaginary tones but in tangible terms of a cleaned-up version of this life.

In making an explicit link between martyrdom and a well-defined reward in heaven, Irenaeus may have taken his cue from the many pagan religions which were still strong throughout northern Europe in this period. If the martyrs were seen as warriors for the Christian cause, then there was a clear parallel with the warriors of the Teutonic mythological system, which continued to dominate on the German plane and in Scandinavia. It taught that those who lost their lives in battle for their gods would enjoy eternal life in Valhalla, a great palace presided over by Odin, the god of war and wisdom. Valhalla was a martial heaven, its rafters made of spears and its roof of polished shields. It had 540 doors, each wide enough to accommodate 800 warriors marching abreast into battle with the devil-like Fenrir and the powers of the underworld. When they were not fighting, the warriors were singing battle songs, recalling great generals, feasting on a magic boar, Saehrimnir, and drinking the mead of the she-goat, Heidrum, served to them by valkyries, armour-clad maidens who were at their disposal. Physically far removed from any Christian notion of heaven, Valhalla's importance was more psychological than physical, an example to Irenaeus with a proven track record of how to use a tangible afterlife to inspire his troops in what was, in these times of persecution, a fight to the death for their faith.

The world itself was not flawed, Irenaeus taught. It had been, and remained, God's creation. The problem was the Romans. His road map of heaven removed them from the picture, along with all other tormentors and sources of grief, but left the basic terrain as it was on earth. Often described as the greatest theologian of the second century, Irenaeus decanted much of his thinking into *Against Heresies* which survives complete in a Latin translation. It details a three-stage plan of eternal life, one following the other: the here and now, the Kingdom of the Messiah, and the Kingdom of God the Father.

In the present, there was persecution, brutality and a time of trial, but that was created by man and not by God. Principally, it was the Romans and their pagan allies who were at fault, but on a more philosophical level, Irenaeus identified original sin, the betrayal of God's creation by Adam and Eve in the Garden of Eden, as having left all of humankind with an openness to choose evil over good in this life.

As a counterbalance to this persecution, Irenaeus then allowed for a world stripped of such negative influences – the Kingdom of the Messiah. This was the equivalent of the thousand-year rule of the Messiah over the earth predicted in Revelation – which historians suggest was a Christian text far more important to apocalyptic minds in the second century than the Gospels – and Irenaeus was again keen to stress to his readers that such passages should be taken literally, not as some sort of metaphor. In his reading of Revelation, Irenaeus found an explanation for the delay in the Second Coming. For first, the book predicted, there must be a battle between good and evil on earth. The struggle of the Christians with their Roman persecutors was, for Irenaeus, just that. The many martyrs were therefore the preface to a second coming and the establishment of a messianic kingdom. 'For it is just,' he wrote in *Against Heresies*, 'that in the very creation in which they toiled or were afflicted, being proved in every way of suffering, they should receive the reward of their suffering. In the creation in which they were slain because of their love of God, in that they should be revived again.'

In this heaven on earth, the martyrs would be among the elite; women would be endlessly fertile, sickness abolished, wine and grain free-flowing, and work unnecessary. Original sin would be banished and there would be no old age and, of course, no death. In short, human beings would become akin to gods – Jesus Christ 'became as we are that we might become as he is'.

This heaven of the early Church was fashioned with reference to ideas of order, government and power. It was often too, by association, an urban place – far removed from the imagery of a garden favoured by Virgil. This preference had three roots, two of them interconnected – the first being the powerful image of the new Jerusalem used by the Book of Revelation, and the second (which may indeed have led to that enthusiasm for the new Jerusalem by the writer of Revelation) the fact that Christians at this time were very largely concentrated in urban areas. In the country, older pagan practices were to be much more resistant to change. And the third was that any effort to imagine a heaven which would symbolise the ultimate power naturally took its model from the Roman system which favoured a very urban structure of authority. Augustine was later to place his seal on this notion when he penned *The City of God*.

Irenaeus was a convinced millennarian. So, as the final stage in his triptych, he taught that after a thousand years, this earthly paradise would be succeeded by the spiritual Kingdom of God the Father. This third age, however, was not extensively detailed. It was enough that those who believed 'shall see God, that they may live, being made immortal by the sight', he wrote in *Against Heresies*. Their final destination would be somewhere, to quote St Paul (1 Cor 2:9) 'which neither the eye has seen, nor the ear has heard, nor has thought concerning them arisen within the heart of man'. Irenaeus was not going to chance his arm by attempting to describe it, especially since his avowed purpose in writing was to offer immediate hope to those facing martyrdom in the form of a post-mortem reward or compensation for their sacrifice. What would happen a thousand years down the line, seen in the context of a situation where Christians were being killed daily, must have seemed of only academic interest. It was enough that the Kingdom of God the Father was mentioned, to reconcile Irenaeus's teaching with the tradition of the scriptures and, most importantly, with the final chapters of Revelation.

There was, however, more to *Against Heresies* than simply a rallying cry to potential martyrs. Irenaeus had in his sights a particular group within the expanding Church – the Gnostics. The term Gnosticism, based on the Greek word *gnosis*, meaning knowledge, is used by historians in many contexts. As Paul Johnson remarks in his *History of Christianity*, 'No-one has yet succeeded in defining "Gnosticism" adequately, or indeed demonstrating whether this movement preceded Christianity or grew from it.' There were, in fact, two separate phenomena – a widespread spiritual and philosophical movement known as Gnosticism, which may predate Christ but which certainly existed in his time and afterwards, and a substantial minority within the emerging Christian Church who took on board broadly Gnostic ideas. It was this second group that Irenaeus was targeting.

Their belief was that this world was irredeemably evil. Their reaction to the persecution of the early Church was to reject not just the Romans but also the earth and earthly bodies, as the creation of the Devil, and therefore an equal and opposing force to God. Only the spirit, coming from the invisible world of light, i.e. heaven, was good. Gnosticism was a deeply pessimistic credo and its adherents distanced themselves from all social conventions and rejected all temporal authority. They positively courted death as the prelude to something better and more godly. Their introspection, Irenaeus believed, would bring the Church to fragmentation and ruin. Yet he could also appreciate the appeal Gnosticism held for a persecuted Christian community. Hence his very tangible heaven on earth was in direct contrast to the Gnostics' dreams of a shapeless, spiritual at-oneness with God in the afterlife world they believed He had created.

Subsequent writers, such as Lactantius (260–330), took up Irenaeus's portrait of an earthbound heaven, and added their own touches. Lactantius is credited with introducing the palm tree into heaven, associating it with the Roman palm of victory and the palms that were spread out before Jesus as he triumphantly entered Jerusalem on a donkey just a week before his crucifixion. More significant, Lactantius was one of a number of writers who conceded that Jews who had remained faithful to the Old Covenant, before Jesus had instituted the second, might also attain paradise. However, those who had seen but rejected Jesus were excluded, along with pagans and sinful Christians.

Other writers were even more generous. Tertullian (*c.* 160–225), who wrote the first Latin book about heaven, entitled *About Paradise* (but which is now lost), was one of several who argued that the virtuous pagan might be saved, especially if they had not had the chance to hear the word of God. In keeping with Irenaeus's special concern for martyrs, Tertullian held that such figures would go straight to heaven, entered through a purging layer of fire, while all other candidates would have to wait until Judgement Day. Tertullian used the term *refrigerium interim* (roughly, an 'interim coolness') to denote this state of waiting – one which would be followed by fire, a reheating if you like – but he later refined this to the more inviting concept of resting 'in the bosom of Abraham'. It was this interim state that later was to develop into purgatory, though for Tertullian it was not a trial, but rather a time of joy, save for the absence of the body.

Cyprian, the first African bishop, who was martyred in 258, was another to make a distinctive contribution to the 'heavenscape' by urging his followers to live chaste lives. If they did, he said, they could aspire to join the angels who had figured so prominently in apocalyptic literature at God's right hand. 'While you remain chaste and virgins, you are equal to the angels of God,' he wrote. Ambrose, fourth-century Bishop of Milan, agreed in his treatise, *About Paradise*: 'For chastity,' he noted, 'has made even angels. He who has preserved it is an angel; he who has lost it is a devil.' Heaven and hell were being visited on earth. More significantly, in promoting heaven as a place of sexual renunciation, the Church Fathers were once again setting it up in direct contrast to most people's lives on earth. Greco-Roman society set a high store by sexual freedom. Sex was regarded as being on a par with eating and sleeping. The Greeks even called the penis 'the necessity'. However, unlike previous attempts to depict heaven as a place where all the ills of this world were banished, the Church Fathers were this time taking away something no doubt considered by many to be one of life's pleasures. 'In a world where individuals seemingly had little control over how their lives unfolded,' writes Elizabeth Abbott, 'the human body seemed the one place they could exercise free choice ... If Christians could harness their sexual urges and maintain lives built on chastity and a new way of living, they would be living proof of the end of an age.' (from *A History of Celibacy*)

No longer was the Second Coming something to wait for patiently; it could be hastened either by martyrdom or by your own efforts at self-denial. However, the second key figure of this period, Origen (*c.* 185–*c.* 254), favoured a different approach which emphasised emerging Christianity's debt to Plato. As a young man, Origen had sought to die alongside his father, one of the early Church martyrs, but his mother had saved his life by hiding his clothes. Later, he turned from such a violent renunciation of this world towards a theology that emphasised the continuity of God – rather than heaven – with the world. All of humanity, Origen argued, has a natural and in-built desire to seek God. By a highly allegorical reading of the Bible Origen took the Virgin Birth as the birth of divine wisdom, *Logos*, in the soul. Thereafter, each individual was on a journey towards union with *Logos* and that long, slow ascent encompassed death and the abandonment of all bodily things (including the incarnate Jesus, a view which later led to Origen being declared a heretic) until the soul finally became pure spirit. In imitation of how things had been before the Fall, there would be a growing knowledge of God that ultimately would bring the soul itself divinity. God was beyond any human imaginings, but the soul, when liberated from the body, which was little more than its temporary carrier on the trek back to God, had the capacity to attain divine nature. As a demonstration of his own disregard for all things bodily, Origen underwent an operation that castrated him.

Origen followed Plato in believing that knowledge, and the individual's striving after that knowledge, was the key to salvation, not Jesus' sacrifice on the cross. This intellectual heaven was enough to put him out of step with his contemporaries and with subsequent Church teaching which came increasingly to reject overt Greek influence. Moreover, his uninhibited use of allegory and symbolism in regard to afterlife made him a controversial and often despised figure for many centuries, though, of course, his views fit much more comfortably with religious teachings in our own times. His sidelining of any literal view of heaven and his concentration on God alone became deeply unfashionable, though the concept of the soul seeking union with the divine against a blank and irrelevant backdrop lived on as part of the mystical tradition that upheld a theocentric afterlife.

*   *   *

Once the Emperor Constantine had formally acknowledged Christianity as one of the religions of the Roman Empire in 313, the age of the martyrs was effectively at an end. Dying for your faith was no longer an everyday possibility, and so the consolation of Irenaeus's heavenly messianic kingdom on earth necessarily lost much of its glitter.

The century of peace that followed gave zealots within the newly recognised Church the luxury of developing alternative models to martyrdom to cement their closeness to their maker. The favourite option to emerge was to flamboyantly reject the worldly trappings of success and excess which characterised a declining empire by attempting to live a pared-down, aesthetic existence on the earth in the manner of the Essenes. The ideal was to join one of the new monastic communities which were a feature of this era, but whether within a monastery or outside it, men and women were urged to concentrate on prayer and contemplation of God; a fitting preparation, it was believed, for what was awaiting them after death. Without persecutors, the faithful, then, were still being urged to put themselves through the mill physically in order to earn God's eternal favour in heaven. The difference being that the punishment was self-inflicted. Moreover, the emphasis had changed – from heaven being in stark contrast to earth, and by way of compensation for it, to earth and heaven now merging seamlessly.

The ascetic movement – from the Greek *askesis*, meaning training or discipline – was a powerful one within the church at the start of the fourth century. Human strategies were developed for spiritual living in this world – and by association for enjoying the beatific vision in the next. The best-known advocate of this philosophy is

St Augustine, our third key figure. Born in 354 into a pious home in what is now Algeria – his mother Monica was subsequently also declared a saint – Augustine at first rebelled against his upbringing and lived what he later came to see as an appallingly dissolute life. He then became involved with a pagan cult – Manichaeism, which took its name from its founder, Mani, and which was Gnostic-influenced but reserving its greatest approbation for the body and flesh – before his mother followed him to Italy where she tried to take him in hand. In 386, she persuaded him to leave his mistress and son. The following year he was baptised as a Christian.

It was soon afterwards, while staying with his mother at a villa at Ostia, then the sea-port of Rome, that, according to his autobiographical *Confessions*, mother and son shared an ecstatic vision that links Augustine with Jewish Throne Mysticism. It developed out of a discussion they were having as they leaned out of a window and surveyed the garden:

> The conversation led us towards the conclusion that the pleasure of the bodily senses, however delightful in the radiant light of this physical world, is seen in comparison with the life of eternity to be not worth considering. Our minds were lifted up by an ardent affection towards the eternal being itself. Step-by-step we climbed beyond all corporeal objects and the heaven itself, where sun, moon and stars shed light on the earth. We ascended even further by internal reflection and dialogue and wonder at your works, and we entered into our own minds. We moved up beyond them so as to attain to the region of inexhaustible abundance where you feed Israel eternally with truth for food.
>
> There life is the wisdom by which all creatures come

into being, both things which were and which will be. But wisdom itself is not brought into being but is as it was and always will be. Furthermore, in this wisdom there is no past or future, but only being, since it is eternal. For to exist in the past or in the future is no property of the eternal. And while we talked and panted after it, we touched it in some small degree by a moment of total concentration of the heart. And we sighed and left behind us the first fruits of the Spirit, bound to that higher world, as we returned to the noise of our human speech where a sentence has both a beginning and an ending.

Therefore we said: if to anyone the tumult of the flesh has fallen silent, if the images of earth, water and air are quiescent, if the heavens themselves are shut out and the very soul itself is making no sound and is surpassing itself by no longer thinking about itself, if all dreams and visions in the imagination are excluded, if all language and every sign and everything that is transitory is silent – for if anyone could hear them, this is what all of them would be saying, 'We did not make ourselves, we were made by him who abides for eternity' (Ps 79:3–5)* . . . That is how it was when at that moment we extended our reach and in a flash of mental energy attained the eternal wisdom which abides beyond all things. (*Confessions* IX: 24–25)

Eternal wisdom which abides beyond all things excludes at a stroke any effort to see this as a naturalistic journey to some external heaven. The description of the episode as something that happened to Augustine and his

---

* [sic] Henry Chadwick, in his translation, notes that Augustine often gets the numbers wrong.

mother – 'our minds were lifted' – rather than something they initiated points to a mental ascent to a reality within. It might almost be that he is describing the consequence of certain techniques of concentration. And in Augustine's inability to describe the God that he and his mother encounter is a further link to the Jewish mystics.

For Monica, it was the immediate preface to her own death. She could, as her son recounts, now find 'no pleasure in this life' and five days later fell ill and passed away. Her grave was uncovered many centuries later amid the rubble that is now Ostia Antica. For Augustine, the vision led him to describe heaven in mystical terms as a shapeless domain of the spirit, a place of self-knowledge and timelessness that was beyond words. Augustine was well-aware of Gnostic openness, in rejecting this world, to a mystical experience of sacredness in the depths of the self. Here, it could be argued, he was attempting to integrate it with the ascetic lifestyle he promoted on earth into a powerful vision of the divine that stood in direct counterpoint to the images of the bricks-and-mortar heaven on earth that Irenaeus had drawn up.

Augustine did have a propensity to change his mind as often as he changed his sexual proclivities. Appointed as bishop of his native Carthage in 396, he was forced to turn his back on renunciation of this life and mystical contemplation of God and to confront more practical questions. In 410 the Goths sacked Rome and the existing imperial social order all but collapsed. Faced by such a calamity, Augustine felt obliged to say something to inspire and sustain Christian life in this insecure and frightening new world and so, over the next fifteen years, he produced the twenty-two books that make up his powerful evocation of a much more literal heaven, *City of God*.

'Augustine wrote [this text], at a first level, to dethrone the idea of Rome from its place in people's minds,' says his biographer, Garry Wills. 'It was never the city that could satisfy human hearts. Only the City of God can do that.' At an immediate level, Augustine was debunking the description in Virgil's *Aeneid* of the gods creating Rome as a place of divine justice. Only the City of God, he said, could be such a place. By association, in taking up the urban metaphor of the new Jerusalem, Augustine was also discrediting it. No earthly city could be cleaned up by a messiah, he suggested. The City of God was somewhere entirely other and had a permanence that no political capital could ever achieve.

His characterisation of heaven as a city meant that it was no longer the blank landscape of his earlier vision. Moreover, Augustine now described heaven as a community of high and low, of the great (the saints and martyrs) and all those who led good lives and resisted the blandishments of the Devil who, Augustine was sure, lurked around every corner. It was an ordered, civic society, but still had a mystical dimension. What united its inhabitants was the vision of God Himself. 'Augustine distinguished between knowing and seeing,' writes the historian Jeffrey Burton Russell in his *History of Heaven*. 'We cannot know God in Himself, but we can in some way see Him ... Our earthly eyes see God only darkly through a mirror, but our resurrected eyes will have an unmediated ability to see God just as the mind will have an unmediated ability to understand Him. This power in our resurrected eyes and mind is a spiritual power, a miracle. The beatific vision is a grace given to the deepest part of the personality, which enables us to find our true selves in God.' Vision, in this scenario, becomes an active force.

Yet if Augustine was rejecting the proposition of a messianic kingdom on earth, to be jump-started by the Second Coming, he had much to say about the fate of those who had died and were awaiting judgement day for their entry into heaven. Augustine softened this time lapse that has its clearest advocate in the Book of Revelation by suggesting that the souls of those who are saved are judged at once on death and either go up or down. For those who go up to heaven, however, enjoyment of their good fortune is tempered by the absence of their resurrected body which will only come once the Devil's defeat is final and eternal.

In heaven, Augustine promised in *City of God*, once Satan had been finally defeated, there would be an eighth day of creation when 'we shall rest and see, see and love, love and praise. This is what shall be in the end without end.' The symbolic link back to the Garden of Eden – created by God in seven days and then destroyed by Adam and Eve's sin – was clear. Its first custodians had exercised free will to their cost, and that ability to sin or to choose the Devil over God in life would, Augustine predicted, have no more place in heaven. God's nature, as revealed to the chosen in heaven, is such that it is impossible to choose to sin again. But here on earth, we are, because of free will, able to accept or reject the promise of salvation in heaven.

For all his talk of the soul Augustine now anticipated a heaven with risen bodies. The distance he had travelled from his vision in Ostia was great. In *City of God*, he foretold that heavenly bodies would be 'of that size which [they] either had attained or should have attained in the flower of youth', that they would be in proportion, and possess 'a certain agreeableness of colour', and that no-one would fart because under God's gaze even bowels would be beautiful. Only the martyrs would carry blemishes – as a sign of their earthly sacrifice and of their special place in celestial society. There would be no sex at all – but here Augustine was simply echoing the early Church Fathers and, indeed, Jesus, who held that there was no marriage in heaven (Mk 12:25). With his own trademark obsession with the wicked lure of female flesh, Augustine pondered long and hard in *City of God* on whether women would have breasts. Were Adam and Eve not naked in the perfect state of the Garden of Eden?

> So all defects will be taken away from those bodies, but their natural state will be preserved. The female sex is not a defect, but a natural state, which will then know no intercourse or childbirth. There will be female parts, not suited to their old use, but to a new beauty, and this will not arouse the lust of the beholder, for there will be no lust, but it will inspire praise of the wisdom and goodness of God, who both created what was not and freed from corruption what he made.

As he grew older, the same Augustine who had once been so dismissive of the body became ever more fascinated by its simple functions. This may just have been a product of age – Augustine died in 430 at the then great age of seventy-six. But the ambiguity in Augustine's thoughts on heaven is more than simply the ramblings of an old man. In *City of God*, he explicitly ruled out the recreation of family ties and household bonds in heaven. There would be, to borrow a phrase from later generations of religious institutions, no special friendships but equally no strangers. Though there were manifestly to be relationships between those in heaven, Augustine's picture was of a world dominated by the spirit and centred on the all-embracing relationship with God. Hence he had ruled out the anthropocentric position. Yet in 408, he was writing to Italica, a wealthy Roman widow:

> You should not grieve as the heathen do who have no hope. We have not lost our dear ones who have departed from this life, but have merely sent them ahead of us, so we also shall depart and shall come to that life where they will be more than ever dear as they will be better known to us, and where we shall love them without fear of parting.
>
> (*Saint Augustine's Letters*, edited by Robert Enno)

Heaven then was not just about the bond with God. There was an overlap with this world. Italica would meet her husband again, a promise reinforced by Augustine's acceptance of Irenaeus's assertion that those in heaven would remember their past life and their sins. In later life, Augustine looked forward to lunching in heaven with his old friends. Perhaps he was offering comfort to a woman in the terms in which he knew she would want to hear it; his words to Italica may have been prompted by a desire to see his own beloved mother again (the novelist Rebecca West once rebuked Monica for stopping her son ever becoming a man: 'Evidently Christianity need not mean emasculation, but the long struggle of Augustine and Monica simply [meant] that in her case it did.'); or Augustine may simply have been attempting to build a bridge between that internalised spiritual map of afterlife he had seen at Ostia and the more physical place called heaven favoured by many Christians of the time.

Apocryphal texts from this era – such as the *Ascension of Isaiah* – adopted the familiar approach of reporting a dream-like journey upwards to a garden or meadow of brilliant light where those who had died recreated earthly relationships, though always in a world dominated by the saints and martyrs. While the Church Fathers did not encourage such exercises in fantasy, they were popular with the minority of Christians who could read.

As a model for the eventual reconstituting of families, the togetherness in heaven of Christ and his mother was an increasingly regular motif in this period. In the third-century *Gospel of Bartholomew*, Mary's ascent body and soul into heaven to be with her son (only confirmed by papal decree into Catholic doctrine in 1950) is hinted at, and by the sixth century, it had become so accepted that it was marked in the Church's calendar by its own feast day, 15 August. Pictorial images of Christian ideas became common from the fourth century onwards – with persecution by Rome removed – and icons started to appear of Christ and Mary in heaven, in the company of the angels and saints. For largely illiterate populations, these conveyed more about heaven than any theological debate could. Complex ideas were boiled down to simple symbols. Heaven as a mystical place of radiant light was reduced to something much more crude and led to first Christ, then Mary, the angels and saints, being painted with haloes.

Taken from the Latin word for clouds, haloes were, for an illiterate audience, the unmistakable badge of a leading citizen of heaven. They were not, however, a Christian invention: in Mesopotamian seals, dating back to 3000 BC, similar rings can be seen hovering above the heads of god-kings, and the Greeks often depicted Apollo with similar millinery.

The haloes the early Christian artists employed originally had specific shapes – God the Father was allotted a triangular one, Jesus a cross-shaped one, and Mary, the saints and angels were allotted circles. If living people were included in a vision of heaven – possibly a visitor in a dream-like sequence – they would be given a square halo, the equivalent of a temporary pass. Gradually such distinctions, whose origins are obscure, were abandoned and the circle became ubiquitous, though it slipped from view during the Renaissance when artists were keen to emphasise the human joys of heaven over its divine consolations.

The Renaissance naturalists also did away with other traditional decorations of heaven, such as auredes, glories and mandorlas, which were seen from the fifth century onwards – there are some excellent examples in the church of Santa Maria Maggiore in Rome – when depicting the Holy Trinity or the Virgin. The aurede was a solid dish of light, with defined edges, behind or above the head; the glory was, by contrast, more of a burst of light-rays; while the mandorla was a kind of vehicle of ascension – a plaque usually seen behind the whole of Mary's body, which seemed to be supporting and lifting her upwards to the clouds.

Augustine's change of heart is profoundly symbolic for a changing attitude within Christianity towards afterlife. The switch from the exaltation of his mystical experience at Ostia to his later musings on whether or not women had breasts in heaven and whom he'd have lunch with illustrates quite how literally Christians now perceived life after death. And, it might be added, quite how banal their concept was. The theology of the afterlife was exchanging a challenging but potentially enriching spirituality for a mundane and dreary practicality. The difference is rather like contemplating Queen Elizabeth II and concentrating on whether, like the rest of us, she makes her own cup of tea at breakfast rather than considering the political, constitutional and symbolic importance of the monarchy.

While the mystical tradition had not been lost for ever, it became an undercurrent in a church where the mainstream sidelined any hint that concepts such as heaven might be myths or symbols by which a deeper but unfathomable truth might be approached. The official line was that they had to be taken literally.

CHAPTER FIVE

Fly Me to the Moon

Muhammad ibn Abdallah (570–632) was an Arab businessman, trading in skins and raisins in and around Mecca. He was also a devout man and every year he would retire to a cave on the summit of Mount Hira, just outside the city, to pray and fast. In 610, he experienced such a powerful vision while in that cave that he came back a changed man. Two years later, it inspired him to begin to preach publicly and in the process he founded Islam. Its tradition teaches that Muhammad was visited that night in the cave by the angel Jibril (Gabriel), a messenger from Allah, the highest god in the pantheon worshipped by his tribe, the Quraysh. Muhammad was told to recite, and when he did he heard pouring from his lips the first words of a new Arabic scripture. This was to become the Qur'an, laid down by Allah and dictated over the next twenty-one years verse by verse to Muhammad from a perfect copy kept in *djanna*, the garden paradise that is Islamic heaven.

Muhammad's teaching about Allah was not radically different in its main points from existing ideas amongst the Quraysh. Many already saw Allah as the creator of the world and some expected that He would judge them in the last days. Muhammad's monotheistic focus was much stronger and more exclusive than had existed before, but the influence of Judaism and Christianity, with their insistence on a single, omnipotent God, had already infiltrated thinking in the region. Indeed, many of the first batch of converts were won over not by the radical content of the Qur'an, but by its sheer beauty, giving voice to their deepest yearnings and inspiring them, at all levels, to reassess their lives.

Islam literally means surrender, and those who followed it were surrendering their entire beings to Allah and His principal concern, as passed on via Muhammad, for justice and equity. It was first and foremost a powerful social gospel (rather like Jesus' teachings as set out in the Gospel accounts), centred on the supreme importance of the community (*ummah*) and of practical compassion. Theological speculation about abstract ideas – into which category heaven might be placed – was not dealt with at any length in the Qur'an and could arguably fall into the category of what it describes as *zannah*, self-indulgent whimsy. Allah could, after all, be experienced in daily life by building a strong community. Why make Him an abstraction or relegate Him to another place?

Muhammad did, however, place great stress on the Last Judgement and consequently also concerned himself with what would come afterwards for those judged favourably. Like most monotheists who thought in similar terms of last days, he saw the need for a heaven where the all-powerful God could be experienced by the faithful beyond this life as well as in it. The promise of resurrection – *qiyama* – runs explicitly through the Qur'an and is open to all who have embraced Allah's wisdom. Those who have not will be annihilated. At the moment of resurrection, it is foretold, Allah will personally retrieve the bodies of the dead and join them to their respective spirits. Angels will lead the faithful across a bridge – an image which may have been borrowed from Zoroastrianism – spanning a void. For the virtuous, that bridge will be wide and well-lit. For wrongdoers, it will narrow to the width of a sword's edge and they will plunge, in imagery that evokes the Book of Revelation, into eternal punishment.

> *When the mountains shall be set moving,*
> *When the pregnant camels shall be neglected,*
> *When the savage beasts shall be mustered,*
> *When the seas shall be set boiling,*
> *When Hell shall be set blazing,*
> *When Paradise shall be brought nigh,*
> *Then shall a soul know what it has produced.* (81:3–14)

One of the main reasons why Muhammad initially received so much hostility from his contemporaries in Mecca was precisely the Qur'an's insistence on the resurrection of the body. 'The Qur'an time and again gives what could be taken as the *ipsissima verba* of his opponents,' writes the Islamic scholar, Professor Anthony Johns, 'to the effect "what, when our bones have rotted away, are we to be resurrected, what a waste of time!" Time and again those who do not believe in the Qur'an are rebuked for this and described as "those who have no hope of seeing us".'*

So, though Muhammad taught of the power of living a good life on earth and of the possibility of experiencing transcendence as a result, he did not leave it at that. The

---

* In correspondence with the author.

Qur'an promised (10:26) 'those who do good' that 'a most happy state' would be theirs but went on to include 'something in addition'. In the exegetical tradition that 'most happy state' is taken as paradise, and the 'something in addition' as the vision of God.

Such a spiritual line was taken, for example, in the oldest extant commentary (written in AD 789) on the Qur'an when considering this verse. It talks of looking on the face of God. This was a controversial message since the Quraysh had little time for a detailed afterlife. They balked at the criteria by which Muhammad said they would be judged. Mecca had grown rich as a thriving mercantile city, but Muhammad was pointing to a consequent loss of moral and community values. On the Last Day, he warned, wealth and power would be of no use. Each individual would be asked what had they done for the poor in imitation of Allah, the Compassionate One.

In terms of a precise imagery of *djanna*, the Qur'an is relatively brief. Those who reach it, it foretells, with echoes of the Book of Isaiah, will enjoy a banquet with Allah of finest foods in a place of peace and tranquillity. They will also be greeted by angels, an essential part of Islam as well as Judeo-Christianity, and houri, beautiful virgins rather like Valkyries, whose purpose was to pleasure the newly arrived warriors in Valhalla. *Djanna* was a decidedly more sensual and erotic place than any parallel description of the Christian paradise where asceticism and overly acute awareness of sin had taken their toll. The Qur'an is thought by scholars, in this regard, to have been strongly influenced by Syrian Christianity in the first centuries AD, in particular by Ephraem Syrus (*c*. 306–373), a theologian and poet whose *Hymns of Paradise* unashamedly presented salvation as unlimited fulfilment of highly primitive and sensual desires.

Western travellers to Islamic lands were later so struck by the eroticism of *djanna* that embellished accounts of Muhammad's paradise made their way into print in thirteenth-century Europe. The most significant, the *Liber Scalae*, or *Book of the Ladder*, in 1264 told of a place with ruby-encrusted walls where virgins lay waiting to satisfy the whims of newcomers in pavilions of pearls and emeralds, set amid fruit trees and tables laden with everything one could possibly crave by way of food and drink. (Women newcomers, however, were apparently left to their own devices.) The distortion of *djanna* in such books is believed to have influenced the popular medieval fantasy land of Cockaigne, an earthbound paradise of plenty, well-known and recorded in the late Middle Ages.

Islamic tradition subsequently embroidered this basic outline with more detailed descriptions. It embraced what Augustine had described, and what Christian scholastics later debated, as the 'beatific vision' – namely, that the resurrected shall see God and He will look on them. The favoured geography was the antithesis of the Arabian terrain – a garden set amid rolling, verdant hills, planted with fruit trees and topped by the *Sidret-el-mounteha* – the tree of life – with emerald branches and leaves on which were written the name of every human being. There were rivers of milk, water, honey; wine which does not intoxicate or produce a hangover; and robes of gold for everyone. The houri were given ebony eyes and creamy complexions and each man was promised seventy-two of these handmaidens. (Muhammad himself was someone who clearly liked and respected women and such calibration may not have been to his taste.)

Such abundant imagery (much, though not all of it,

with echoes of Greek and Judeo-Christian ideas) can, however, give a mistaken sense of how the place of heaven stood in Islamic thought. Muhammad's main focus was on this life, not the next, and it is significant that it was other writers who conjured up *djanna* rather than the Prophet himself.

The confusion increases with the wealth of Islamic literature given over to Muhammad's visions of God, mentioned only briefly in the Qur'an. One may have occurred when Jibril visited him in the cave; another sometime later, possibly in 620; and the timing of the third, if it took place, is wholly unknown. If we rely solely on the testimony of the Qur'an, it is impossible to work out any time scale. Verses 53 and 81 both speak of a vision of Allah, but mainly do so in the context of defending Muhammad's claim to be a prophet.

By the star when it goes down, your companion [the Qur'an has a confusing habit of changing narrator but this refers to Muhammad] has not wandered nor has he erred, nor does he speak of his own inclination. It was nothing less than inspiration that inspired him. He was taught by one mighty in power, one possessed of wisdom, and he appeared while in the highest part of the horizon. Then he approached and came closer, and he saw at a distance of two bows lengths or closer. And he inspired his servant with what he inspired him. His heart did not falsify what it saw. Will you then dispute with him over what he saw. Indeed he saw him descending a second time, near the lotus tree that marks the boundary. Near it is the garden of the dwelling, and behold, the lotus tree was shrouded in the deepest shrouding. His sight never swerved, nor did it exceed its limits. Indeed he saw the signs of his Lord, the Greatest. (53:1–18)

There is some difference of opinion among readers here between Allah being himself, and Allah being represented by Jibril. Islamic scholars have traditionally taught that it is Jibril, but this is not stated in the Qur'an. Furthermore, whether the lotus tree was real or imaginary is again open to interpretation. Verse 81 does not bring much more clarity:

Truly it is the speech of a noble messenger, one possessing power with the master of the established throne, obeyed and trustworthy. Your comrade is not *jinn*-possessed [jinns are often mischievous spirits]. He saw him on the clear horizon; he does not withhold knowledge of the unseen, nor is it the word of a stoned Satan. So where will you go? Is it nothing else than a reminder to the worlds? (81:19–27)

There is the same mention of the horizon, linking the two visions, and tradition again has seen in the word 'messenger' the figure of Jibril. Finally, in verse 17 there is the most distinct reference:

Glory be to Him who carried His servant by night from the sacred shrine to the distant shrine whose surrounding we have blessed, that we might show Him some of our signs. (17:1)

Even if the translation obscures it (it is sometimes said of Arabic that while with other languages one reads in order to understand, with Arabic one has to understand in order to read), God here is the subject, Muhammad the object of the nocturnal visit, and the sacred shrine is a reference to Mecca. But where is the distant shrine? Some parts of Islamic tradition hold that it was heaven.

Others that it was Jerusalem, and others still that it was first Jerusalem, then heaven. In this line of thinking, the golden-topped Dome of the Rock Mosque on the Temple Mount in the old city of Jerusalem marks the spot where, supposedly, a ladder came down so that Muhammad could ascend to the heavens. The Dome of the Rock Mosque was built in 691 to commemorate his ascent, though for a building so linked with an historical event it contained no figurative art to distract worshippers: as a counterbalance to those who would give heaven too much importance, transcendence was held to be beyond human imagery.

In the *Ascension of Muhammad*, typical of the later stylised versions of Muhammad's night journey, the prophet is accompanied by Jibril and rides a mystical white mount – half-mule, half-donkey with wings and a woman's head – traditionally called Borak (lightning). Heaven, once reached via the ladder, is made up of seven layers: the first consisting of moon and stars, where Muhammad meets Adam, the next being the place of Jesus – regarded as a prophet by Islam – and so on to a lotus tree, with leaves as broad as elephants' ears, which is the throne of Allah. Muhammad does not see Allah, but senses Him in his heart as a radiant sweetness. They communicate only through the angel.

This story has been told in many variations down the ages. As-Suyati (1445–1505), an Egyptian Moslem writer of commentaries on the Qur'an and on the prophetic tradition, depicts Muhammad, in a first-person account, *al-La'ali al-masnu*, as floating upwards through the layers of heaven on a silken cloth or *rafraf*:

That rafraf floated me into the [presence of the] Lord of the Throne, a thing too stupendous for the tongue to tell of or the imagination to picture. My sight was so dazzled by it that I feared blindness. Therefore I shut my eyes which was by Allah's good favour. When I thus veiled my sight Allah shifted my sight [from my eyes] to my heart, so with my heart I began to look at what I had been looking at with my eyes. It was a light so bright in its scintillation that I despair of ever describing to you what I saw of His majesty.

(from *Muhammad and His Religion*, translated by A. Jeffery)

This rich imagery can be viewed in a number of ways. If the journey it describes did in fact take place in 620, as some Islamic biographers of Muhammad have suggested, then it could be referring symbolically to the actual events around Mecca. This was the point at which hostility to Muhammad was so great in Mecca that he made his *hajj* to Medina. The night journey depicted may merely be a way of cloaking that seminal pilgrimage in godly terms. If, then, it was an imaginary and not a literal journey, there is a strong case for linking it to the tradition of Jewish Throne Mysticism, for it contains some characteristic features – a throne, looking within, and a lack of a specific final vision of Allah.

Islam has never embraced quite the literalism that Christianity later came to promote regarding heaven. Instead it retains a lack of precision in its dealings with matters beyond this life. It was, and is, a creed with a strong sense of the symbolic. Verses in the Qur'an which speak of Allah as having hands, a face and an eye, are taken to be referring to His powers, and not to actual body parts.

The Sufi tradition amongst Sunni Moslems from the

ninth century onwards was a mystically based reaction against too narrow and literal an interpretation of the Qur'an, urging instead a greater concentration on Muhammad's pleas for justice, compassion and love in this life as the keys to transcendence and, therefore, the route to Allah. Some fringe Moslem groups have even taken this a stage further: the Druze people, a sect founded in the eleventh century in what is today Syria and the Lebanon within the Shi'a tradition of Islam, believe in reincarnation – an aberrant view to main-stream Islam because it denies Muhammad's explicit emphasis on death and resurrection.

As Christianity evolved, it would constantly change its view of heaven. Islam, likewise, has not enjoyed unanimity over the question of life after death. There are even some passages in the Qur'an itself which seem to deny the validity of the notion of a heavenly journey altogether, and to emphasise instead that revelation and transcendence is found here on earth:

They say: 'We shall not believe you until you cause a spring to gush forth for us from the earth ... or you cause the sky to fall to pieces, or you bring God and the angels before us face to face. Or you have a house adorned with gold, or you mount a ladder into the skies. No, we shall not even believe in your mounting until you send down to us a book that we could read.' Say: 'Glory to my God! Am I aught but a man, an apostle?' (17:90–93)

PART TWO

And the Soul Goes Marching On

CHAPTER SIX

Safe in My Garden

The attraction of imagining the hereafter as somewhere where one's suffering will be dispelled and made good is obvious. Those who take this option and imagine a literal heaven are also telling us a great deal about the age in which they live, and what they aspire to. Heaven becomes a mirror. This pattern recurs throughout history in all faiths which teach of heaven, but was never more clearly seen than in Christianity in the medieval period. The differing guidelines drawn up by the early Church Fathers were enduring ones for this new generation of travellers. Each of the three main schools of thought on the nature of heaven had its champions in the medieval period and each, at different times, held sway depending on the circumstances in which the Church and the God-fearing found themselves.

From the sixth century onwards, monasticism grew rapidly, principally under the influence of Benedict of Nursia (480–547). His *Rule* was heavily promoted by the papacy, especially by Gregory the Great (590–604), the first pope to be a monk, as a means of bringing leadership, order and discipline to a disparate Church.

Monastic communities inspired by Benedict developed all over Europe, doing much to place the Church at the centre of people's lives, in what was a brutal and often lawless period, up to and including the Dark Ages of the ninth century.

Benedict's view of heaven in his *Rule* was a simple and decidedly unmystical one, geared more to behaviour here on earth and how to ensure one got to heaven, rather than what it would be like when one got there. 'Just as there is an evil, bitter zeal which separates from God and leads to hell, so there is a good zeal which separates from vices and leads to God and to everlasting life.'

The most striking image of the *Rule* is that of Jacob's ladder, taken from Genesis. Benedict writes that to join the angels on this stairway to heaven, it is necessary to achieve the qualities characterised by each rung. These range from selflessness, self-giving, obedience, and patience to more restrictive virtues. The tenth rung symbolises the absence of laughter. 'The fool raises his voice in laughter,' Benedict warns. His heaven would be a very sombre place.

Many of the monks who followed this plain formula would have spent the majority of their lives working unpromising monastery lands, which often would have been chosen by founding fathers because of the challenge they posed to restore an Eden-like fertility. For example, Bernard of Clairvaux, the twelfth-century founder of the Cistercians, insisted that his order's abbeys always be located in the most stubborn wilderness on seemingly intractable terrain so that the thorn bushes, to which Adam and Eve had condemned themselves, could be transformed once again into a godly, abundant paradise garden. So, when these monks imagined what was at the top of the ladder, it is no surprise that they envisaged a perfect garden, fruitful, verdant, and probably low-maintenance.

'There lilies and roses always bloom for you, smell sweet and never wither,' wrote Otfrid of Weissdenburg, a ninth-century German monk, in his *Book of the Gospel*. 'Their fragrance never ceases to breathe eternal bliss into the soul.' One particular feature of the garden, often mentioned by such scribes, was the absence of thorns. It had a specific symbolism: by depicting heaven as without thorns, the monks were demonstrating that in the after-life God would take back the punishment he had meted out at the dawn of humanity. The link between the garden of paradise, and the Garden of Eden which Adam and Eve had lost for the subsequent generations of humankind, was explicit.

Garden imagery was also popular with those outside the monasteries. Pope Gregory was a great encourager and harnesser of popular devotions. He penned sugary lives of saints as a sideline to provide role models for the faithful to follow. It was part of his drive to make the Church more centralised by bringing under its wing those on its fringes who clung to older rituals. Thus he sanctioned a revival in the apocalyptic tradition of vision literature, with its inspiring tales of the heaven that would be the eternal reward of those who did as he told them. Once again, he led by example. In *Dialogues*, Gregory tells the tale of a soldier who almost died of the plague but who came back from the brink. The soldier then recalls what he saw during his travels on the cusp of life and death. The language and imagery of travel, it is worth noting, was ever present in such accounts:

Across the bridge, there were green and pleasant meadows carpeted with sweet flowers and herbs. In the fields groups of white-clothed people were seen. Such a sweet scent filled the air that it fed those who dwelt and walked there. The dwellings of the blessed were full of a great light. A house of amazing capacity was being constructed there, apparently out of golden bricks, but he could not find out for whom it might be.

In its emphasis on precision and detail, there is little in this style of vision to link it with the internal ascents of Throne Mysticism and Augustine's experience at Ostia. Gregory's description was indeed a perfect inversion of the life of even the privileged few who could read it. Towns and cities, with little by way of sanitation, public health provision or even adequate building materials, would certainly not have been sweet-smelling or fashioned of golden bricks. Only leading churchmen would have floated around in white robes because they had the money and the staff to keep up such exacting sartorial standards amid the filth of urban living. For the mass of the population, primitive grey clothing was the order of the day. They would be crowded together, cheek by jowl, in damp homes with narrow doors and earth floors and not so much as a window, let alone a view of meadows. The image of dwellings filled with light would have been nothing short of miraculous.

Gregory's heaven was aspirational, but in equal measure it was a compensation for this world in a way that, for example, vague talk of oneness with God could never be. It was also astutely political. The promise of heaven was set against the threat of hell. As well as the story of the soldier who had been to the paradise garden, *Dialogues* included tale after tale of overactive demons lurking in the undergrowth.

One of the most often repeated concerned a nun who

had succumbed to the deadly sin of gluttony. Wandering around the monastery garden, she hungrily spied a lettuce. She gobbled it up without so much as making the sign of the cross (a primitive form of exorcism) only to discover that in her haste she had eaten a demon who then began to torment her.

This new wave of vision literature also enabled specific problems that had troubled the early Fathers to be tackled – for instance, whether the dead had to wait until judgement day to achieve heaven. Its favoured solution was taken from the later Augustine – the souls of the faithful departed could go straight there, but their bodies had to wait until the end of the world. What happened to the bodies in the meantime was unclear. In another story from *Dialogues*, Gregory the Great tells of a bathhouse attendant who declines a piece of bread from a visiting priest because he is dead. His body, he explains, is awaiting God's judgement, and he asks the priest to offer sacrifice to God on his behalf. This the priest does and when he returns to the bathhouse the attendant is gone. Gregory here appears to be writing of what in medieval thought was to become purgatory, albeit in this case unusually here on earth.

In similar vein, the Venerable Bede (*c.* 673–735) recounts in his *Ecclesiastical History of the English People* the heavenly vision of a Northumbria man called Drihthelm, who was close to death but who recovered. Drihthelm talks of being taken by an angel first to hell and later to the top of a high wall.

> Within it was a vast and delightful field, so full of fragrant flowers that the odour of its delightful sweetness immediately dispelled the stink of that dark furnace which had pierced me through and through [hell]. So

great was the light in this place that it seemed to exceed the brightness of the day, or the sun in its meridian height. In this field were innumerable assemblies of men in white, and many companies seated together rejoicing. As he led me through the midst of those happy inhabitants, I began to think that this might, perhaps, be the kingdom of heaven, of which I had so often heard so much. He answered to my thought, saying, 'This is not the kingdom of heaven, as you imagine.' When we had passed those mansions of blessed souls and gone farther on, I discovered before me a much more beautiful light, and therein heard sweet voices of persons singing, and so wonderful a fragrancy proceeded from the place that the other which I had before thought most delicious then seemed to me but very indifferent; even as that extraordinary brightness of the flowery field, compared with this, appeared mean and inconsiderable. When I began to hope we should enter that delightful place, my guide, on a sudden stood still, and then turning back, led me back by the way we came.

(from Bede's *Ecclesiastical History of the English People*)

Here again is an early glimpse of purgatory – although it fits better with later ideas than Gregory's image of the walking dead on earth. The ante-chamber to heaven, though not embedded in doctrine until three centuries later, was apparently already part of the popular landscape of life after death. Bede, however, makes one subsequent reference, which demonstrates how confusing and contradictory any attempt to delineate exact positions on afterlife can be. He writes that life on earth is like the flight of a sparrow through a great hall. While inside, the sparrow escapes the wintry storm. When it leaves, 'it returns to the winter whence it came . . . Man's life is similar; and of what follows it, or what went before, we are utterly ignorant'. Having plotted it exactly with Drihthelm, Bede then dismissed those plans in favour of the line that heaven is beyond our imagination.

Bede had the relative security of a monastery within which to fashion such abstract ideas. For others less fortunate, everlasting life in a walled garden would have had a distinct appeal as a haven, as Europe was then awash with predatory armies which would sweep through villages and towns with little thought for their defenceless inhabitants.

Until the birth of nation states in the nineteenth century, much of continental Europe was made up of an ever-changing patchwork of feudal loyalties, ecclesiastical sees and antagonistic ethnic groups. For long periods, the social order appeared to have collapsed. In the tenth century, after the death of Charlemagne, who had brought unity to great swathes of continental Europe and cemented an alliance with the papacy, his successors lost control, giving way in France and Germany to local barons, who were answerable to nobody. They rode out of their fortified castles to plunder from the peasantry as they pleased. Any resistance was met with violence. Fighting was the great game of Europe until at least the fourteenth century, when the crusader movement finally ran out of steam. Warriors were celebrated by name as the sporting icons of their day in epic verse like the *Chanson de Roland* (c. 1100). This was, of course, fine for the warriors, but for the mass of the population it meant that life was lived in a constant state of fear. For them the parallels between their lives, their world and the Book of Revelation's description of the last days would have been clear. As would have been the book's promise of reward and justice in heaven.

Not all monks, however, were drawn to the heaven-as-a-garden school of thought. Those whose lives were less to do with farming and more concentrated on contemplation and prayer each day concentrated instead on union with the divine. Their preference was the internalised spirituality that regarded paradise as the logical end of that journey – not as a place, but as oneness with God. This approach had its most eloquent advocate in a sixth-century Syrian monk known by the nom de plume Dionysius the Areopagite, or Denys.

Dionysius is credited with coining the term 'mystical theology' and clearly set out the distinction between the literal and the symbolic, especially important in the case of heaven. The Christian tradition, he wrote, 'has a dual aspect, the ineffable and mysterious on the one hand, the open and more evident on the other. The one resorts to symbolism and involves initiation. The other is philosophic and employs the method of demonstration.' This distinction between the ineffable (*dogma*) and what can be expressed (*kerigma*) is absolutely standard in the Orthodox tradition of Christianity where Dionysius is regarded as an immensely important theologian and where his work has almost canonical status. It favours, as a consequence, the mystical approach to afterlife and has little truck with efforts to construct palaces in the sky.

Dionysius was resolutely pragmatic in his realisation that not everyone would be up to grasping the ineffable and so he endorsed the use of more tangible imagery to satisfy their curiosity about the hereafter. In *On Celestial Hierarchies*, he wrote:

We might even think that the celestial regions are filled up with herds of lions and horses and re-echo with roaring songs of praise and contain flocks of birds and other creatures, and the lower forms of matter, and whatever other absurd, spurious, passion-rousing and unlike forms the scriptures use for describing their semblances . . .

But they are, he argued, just symbols which both reveal and conceal heaven. For those able to understand the symbolism, they were revealing, for those without the knowledge or the ability to apply it, they provided an alternative, if shallow, imagery.

It must be said that the reason for attributing shapes to that which is above shape, and forms to that which is beyond form, is not only the feebleness of our intellectual power, which is unable to rise at once to spiritual contemplation and which needs to be encouraged . . . but it is also most fitting that the secret doctrines, though ineffable and holy enigmas, should veil and render difficult for access for the multitude the sublime and profane truth of the Supernatural Mind: for, as the Scripture declares, not everyone is holy, nor have all men knowledge.

(*Pseudo Dionysius: The Complete Works*, translated by Colm Luibheid)

In trying to tease out the ineffable for his most discerning readers, Dionysius described in *On Celestial Hierarchies* how souls are one with God in paradise, but, despite this closeness, God remains wholly other. (He was not particularly fond of the word God at all, feeling it had been used too literally in the past.) Souls, then, are unable ever fully to understand the divine. For Dionysius, God knew no boundaries – He was 'not one of the things that are'. Therefore everything we say and know and see about Him here on earth and after death is metaphorical. Humanity, misshapen as it is by sin, has simply to accept, even if we cannot comprehend it, the secret at the heart of the world – namely the mutual longing between God and the cosmos.

Dionysius was not afraid, as Augustine had been, to use physical, even sexual, imagery to explore afterlife metaphorically. In conjugal love this unusually un-buttoned theologian saw a partial reflection of God's passion for the world. 'This Divine Yearning brings ecstasy so that the lover belongs not to self but to the beloved,' he writes in *The Divine Names*. Humanity's most basic instinct is, he held, to seek oneness with God, and the conclusion of that search lies in heaven where the blest will be:

> . . . filled with the light of God shining gloriously around us as once it shone for the disciples at the divine trans-figuration. And there we shall be, our minds away from passion and from earth, and we shall have a conceptual gift of light from [God], and somehow, in a way we cannot know, we shall be united with him and, our understanding carried away, blessedly happy, we shall be struck by his blazing light.

Dionysius wrote of each individual's potential for ecstasy – not as an alternative form of consciousness, but as something reached by prayer and tapping into the divine power that enables us to ascend to God Himself – a process he called theurgy. 'As we plunge into the darkness which is beyond intellect, we shall find our-selves not simply running short of words, but actually speechless and unknowing.'

While this style of metaphorical, mystical imagery was influential in Dionysius's own times – even Pope

Gregory the Great, for example, used the image of conjugal rights in his text, *Moralia*, to describe the reunion of the elect with God in a heavenly bridal chamber – it was not taken up in the Western Christian Church with anything like the same intensity as in Orthodoxy, where it remains to this day the standard approach to the subject of heaven.

Before moving away from Dionysius, it should be added that he did make an uncharacteristic contribution to the literal view of heaven by drawing up a 'sacred order' with three ranks of angelic beings. These might be seen as the attendants outside and around the bridal chamber. In the first group, he placed the seraphim, cherubim and thrones, the manifestations of spiritual intelligence that were closest to divine perfection in their oneness with God. Their characteristics were order, knowledge and presence. Traditionally, following Dionysius's pattern, they were depicted with six wings, two pointing to above their heads, two down to their feet, and two fully extended, so they could fly. In the second group, he put the dominions, virtues and powers, who spread God's light to the world beneath them. Finally, on the bottom rung, he located the principalities, archangels and angels who were spiritually pure, but nearest to humanity and so could guide those on earth away from temptation and towards a heavenly reunion with God. Artists took this more mundane function as an excuse to clad this final group in workaday warriors' garb.

Dionysius was doubtless using these ranks of angels symbolically, to emphasise the importance of spiritual intelligence over pondering the practicalities of heaven. While we may know the sacred, transcendent order, he wrote in *Celestial Hierarchies*, 'it is not possible to know the mystery of these celestial minds or to understand how they arrive at most holy perfection. We can only know what the Deity has mysteriously granted to us through them, for they know their own properties well.'

He lent weight to the approach that saw earthly hierarchy mirroring arrangements in heaven. His classifications were increasingly taken up as the medieval Church moved inexorably towards the high point of its temporal power as the dominant and almost unrivalled power in Europe in the thirteenth and fourteenth centuries. Angels, ill-defined figures in the Old and New Testaments, though the leading characters in apocalyptic literature of the inter-testamental period, assumed a definite political purpose. In their jockeying for position, they replicated and endorsed the niceties and distinctions of the Church's own hierarchical set-up.

It was not only the angels that mirrored the Church's ambitions to be in charge on earth. The *Acta Sanctorum*, one of several holy chronicles of this period, recalls a nun called Gerardesca who lived as a recluse in Pisa until her death in 1269. Her literal vision of heaven as a city-state had all the precision of an Ordnance Survey map: in the city proper resided the Holy Trinity, the Virgin Mary, the choir of angels and the saintliest of the saints. 'All the streets were of the purest gold and the most precious stones. An avenue was formed by golden trees whose branches were resplendent with gold. Their blossoms remained rich and luxuriant according to their kind, and they were more delightful and charming than anything we can see in earthly pleasure-gardens.' Then there were seven castles encircling the city, home to distinguished, but not quite distinguished enough, souls. These castles were visited three times a year (Gerardesca

saw heaven as having an earthly calendar) by the aristoc-
racy from the city, rather as a bishop would travel with
great pomp to visit the outlying areas of his diocese.
Finally, there was a whole series of minor fortresses
where the lower orders of heaven lived.

Sister Gerardesca's heaven was an intriguing combination of city and garden, urban and pastoral. It reflects
what was happening around her – the growth of towns
across Europe. Between 1150 and 1250, historians of the
medieval period estimate that the number of urban
settlements in central Europe had increased from 200
to around 1500. The Pisa nun's interest in the Book of
Revelation's new Jerusalem may well have been fired by
this development. The same town and country combination is seen in the vision of Gunthelm (as quoted in
Jeffrey Burton Russell's *History of Heaven*), a twelfth century English Cistercian monk. The paradise he glimpses
in a dream has the outward appearance of a city but
houses within its walls a garden. The popularity of this
two-layered heaven extended beyond books. In the
public festivals which marked the feasts of patron saints,
towns and cities would often garland their walls or great
buildings to represent this sweet-smelling oasis in the
heart of a conurbation.

Gunthelm described two heavens – the second had a
chapel at the centre, presided over by the Virgin Mary
who shone like the sun in her golden robe. The high
middle ages – the twelfth and thirteenth centuries – saw
a flowering of intellectual, liturgical, artistic and
devotional interest in Christ's mother, so finding this
flesh-and-blood figure so much at the centre of the literal
heavenly tableaux of the time comes as no surprise. Gunthelm's positioning of Mary within a chapel fits neatly
with the Gothic period which produced great cathedrals

like that at Chartres (completed in 1240) dedicated to the mother of God. 'Even before the Middle Ages,' write the historians of heaven, Colleen McDannell and Bernhard Lang, 'Christian liturgy and speculation identified the church building with the heavenly Jerusalem. The hymn *Urbs Hierusalem beata*, sung on the feast of the church's dedication, compared the earthly building to "the city of Jerusalem, the blessed", whose "gates shine with pearls". At the original dedication, the priests read the biblical text on the new Jerusalem which descends from heaven "prepared as a bride".'

The precise imagery of heaven, as it developed in this period, was largely drawn from biblical sources. The pearly gates, for instance, relate both to Revelation's depiction of the New Jerusalem as surrounded by twelve gates, and to the passage in Matthew's Gospel (13:46) in which Jesus likens the kingdom of heaven first to a hidden treasure and then to 'a merchant looking for fine pearls; when he finds one of great value he goes and sells everything he owns and buys it'. Taken together with a later passage in Matthew's Gospel (16:18–19) where Jesus says to Peter, 'I will give you the keys to the kingdom of heaven: whatever you bind on earth shall be considered bound in heaven; whatever you loose on earth shall be considered loosed in heaven', the two led to depictions of the first Pope waiting at the glittering gates of heaven, judging each and every new arrival.

Traveller's Tales: 2

~~~

Saffron is a retired literary agent from London. A strong-minded, independent and immensely practical woman, her own view of heaven could be, she said, summed up in a phrase from Caryl Churchill's play *Top Girls*: corporate immortality. 'It is a phrase which I hold dear as I feel it has some comparison with being in the chorus for *The Messiah*, individually of no use, but collectively vital,' she told me.

Saffron's traveller's tale is second-hand. She observed a friend in purgatory: 'He was in hospital following a major heart attack. I had been visiting regularly and I went into his room one morning to see that all the life-saving devices had disappeared. The doctor told me, very sympathetically, that if they could keep him alive, he would have a life he would hate. I was so grateful that they didn't ask me to make the decision.

'He was alive, but completely out of it. But he was worried and restless, plucking the sheets and murmuring the whole time. He seemed to be reviewing his life and I can only describe his behaviour as being that of a soul in torment. He kept saying that he knew how bad he'd been, that he'd made a lot of people unhappy, and that he was sorry. This went on for several hours and we could do nothing to calm him.

'Towards evening, things changed; no more tossing and turning, the frown left his face and he said quite clearly "I am at peace now." He slept peacefully and said no more, dying at seven the next morning.

'I was glad to have been there. It gave me such comfort to see this evidence that he had made his peace with God. I can't think of any other explanation.'

CHAPTER SEVEN

———— ∞∞ ————

Space Oddity

U ntil the dawn of the twelfth century, the cardinal rule of architecture was a simple one: ensure there was sufficient weight on the ground to keep everything above upright. From the time of the pyramids in Egypt, people knew that to build more than a single floor, it was essential to start with a huge base and then gradually taper off as the edifice grew taller. Subsequent generations may have brought in their own tastes in materials, adornment and even tapering, but they stuck to the basic principle that construction was all to do with stability and spreading the load. It made for resolutely earthbound castles, churches and palaces.

The Gothic style, with its flying buttresses, high-pointed arches and clustered columns passing without interruption, hesitation or repetition into the vault was an architectural revolution. From 1100 onwards, architects could suddenly fashion something very tall and very slender with a base that was no larger than its roof; an achievement which we may take for granted today, but which, by the standards of the time, must have seemed miraculous. Stone was rendered weightless as the towers and spires of cathedrals and abbeys began quite literally to reach for heaven. Walls were strong enough to support large, often ornate windows, which at a stroke imported light – long believed to be the paramount virtue of paradise. Inside, great vaulted naves recreated for the first time a tangible vision of the hereafter as a place of space and tranquillity.

Chartres Cathedral is the much-imitated masterpiece of this early Gothic style. It was once a firm favourite on the medieval pilgrim routes, on account of its resident relic, allegedly part of the tunic the Virgin Mary wore at the time of the Annunciation – when she was told by the Angel Gabriel that she had been chosen to bear God's child. It seemed an obvious jumping off point for my pilgrimage to heaven.

Even in an age of skyscrapers and tower blocks, Chartres Cathedral is still impressively massive. As the suburban train chuntered along in the flatlands to the west of Paris, I could see the two very different towers of the cathedral's imposing west front at least fifteen minutes before I pulled into the station. The smaller tower, older and more beautiful, was completed in 1145, and moves up from a square base to an octagonal spire, all its arches guiding the eye ever upwards. In 1194, the whole church burnt down. Only the Romanesque crypt, the remains of an earlier building on the site, and west front were spared. At the time, the two towers more or less matched, but in the early sixteenth century the north tower had its upper reaches replaced by something taller and much more flamboyant – less an austere hint to look up to paradise and more the equivalent of a flashing neon arrow proclaiming 'God this way'.

It is a five minute walk up from the station. There

doesn't appear to be anything much to Chartres other than its cathedral and so the town planners have framed their only asset with open space, creating a pedestrian zone with umpteen bollards and countless rather suburban pots of conifers. All very laudable, if anachronistic, given the backdrop, and the uninterrupted vista of the cathedral that has been created is certainly breathtaking, the harmony of its proportions a tribute to the mathematical calculations of its builders, its mighty buttresses lining up like giant spiders' legs behind the towers to support the nave.

What it seemed to lack, however, from my particular viewpoint, was a sense of how much more miraculous this huge building would have appeared in medieval times, rising out of a squash and squeeze of timber houses, some grand, but many basic, piled one next to the other, tumbledown, dark, earthy and insanitary. It could only have been, I imagined, the equivalent of a spaceship landing in the middle of a contemporary crowded city.

One of the reasons the west front seems so massive is its flatness. The recess between the two towers is unusually almost flush with their outer edge, creating the impression of a sheer mountain face. Standing at the foot of the old spire, peering up, I found it all too easy to believe it was about to come tumbling down on my head when, in reality, it had remained standing for almost a millennium, pock-marked but unbowed by fire and war, revolution and restoration.

The intricately carved three-bay portal which joins the two towers is, according to the historian Kenneth Clark, 'one of the most beautiful congregations of carved figures in the world'. He was, admittedly, a bit of a Chartres buff. In his celebrated television series, *Civilisation*, he called the interior of Chartres Cathedral and that of Saint Sophia in Istanbul the greatest covered spaces in the world. On the right-hand bay of the portal, in a tribute to Greek philosophy, are Aristotle and Pythagoras, in vogue here at Chartres with both stonemasons and clerics as it became a centre for Scholasticism which in the twelfth century turned back to ancient Greece to sweep away many medieval theological notions. It was the centre bay, though, that caught my eye. It shows the elders of the Book of Revelation, ubiquitous in most attempts to conjure up heaven, surrounded by the faces of unknown kings and queens who stare out serenely, as if obeying a higher order. It is as if they are in heaven already and so, as I walked through the doors below them, I too was entering the mystery that they had already discovered, albeit, as befitting the medieval order of things, in my proper lowly place in a rigidly hierarchical world.

Once inside, I experienced something decidedly otherworldly about the interior – dark, hushed and filled with indistinct figures wandering randomly around while all the time avoiding eye contact. To my modern imagination, shaped by too many sci-fi adventures, I had an impression of walking up a ramp into a spaceship. To medieval visitors, though, the signposts would have been clear: this was heaven. The story of the rebuilding of Chartres after the fire of 1194 belies any doubt about this. The Virgin Mary's tunic escaped the inferno unscathed. Many took this as a sign of God's presence and so, when the reconstruction began, the faithful lined up to pull the carts that delivered the stone – not just up the incline to the site, but all the way from various quarries around France. Not only the lower orders, but also pious noblemen and women sullied their hands with this hard manual labour, firm in the belief that they were contributing to the building of God's kingdom here on earth. Many of the small army of glass workers who made the 170 windows of the cathedral travelled from all over the country just to be part of the project. They sincerely believed that they were sharing in constructing the pre-eminent home for the Virgin Mary on earth, as close a representation of heaven, where they knew she resided, as had ever been attempted before. It was tempting, as I grew accustomed to the light, to label it a people's cathedral, but that would miss the point. For those who gave their services for free, the result was something entirely beyond them and their world.

The initial effect of the soaring Gothic style of the interior is to make the visitor feel very small. Humankind's physical insignificance before God is an oft-repeated biblical theme. As I started to walk along the aisle, there was the almost constant imperative (all the more striking because I am six feet, four inches tall and therefore used to looking downwards when meeting people) to look up. Like its old spire, the whole momentum of Chartres Cathedral is to direct the eye upwards, in the medieval view of the universe, towards heaven. Details such as the altar piece – a flashy eighteenth-century addition of the carbuncle variety – become insignificant. Those cavernous, misty upper reaches of the cathedral seemed to take on their own mystery and life, far beyond anything I could touch, see or even comprehend. As a symbol of heaven, it was a neat fit.

Unlike the thirteenth-century visitor, I was able to make comparisons – with the scale of other buildings and with the underpinned, building-regulated, surveyor-approved permanence of my own home. Those who came to see when the cathedral was completed in 1230 might as well have been living in tents for any points of reference they possessed. In awe, they must have descended to the ancient crypt to see the relic of the Virgin's tunic and touched the deeply embedded foundations of the cathedral, the symbolic link to the past and the practical means of its stability.

Both Chartres Cathedral and the nameless medieval cathedral at the centre of William Golding's 1964 novel, *The Spire*, share an obsession with reaching to the skies, but they have one important difference. Where Golding's central, paradoxical character, Dean Jocelin, tried to send up a tower to the heavens without adequate foundations, convinced that God had blessed the scheme and so would make certain it didn't fall, the anonymous builders of Chartres knew enough of geometry to be pragmatic. They built down as well as up and so ensured that it has remained standing for almost a thousand years.

Chartres is rightly famous for its stained glass, bland and blank on the outside, but wonderfully colourful and illuminating on the inside. Again, there is that parallel with heaven, the mystery which only reveals itself once one is on the inside. All along the nave, cutting across the murky light of a dark autumnal day, were shafts of light. As I turned from the south transept towards the north, its great round window felt like a cinema screen, the vibrant colours of its diamond-shaped panels bouncing back through the black air at the audience. Here was that quality of light that had figured so largely from the earliest accounts of heaven.

The north window is not as detailed as others in the cathedral – especially the twelfth-century rose window and three lancets above the west portal. These tell biblical stories in intimate detail. Even with the help of a guide,

I found them hard to follow, the figures too small, the panels too crowded, but that did not seem to signify. Next to paintings on canvas, or the wall illustrations which would have been standard elsewhere in churches in the twelfth century, these windows had a depth of colour, an animation and a power that spoke directly to the emotions.

The craftsmen who laboured to make them of course had in mind another purpose entirely: at a time of widespread illiteracy, the windows were teaching tools, passing on stories, dramatising the events of Christ's life, making them seem real. This is the gulf that separates us from them. We have lost all sense of cathedrals as places of learning. They are variously museums, tourist attractions, landmarks, a suitable backdrop to ecclesiastical egos, but rarely a school or a treasury of stories, and never in and of themselves a representation of heaven.

CHAPTER EIGHT

———— ⦿⦿⦿ ————

Star-Man

Around the medieval cathedrals centres of learning grew up which would ultimately become the first universities – at Paris, Rome, Bologna, Oxford, Cambridge. They gave rise to the scholastic movement in Western Europe in the twelfth and thirteenth centuries, injecting a theological vigour into a Church which, since the age of Augustine, had largely lost sight of such finer details, taken up as it had been with political manoeuvrings and, at times, sheer survival.

Among the neglected and unresolved issues the scholastics tackled was that of heaven. 'As a broad intellectual trend,' writes Professor David Chidester in *Christianity: A Global History*, 'scholasticism represented a range of critical methods in the science of logic that were devoted to the analysis and demonstration of the truth of propositions. Commonly referred to as dialectics, these logical methods that were derived from ancient Greek philosophy investigated the validity of truth claims.' Simply put, scholasticism believed that everything could be classified and that many things could be understood by humanity's own powers – hence its rediscovery of the wisdom of Greece – rather than relying on divine revelation of the type seen in vision literature. So, it was suggested, one could prove that heaven existed without God sweeping people up there for a foretaste in a dream.

Part of the problem, the scholastics felt, was that the exact location of heaven remained unknown. How could people believe in something that couldn't be pinpointed anywhere? So they turned to Ptolemy, the second-century Egyptian geographer, who held the debatable theory that the world was round. In his basic scholastic manual, *Four Books of Sentences*, Peter Lombard (d. 1160), the Bishop of Paris, adapted Ptolemy's depiction of the earth as a sphere to create a cosmos-scape with a round earth at the centre of several concentric spheres containing the moon, sun, stars and other planets. Beyond all of these, Lombard said, was a firmament or shell enclosing the whole. And outside the firmament was the spiritual heaven or empyrean, the dwelling place of God, or at least of His visible form. The word empyrean had its origins in pagan beliefs – as a supernatural realm of fire and light – but had great resonance as a place of light in medieval Christian thought about heaven. It had gradually been annexed by Christianity as part of its drive to expunge pagan practices from Europe by a two-fold policy of repression and what was called transformation, adapting existing rituals, imagery, vocabulary and even feast days to the Church's practices, theology and calendar.

Such a characteristically detailed and precise schema had the effect of making heaven, previously either a place of dream-like proportions or somewhere reached by an interior mental ascent, seem ever more real. Medieval astronomers would accordingly gaze up at the stars in the hope of catching, through a break in the clouds, a glimpse of the souls of the faithful departed at play with the saints. They were seeking both tangible proof of an afterlife and a bridge between earthly life and divine eternity. All the efforts of the mystics and monks to stress the symbolic and imaginary nature of heaven, essentially a place beyond the ken of humankind, were being discarded by the new movement.

Scholastic theologians like the Dominican Albert the Great (1200–1280) developed complex theories about the nuts and bolts of heaven. What was it made of, he asked? Since it was God's realm, he suggested, it couldn't be simply earth, fire, air and water. It had to be something better than earth, fashioned of a fifth element known as the *quinta essentia* or quintessence. Another topic of debate was whether it was only Christians who travel to experience this *quinta essentia*. Some scholastics held that the admission terms to paradise were more broadly laid down. There could co-exist explicit faith – lived out as a member of the Church – and implicit faith, a desire for God that was not catered for on earth and indeed which may not even have been known to the person themselves, but which was evident to God. Natural virtue or the intervention of a saint were other means suggested by which pagans could join the elect.

One of the most contentious issues for the scholastics was whether, once in heaven, you would be able to see God – the so-called beatific vision first mentioned by Augustine. The scholastics got stuck on this detail because of a passage in St Paul's First Letter to Timothy (6:16) which described God as the one 'whom no man has seen and no man is able to see'. In the face of such a clear biblical statement of God's invisibility, various devices had to be constructed. In his *Commentary on the Celestial Hierarchy*, Robert Grosseteste (1175–1254), the polymathic Oxford philosopher who became Bishop of Lincoln, distinguished between God Himself and His essence: 'We see Him face to face, and He is truly understood, and His essence is understood.' But the essence is not God Himself and therefore 'the totality of His essence is not penetrated'.

Grosseteste was getting back to Dionysius's description of the dual aspect of religion, the ineffable and what can be expressed. In Orthodoxy, the distinction between God's essence and the part of God that can be experienced and known is absolutely central. In Western Christianity, it has been much less clearly understood. Grosseteste's theorem was therefore far from universally accepted, and in 1241 the University of Paris intervened in the argument to decree that God in heaven would be seen in both His essence and His substance. The vexed question later preoccupied the supreme scholastic, Thomas Aquinas (1225–74) whose *Summa Theologiae*, a giant Highway Code of Christian theology, remains influential in Church circles to this day. God's essence, Aquinas remarked, was His Being; the two could not be divided. Such a split nature was the lowly lot of humankind who are both matter and essence. Only with the light of glory can we see God.

Aquinas viewed both individual life and the collective experience of humanity on earth as a journey – again the metaphor of travel – which began with God, was dominated by the desire to return to God, and which ended with the promise of that return. Adam and Eve's upsetting the apple cart in the Garden of Eden had spoilt the beginning, and the stain of that original sin now blocked our path back to the paradise garden. Only by wiping it clean could heaven be attained. This was done principally by resisting temptation. Aquinas had a highly developed demonology to provide plenty of occasions of temptation.

With a scholastic's determination to iron out any doctrinal inconsistencies, Aquinas also turned his attention to the grey area of whether the righteous dead went straight to heaven, there to behold God, or whether they had to wait until the Last Judgement. His chosen approach was to run the two together rather as Augustine had, but Aquinas's solution was cleverer by half in that it was all things to all men. By describing an eternal moment when both particular judgement and the Second Coming would happen as if at once, he effectively disabled any questions about timing: the two would not be simultaneous, but would be on the same plane. If in one sense God would be seen at once, in another sense there would still be some sort of wait.

And this wait could be unpleasant. Aquinas described it in *Supplement*, a volume composed by his disciples from his notes after his death, as a place where the least degree of pain 'surpasses the greatest pain that one can endure in this world'. Yet rather than dwell on a formal purgatory, Aquinas preferred to depict a lower level of heaven with God still visible and presiding. This, though, was no glorified waiting room for the hoi polloi. He believed that only Jesus and Mary had made it into the upper echelons of heaven in advance of the Last Judgement. Everyone else – even those reported by the Bible to be on a fast track like Enoch and Elijah – had to pause in their journey before final fulfilment.

Among this group were the saints. It is to Thomas Aquinas that heaven owes the image of a communion of saints – acting collectively as a body rather like a trade union. 'Since all the faithful form one body,' Aquinas wrote, 'the good of each is communicated to the others

... The riches of Christ are communicated to all members, through the sacraments.' (While it is clear that Aquinas had in mind an over-arching body of all the faithful – living and dead, thereby sanctifying lesser mortals who followed God's commands – the term has traditionally been used to depict an exclusive club within heaven of the elect, on the grounds of virtue.)

It is easy in an age of rather more fluid and spiritual Christian doctrines to underestimate how such questions as these could become matters of life and death in the thirteenth-century Church. Yet it was an issue around which popes, cardinals and even temporal rulers came to blows – metaphorically, and sometimes also literally. Pope John XXII (1316–34), in a series of four sermons in the winter of 1331/2, questioned Aquinas's running together of death and final judgement. The two were, the Pope said, entirely separate. The University of Paris in its turn immediately condemned his view, as did most of the leading theologians of the day. It then became something of a political football (the papacy was at this time in exile in Avignon), with the Pope's political enemy, Louis IV the Bavarian, trying to get a general council called to rebut and depose John XXII.

In the midst of it all, the pontiff fell ill, convincing many that this must be heaven's judgment. On his death-bed, he was finally persuaded to issue a partial retraction – the souls of the blessed could see the divine essence face to face as clearly as their condition allowed. John's successor, Benedict XII (1334–42) accepted this formulation and, in one of the rare occasions on which heaven has been the subject of anything as grand as a papal pronouncement, enshrined it in the constitution *Benedictus deus* of 1336, speaking of 'an intuitive, face-to-face vision of the divine essence'. It was 550 years before there was another official look by the papacy at heaven.

Next to such intricate questions as the beatific vision, the scholastics could not muster much enthusiasm for mundane questions which might interest simple souls in the pews, such as the fixtures and fittings of heaven. Aquinas made no comment on the city or garden debate, though he did rule out the presence of any plants or animals in the hereafter and so, by implication, he did not regard it as a restored Eden. His one major environmental concern was the quality of the light in paradise. The bodies of the blessed, he said, had a special quality of light, different from that of the angels and, again, from that of the saints. Here he was making his own contribution to establishing the hierarchy of heaven.

Scholasticism was an intellectual and theological movement which had great influence, but it caused little excitement in the hearts of those who filled churches and who lacked the basic skills of literacy and education to follow the twists and turns of the controversy. Where scholasticism was largely about library work and precise definitions, the medieval mystics in both their words and their deeds spoke less of heaven the place and more of a highly individual and most attractive relationship with God. Their impact on the medieval mind was one of the high points of a trend in ecclesiastical history whereby individuals moved away from great rituals and from being told what to think by men in mitres, and instead tuned in, through prayer to God and by introspection, to themselves and their own innate ability to make judgements.

Medieval mysticism was about love, not punishment, a world transformed by love not quantified by physics and geography. And as such it chimed well with the secular world, with its obsession with courtly love, poetry, heroic knights and their fair ladies. Arnaut Daniel, a Provençal troubadour who later appeared in Dante's Purgatorio, hailed the love that led to heaven where you worship both your lady and your Lord; 'I love her more than I do cousin or uncle, hence in paradise will my soul have twofold joy, if ever a man through fine loving therein enters.' (*Anthology of Troubadour Lyrics*)

Many of the medieval mystics were women religious. Some were anchorites, which meant that they lived in cells, walled in, within churches or monasteries. Their life was as close to death as they could make it – no distractions, little food, little exercise. The cell was a tomb, and they were striving by prayer, contemplation and their own internal, spiritual resources to get as close to heaven as they could while still on earth. In 1095, Pope Urban II issued a charter urging respect for such women who were, in his words, 'dead to the world' so that they could find their 'eternal spouse'.

Hildegard of Bingen (1098–1179) began her adult life as an anchorite, walled in within the monastery at Disibodenberg in what is now Germany. She was later to correspond with popes and travel around Europe preaching, achieving a celebrity status in her lifetime which has in recent times been rekindled (in 1997 the UK style magazine *The Face* acclaimed her 'the feistiest woman since Boadicea, the smartest since Athena'). Yet she chose to live a tomb-like existence until she was forty. It was in this period that she started to have visions of God. Unlike the seers of apocalyptic literature, her revelations came to her when she was awake. In *The Book of the Rewards of Life*, this prolific author described heaven thus:

> I saw certain ones, as if through a mirror, who were clothed with the whitest garment interwoven with gold and embellished with the most precious stones from their breast to their feet, in the manner of a hanging sash. Their garment emitted a very strong aroma, like perfume. And they were girdled with a girdle embellished with gold and gems and pearls beyond human understanding. On their heads they wore crowns intertwined with gold and roses and lilies and surrounded with pipes of most precious stones. Whenever the Lamb of God used his voice, this sweetest blowing of the wind coming from the sacred place of the Divinity touched these pipes so that they resounded with every type of sound that a harp and organ make. No one was playing this song, except those who wore these crowns, but the others who heard this song rejoined in it, just like a man who could not see previously now sees the brightness of the sun.

Hildegard's favourite image of heaven, however, was that of a bridal chamber. In an elegiac speech she wrote as a memorial to her favourite fellow nun, Richardis, she put it thus:

> *O virginity, you stand in the royal bridal chamber.*
> *O how tenderly you burn in the King's embraces*
> *when the sun shines through you*
> *so that your noble flower shall never wilt.*
> *O noble virgin, no shade will ever find your flower*
>   *drooping!*

The flower of the field falls before the wind,
The rain scatters its petals.
O virginity, you abide forever
in the chorus of the company of heaven!
hence you are a tender flower that shall never fade.
(from Hildegard of Bingen: The Woman of Her Age,
Fiona Maddocks)

Hildegard was not the first, as we have seen, to use the metaphor of conjugal love to describe union with God in heaven. Neither was she alone in her age. Mechthild of Magdeburg (1207–82) wrote of her own visions in *Flowing Light of the Godhead*, a collection of poems, allegories and meditations. She belonged to a Beguinage for much of her life – a community of independently minded women bound by disciplines not as strict as those in a convent and more akin to the senior common room in an old-style, single-sex Oxbridge college – and though she lived a freer life, Mechthild used language similar to that used by Hildegard. She describes heaven as being on three levels – the first was an earthly garden paradise where she met Elijah and Enoch (a debt to Aquinas is indicated here, in showing that scholasticism and mysticism were not rivals, but existed side-by-side); the second, a domed region of singing, dancing and light, with children, and with ten levels of choirs and empty seats vacated by the angels who had fallen with Lucifer and which would be filled by the souls of those who would rise at the Last Judgement; the third level, heaven, was the one on which she concentrated, and this was both God's throne-room and Christ's bridal suite.

Accompanied by some of the holy women from the second level, Mechthild enters this sacred chamber.

She knelt down, thanking him for his favour. She took her crown from her head and placed it on to the rose-coloured scars of his feet and wished that she could come closer to him. He took her into his divine arms, placed a paternal hand unto her breast and beheld her face. And in a kiss, she was elevated above all the angelic choirs.

(McDannell and Lang, *Heaven: A History*)

The image of being kissed by God is a startling one, and overall the imagery makes for uncomfortable reading in the twenty-first century, especially the mixture of paternalism and eroticism – a father with his hand on his daughter's breast in a bridal chamber. However, applying a post-Freudian literalism is bound to distort the medieval mystical mind with its emphasis on a ceaseless outpouring of unconditional love.

Similarly, too narrow an application of the principle that an individual's vision of heaven is often an inversion of the circumstances conjures up only a caricature of sexually frustrated nuns dreaming of physical love with the allusive but divine man in their lives once they get to heaven. Rather, the poetry of love which is the dominant note of Mechthild's writings owes much to then-popular notions of courtly love. In another vision, she sees Christ as a duke, herself as a noble lady, and their palace a 'bed of love'. The Duke tells his lady 'keep, in eternity, only those virtues that are inside yourself by nature. They are your noble lust and your ardent desire; to these I will respond eternally in my boundless tenderness'. Lust, traditionally condemned out of hand by the Church, is sanctified here. The scholastics' beatific vision becomes beatific union.

Mechthild spent her later years in a more conventional Cistercian convent at Helfta in Saxony. There she met

Gertrude (1256–1302), whose own vision of Jesus is far more sugary. She has no trouble looking him in the eye, as she records in her surviving mystical diary, *Herald of Divine Love*: he was 'a handsome youth of sixteen years, beautiful and amiable, attracting my heart and my outward eyes' with wooing, songs and declarations of love.

Yet in all three women's writings, the assumption is that the bride – the soul entering heaven – is virginal and remains so whatever happens next. 'When I love him,' Gertrude writes, 'I am chaste; when I touch him, I am pure; when I possess him, I am a virgin.' The idea first put out by the early Church Fathers that chastity was the way to heaven was being reiterated, albeit in more florid terms.

This necessarily remained a fairly exclusive take on heaven. Most women and men were not virgins. Hildegard, her followers and the Beguines were all well-born women who were able to make choices about how they lived their lives. In less exalted company, their romantic talk of consummation with Christ may have rung as hollow as the scholastics' narrow definitions. For most, the traditional image of heaven as a garden of refuge remained strong and appealing, the eternal promise that lay behind the apocalyptic language of the thirteenth-century Latin hymn *Dies Irae* (day of [judgemental] wrath):

> *Day of wrath and doom impending,*
> *David's word with Sybil's blending:*
> *Heaven and earth in ashes ending.*
>
> *Oh, what fear man's bosom rendeth*
> *When from heaven the judge descendeth,*
> *On whose sentence all dependeth.*

Wondrous sound the trumpet flingeth
Through earth's sepulchres it ringeth,
All before the throne it bringeth.

Death is struck, and nature quaking,
All creation is awaking,
To its judge an answer making.

This sense of impending gloom, of the end of the world, was an integral part of popular medieval Christianity to an extent almost impossible to imagine today.

In the parades, processions and public spectacles of the medieval age, the dominant image was that of Adam and Eve and their expulsion from Eden. Original sin and damnation hung heavy in the air. An all-pervading sense of the loss of a perfect life infused popular culture. For example, in Louvain, in what is now Belgium, the authorities insisted from 1401 onwards that in the annual religious procession through the city the first float had to be the one depicting the Fall. It was, they pointed out, the starting point of human history and the betrayal that had landed all humanity in the mess it now found itself. Thus for two centuries Adam and Eve, in a variety of costumes, headed up the parade. A depiction of their carriage from 1594 has been preserved. The accompanying rhyme sums up the general feeling of abandonment:

Adam, the recalcitrant, is driven
From blissful paradise, filled with delight,
Because to God's command he did not listen.
So daily toil is now the plight
Of one who walked in heaven's peaceful light.

Heaven and Eden were thus conflated. One had been lost and the other was virtually unobtainable. The same angels who guarded the now-locked gates to Eden in the mystery play, *Mary's First Joy*, which was performed every seven years from 1447 onwards in Brussels Grande Place, were also barring the gates to heaven. It was a scene repeated in many such performances across the continent. That sense of doom, decay and division, of a stolen future, with the tangible paradise lost and the alternative so remote that it could only be glimpsed by mystics and scholastics, was augmented by an evermore acute awareness of the presence of the Devil luring the unwary into hell. The evident sickness at the heart of the Church where, from 1378 onwards, there were popes and antipopes installed in Rome and Avignon, contributed to a tide of hopelessness.

If the hereafter was uncertain and ultimate bliss almost unimaginable, then popular culture found a variety of escape routes in the dreamlands that were the heavens of popular medieval culture. Some were more godly than others. The promise of a new Jerusalem here on earth, as outlined in Revelation, was one stand-by. If people could not envisage going to heaven, they could just about imagine it coming to them, albeit with many casualties among sinners in the process. A popular text of the time was the *Sterboeck* – or *Book of Death*. This was a collection of teachings about the sort of behaviour that might win its readers a place in the New Jerusalem on earth which it portrayed – in a 1491 edition – as a city without hunger or thirst, heat or cold, rain or snow. Instead of illness there would be eternal health. All would be perpetually 33-years-old – the age of Christ when he was crucified. Life took place against a backdrop of angels playing such a profusion of musical instruments that there was a veritable orchestra – a scene recreated in the paintings of the period by Flemish artists such as Jan van Eyck (1390–1441) and Hans Memlinc (1430–94).

For others, though, the earthly paradise took on a different, less overtly biblical, form. The medieval fantasy of a land called Cockaigne is well-recorded in northern European literature. A Dutch text of 1458, in modern translation (Herman Pleij's *Dreaming of Cockaigne*), describes this 'land of the Holy Ghost' thus:

> *There no one suffers shortages;*
> *The walls are made of sausages.*
> *Windows and doors, though it may seem odd,*
> *Are made of salmon, sturgeon and cod.*
> *The table tops are pancakes. Do not jeer,*
> *For the jugs themselves are made of beer.*
> *Household plates and platters, I'm told,*
> *Are all made of finest gold.*
> *Loaves of bread lie next to wine,*
> *As bright and radiant as sunshine.*

The Middle English text, *The Land of Cokaygne*, recorded at the beginning of the fourteenth century, and again in the same modern translation, is more precise about the location:

> *Far in the sea, to the west of Spain,*
> *There is a land we call Cokaygne.*
> *Under God's heaven no other land,*
> *Has such wealth and goodness to hand.*
> *Though Paradise be merry and bright,*
> *Cokaygne is yet a fairer sight.*
> *For what is there in Paradise*
> *But grass and flowers and green rice?*

Though there be joy and great delight,
There is but fruit for the appetite;
There is no hall, no room, no bench,
Just water, man's thirst for to quench.

Whatever physical comforts were missing in the sparse heaven of the scholastics and mystics were to be found in abundance in Cockaigne. And whatever people were lacking in their daily lives – food, comfort, rest, pleasure – were there too. The origins of this dreamland are obscure: some have suggested that the sexual licence that was part of Cockaigne was influenced by tales which had reached the West via travellers of the Qur'an's *djanna* paradise with its readily available virgins. Another theory would link it with the pagan heavens of Teutonic and Celtic mythology, still floating around in the popular imagination despite Christianity's heavy-handed efforts to stamp out its rivals. Valhalla, after all, was fundamentally nothing more than one long feast, with the magic boar and goat who provided the food and drink each having the power to come to life once again as soon as they had been stripped to the bone and milked dry. The same quality was enjoyed by the pig that was eaten continually in the Celtic heaven of bruidhean – as described in a prose narrative, traces of which have been found in Ireland and the Scottish Highlands. Bruidhean had at its centre an inexhaustible cauldron and ever-willing women.

Historians have speculated, however, that the fare of Cockaigne was assembled from ordinary people's observations and rare participation in great feasts enjoyed by those higher up the social ladder. For example, on 28 December, the big monasteries would often hold a Feast of Fools and offer a lavish running buffet for local people.

Cockaigne turned this one-off into an everyday event. It was eat as much as you can without ever having to pay, and was mainly a fantasy of the poor, their way of sharing in the feasts and the lifestyle that they imagined their rulers were enjoying while they starved.

But it was also an expression of the remoteness of the heaven preached by the Church. It was an indictment, even a satire, of exaggerated hopes of a new Jerusalem and how unattractive a heaven in the clouds seemed to many. Some 40 per cent of the Cockaigne texts that remain – and it was largely a take that passed through the oral tradition – are concerned with food or food fantasies. Aquinas might have written and taught of light, love and beauty, but, in the pews, were people who wanted reassurance that in heaven they would finally be well-fed and free from the shackles of hard physical labour. Finally, it was an expression of frustration that the long-held promise of a Second Coming still had not materialised.

For most of its adherents, Cockaigne was nothing more than a fantasy, often a childlike one. Because of the emphasis on 'party food', it was presented to children as a land of sweets. When a medieval child died, his siblings would be told that he was 'off to the land of Cockaygne'. The adults knew that, even when they gazed at Pieter Bruegel the Elder's 1567 depiction of this dreamland of fat, bloated figures, too tired and too full to pick up their tools again, they would only ever encounter Cockaigne in their dreams. But what delicious and liberating dreams they were. The appeal of the fantasy may even have been heightened by the very meagreness of their own diets. Death by starvation, while not a daily threat throughout the medieval period as is sometimes implied, did loom large during famines such as that of

1315–17, and thereafter haunted the imagination almost as effectively as Satan. In hard times, the poor in medieval Europe lived on grasses and seeds, including hemp and poppies, both of which have hallucinatory qualities. While no scholar has pinpointed the roots of the word Cockaigne, its verbal link with today's drug culture is intriguing.

If Cockaigne existed only as a fantasy paradise, some believed that an equivalent pleasure garden on earth could be found or at least created. At Hesdin Château in northern France between 1299 and 1553 (when it was destroyed by Charles V), the wealthy owners had created their own imitation of Eden, complete with golden trees that swayed in a breeze artificially created by a complex arrangement of pipes. Binche Château in what is now Hainaut in Belgium was destroyed in 1555, but in its time was an Eden, Cockaigne and heaven rolled into one. For a religious festival in August 1549, the future Philip II witnessed constellations moving across the firmament and planets passing by on floats. The air was sweetened by oil lamps, elaborate tables loaded with food were lowered from the ceiling by cables (in a direct reference from the Cockaigne legend) and the finale was a storm where the rain was orange blossom water and the hailstones sugared almonds. The local bishop, needless to say, condemned the spectacle as the work of the Devil.

Some took this quest for a flesh-and-blood paradise even more literally. It is an indication of the nature of the confused state of late medieval expectations of heaven that when Christopher Columbus made his third voyage of discovery (1498–1500), he explicitly stated that he was going in search of an earthly paradise. It may just have been window-dressing, a way of appealing to the Catholic monarchs who sponsored him, but when he found the Orinoco River, he recorded unequivocally that he had discovered one of the four rivers of paradise. Moreover, on encountering local Indian people, he broke into a song of praise for their (as he saw it then) innocence and natural goodness. He took it as a sign, he wrote, that he had reached the threshold of heaven, though this later did not stop him subsequently recasting his new domains as El Dorado, another fantasy land, dating back to classical times, and then plundering it of its wealth.

The Church was not blind to the appeal of Cockaigne. It came to understand that it had made heaven seem so remote to many as not to be worth considering. Its response was a pragmatic one – the creation and promotion of a poor man's heaven or purgatory, somewhere one step down from the preserve of saints, monks and virgins, with just a hint of hell, lest people thought they were getting off too lightly.

Purgatory had been acknowledged, but not named, in the teaching of Bede in the eighth century (as mentioned already), yet only made its real debut in scholarly books in the twelfth century. The very word, historian Jacques Le Goff argues in *The Birth of Purgatory*, only entered theological discourse in around 1170, and was not used by the papacy until 1254. Perhaps the official hesitancy was because there is little scriptural basis for purgatory, but this did not seem to affect its popularity, especially in the later part of the thirteenth century until the Reformation.

There were several arguments in favour of purgatory, when set against a remote, austere and seemingly unreachable heaven, and the lure of Cockaigne. First, it allowed the faithful on earth some measure of contact with the dead. It created an arena, where reality and imagination could mingle with grief and loss.

If those left behind prayed for the souls in purgatory, particularly on All Souls' Day (2 November), a feast day which was to grow in popularity towards the end of the thirteenth century, they could have an impact on matters in the hereafter. Those in heaven or hell were beyond the reach of prayers. Purgatory, however, was seen as accessible. Often, it was not just a question of praying for deceased family members, but for the whole community as well. In England in medieval times it was customary on 2 November to distribute 'soul cakes', made of bread, to represent each individual from the parish who was believed to be in purgatory and therefore in need of prayers.

Not only was death – whether through famine, warfare or random blows of fate, such as the Black Death, which carried off a third of the population of Europe in the fourteenth century – somehow regarded as your lot in life, and a judgement from on high, it was also very much more present, physically, in everyday life. When worshippers gathered in church, the dead bodies of the higher-born members of the community would be rotting under their feet, sometimes giving off a pungent smell. Corpses would be routinely handled. Even the pictures on the walls of the church seemed to cry out that the border between life and death was close at hand at all times and that, once you had crossed, purgatory would be your first stopping point if you were fortunate.

In the 1180s, an anonymous monk chronicler first recorded the Latin prose treatise, *Saint Patrick's Purgatory*. In a dream vision, the Irish saint discovers, with Jesus' help, the entrance to purgatory at Lough Derg in Donegal. It is explained to him that this is a place of penance and that if he spends a night and a day in there, his sins will be forgiven and he will avoid something so much worse – presumably hell. According to the story, Patrick wakes, builds a monastery on the spot and pilgrims come to repent and enhance their chances of getting to heaven. One of them is Owein, a knight of Northumbria. He plunges manfully into purgatory and enters a stone hall lit with wintry light, where he meets thirteen wise men dressed in white, who tell him to keep God in his heart. The hint of heaven is quickly followed by the haunting of hell. Owein is tormented by devils who attempt to deny the existence and certainly the healing effect of purgatory.

Resisting the demons' blandishments, Owein proceeds through a hell-scape of ghouls and fire, icy winds and dragons, torture chambers and dungeons. Finally, he approaches a bridge, where the demons pelt him with stones and he risks falling into a foul-smelling river. He perseveres, sure that God is with him, and therefore reaches the gates of paradise where he is greeted by a distinctly hierarchical crowd of 'Popes with great dignity/And cardinals great plenty/Kings and queens there were/Knights, abbots and priors/Monks, canons and friar preachers/and bishops that crosses bear'. After spending a night in such distinguished company, Owein returns to the abbey where he emerges a changed and holy man, living for seven years before he goes straight to paradise.

Owein became a role model for those who knew the story, and its influence cannot be underestimated. Literary historian Stephen Greenblatt writes in *Hamlet in Purgatory* that some 150 hand-made copies of the Latin text of *Saint Patrick's Purgatory* survive to this day. In an age when each new version had to be painstakingly taken down with quill pens, this is a very large number indeed. Moreover, Lough Derg itself became a famous medieval site of pilgrimage, evidence that heaven and purgatory no longer belonged only to the realms of the imagination, and on arrival, visitors would clamber into a cave that had been identified as the one used by St Patrick and Owein.

The medieval Church was keen on pilgrimages and the worship of relics, as were the pilgrims themselves. In popular folklore it was believed that if you could touch the bones of a saint, those bones would miraculously reassemble on judgement day and the resurrected saint would lead all who had touched his remains into heaven. Yet despite its popular appeal, Lough Derg was regarded by the Church with a certain amount of suspicion, not least because the whole cult of the place had emerged from a source that was outside the authorities' control. Furthermore, there was the risk of scandal, through bogus miracle cures and of the Church being ridiculed on account of the claims made for the place.

In the late fifteenth century, the papacy moved against its people when Pope Alexander VI had the Donegal shrine demolished, but it quickly rose again, only to be categorically smashed by his successor in 1632. However, Lough Derg remains a place of pilgrimage to this day.

The story of Lough Derg is an unusual one, for the institutional Church habitually exploited anything to do with the popular idea of purgatory to its own advantage. It encouraged prayers, fasts, alms-giving and Masses – suffrages as they were collectively known – for the souls in purgatory and charged a toll for each Mass said. One had to put money into the Church's coffers to profit the dead by moving them more quickly on to heaven. Medieval wills in England were full of such bequests and, according to Stephen Greenblatt, 'virtually all monasteries and churches in the Middle Ages would have been the recipients of donations in exchange for prayers for the dead'.

There was another institutional reason for allowing the popularity of purgatory in the medieval era. It was a way for the Church to rationalise and take control of an ancient pagan belief in ghosts. If you conceded a place of unquiet spirits, yearning to move on to heaven, then you had a ready explanation for persistent reports of the souls who haunted communities. Such interplay between this world and the next may have sat ill with the careful maps drawn up by the scholastics, but it raised the possibility that some ghosts might be essentially good spirits, engaged in a cosmic battle with Satan's demons. 'Commonly such spirits be fiends,' warned the fifteenth-century author of *Dives and Pauper*, but some, he acknowledged, may have been sent by God 'sometimes for to have help, sometimes to show that the souls live after the body, to confirm them that be feeble in the faith'.

In general, though, the Church attempted to stamp out stories of ghosts. In 1397, for instance, an inhabitant of a rural English parish in Hereford was charged with occasioning scandal by publicly declaring that the spirit of his dead father haunted the area at night. By talking up purgatory the Church was admitting the enduring power of such popular ideas. Next to tales of ghosts, dark caves, demons and unquiet souls, heaven must have seemed ever more remote.

But the cult of purgatory soon peaked. The abuse of it, for commercial gain, became a key rallying cry of the

Reformation, as we shall see later. As a young man, Martin Luther had climbed the Scala Sancta in Rome on his knees, pausing on each step to say the Our Father, in the hope of freeing his grandfather from purgatory. Only when he got to the top did he have his doubts, which he later translated into a wholesale rejection of any interim stage between earth and heaven. ('It was,' Professor Keith Thomas writes in his seminal study *Religion and the Decline of Magic*, 'a shibboleth which distinguished Protestant from Catholic [as we shall see later] almost as effectively as belief in the Mass or the Papal Supremacy.')

Before moving on from purgatory, a brief mention should be made of its near relative, limbo – from the Latin *limbus*, meaning the hem of a garment. The Church has never pronounced officially on limbo, but it has been popularly understood in two ways: the first, mainly in the early Church, was as a place where men and women of good will who had not heard the message of Christ could live happily after death. It would be a pale shadow of heaven, but far removed from the torment of hell. The second, was again as a reserved area just short of heaven, but this time containing babies who had died before they could be baptised and cleansed of original sin. Augustine, when challenged on this point, had insisted that since these infants did not fulfil the criteria for heaven, they went to hell, though he did mitigate these harsh words with the caveat that their punishment there would be of the mildest type – presumably stoking lukewarm fires rather than blazing furnaces.

Unsurprisingly, this was not much of a comfort to grieving relatives and in the Middle Ages limbo entered Church folklore, despite the hostility of the authorities.

It was debated at several Church councils (for example at Lyons, in 1274, and Florence, in 1439), but the ecclesiastical bigwigs refused to yield to popular sentiment, sticking to their guns over the paramount importance of original sin.

Some theologians attempted to reconcile the people with the hierarchy. The philosopher Peter Abelard (1079–1142) showed a scholastic precision in adapting Augustine's decree by saying that such infants were punished only in so far as they were deprived of the beatific vision. Their only suffering, then, was that they could not see the face of God. In post-Reformation times, however, limbo gradually faded from use, with theologians arguing that unbaptised children will inevitably be judged kindly by a merciful God.

CHAPTER NINE

Tomorrow's World

They are young, muscular, vibrant and absolutely at ease, though most haven't got a stitch on. Every one of them could easily be a model, an Olympic athlete or a teen idol from a boy band, the sort who thinks nothing of posing, scantily clad, for the centre-spread of a glossy magazine or parading through the changing room of the local gym without so much as a towel while the rest of us cower flabbily and shyly in our cubicles.

They are an intimidating bunch; a picture of physical perfection to die for, literally. For they are the lucky ones at the gates of paradise, about to receive their heavenly reward from angels – modestly attired by comparison in flowing robes – in one of the masterpieces of Renaissance, Luca Signorelli's early sixteenth-century frescoes in the Cappella di San Brizio in Orvieto Cathedral, the most extensive treatment of death, judgement, heaven and hell to be found in Italian art, and also the most sensual, though the guidebooks tend not to mention this, as if hoping visitors might not notice, or at least won't say so if they do. To understand the Renaissance's radical new take on heaven, it seemed like the obvious place to go.

Today, British holidaymakers and second-home owners often equate the Tuscany and Umbria region around Orvieto with heaven itself. I found myself a convert to its Edenesque pleasures as I drove up to Orvieto from Rome. Accustomed to a domestic landscape where, since the Norman Conquest, it has never occurred to anyone to build a settlement somewhere so impractical as at the top of a steep incline, (save in Shropshire, guarding what was once the tricky border with Wales) the sight of a collection of ochre-coloured houses perched precariously on the top of a summit, seemingly in defiance of gravity and probably beyond the reach of a motor car, gladdened my heart.

Even more impressive, was the fact that the Italians had realised that it was not enough just to protect the hill towns themselves against ugly modern developments. They extended the exclusion zone to the circle of land that could be glimpsed from the summit. If one visits a Shropshire hill-town like Bridgnorth or Ludlow, the historic centre is well-preserved, but when you look out across what should be rolling countryside, you see only ugly suburban bungalows and a disfiguring sprawl. By contrast, from the top of the crag on which Orvieto is balanced, you can still see the fields and trees of the timeless Umbrian landscape that Virgil described as paradise in his *Aeneid*.

The Church was at the height of its powers in the medieval age when Orvieto Cathedral was built, and so, appropriately, this giant licorice allsort, its exterior alternating rows of crumbly black-and-white stones, is at the pinnacle of the hill. Once inside, I began to worry that I had made a very long journey and a very steep climb to get to the wrong place: nowhere was there even a hint of heaven. The nave itself was bleak and decidedly terrestrial, rather than celestial. Uncluttered by anything so mundane as pews – where weary pilgrims might rest their tired legs – it was a triumph of understatement, a house of prayer masquerading as a minimalist museum. Such is the secular fate of too many great cathedrals as they attempt to swim with the tide and bring in the tourists to replace the worshippers who have drifted away.

Only the richly decorated altar hinted at this building's eight-hundred-year history as a church. The altar had an austere beauty which made the squeak of my rubber-soled shoes on the shiny floor as I approached it seem unforgivably vulgar.

Then, over to the right, I saw a flash of colour and, relieved, followed this rainbow to the Cappella di San Brizio. It was housed in an extension, built at right angles to the long, slim body of the cathedral. Entering through metal gates, I felt I was trespassing into a realm entirely separate from the cathedral, somewhere subject to radically different laws, for every inch of walls and ceiling was covered with a cacophony of reds and blues and golds. Going in was like plunging into a crowd. Though the figures were all on the wall, they had a living, breathing quality which made them leap out.

As with all crowds, there were some faces that just shouted out to be noticed. Though Signorelli had worked his way through the drama of the Last Judgement in all its various scenarios, it was his vision of the faces of the damned in hell that immediately caught my eye and instantly had me running through in my mind whatever mortal sins I might have committed since my last visit to the confessional twenty odd years ago. The power of this apocalyptical vision owed something to the vivid red flames that lick the poor unfortunates' bodies as the demon ferryman transports them to eternal torment, though perhaps it was more the inescapable burden of pain and terror on their faces as they are beaten, kicked and garrotted on the other side by evil-faced demons. A threat is always, it seems, more potent than a promise.

It is for his hell that Signorelli's work at Orvieto is most celebrated. There was, it has been suggested, a touch of the gallows in his temperament. And it was hell that dominated the area above and to the right of the chapel's altar. But it was his heaven that I had come to see, and this covered the area to the left of the altar, starting with panels of purgatory on the lower part of the wall, building up to the *Coronation of the Elect* above it, moving on to the *Elect Entering Heaven* and, finally, up on the ceiling, to Christ in majesty on the throne of his heavenly kingdom.

Heaven, according to this parade ground of naked buttocks, beatific glances, easy movements, redundant loin cloths (alleged to have been painted in, as with Michelangelo's Sistine Chapel, by a later, more prudish generation of cathedral clergy) and unembarrassment, is going to be one, long, divestment of all earthly inhibition. Not, it should be stressed, that Signorelli imagined some sort of orgy. Taking off your clothes can be a prelude to other things. It is, after all, only our own age that is obsessed with seeing sex in every situation. Signorelli's heaven, by contrast, is a place where perfect pecs, unlined skin or even sex are things too trivial to bother about. Its inhabitants might be unabashed, and they certainly are familiar with each other, but they are not lustful.

Signorelli's take typifies the image of heaven which emerged in the Renaissance. Starting in Italy in the fourteenth century, it was not, per se, an anti-Christian movement, but rather was one which wanted to reform the Church by dispelling fear and pessimism and banishing the sense of being powerless before a wilful and often cruel God which had dominated the medieval mind. Part of Renaissance thinking was to celebrate life as a gift from God and therefore as something potentially pure rather than a burden containing nothing but temptation and sin. Actions were potentially just as noble as prayers, the Renaissance thinkers said, life as holy as death and the world was there to be enjoyed, not renounced.

Part of this humanising process was to humanise heaven itself, most notably by allowing for earthly relationships to carry on once in God's domain. The pendulum was swinging to an anthropocentric setting. Paradise was no longer a place where God sat in judgement on high, surrounded by self-denying saints, but rather a celestial pleasure dome where human friendships would be restored and life's luxuries freely available.

In the evolutionary spirit of the Renaissance, the old medieval view and the new humanised version were often placed side-by-side. So, for example, in his *Compendium of Revelations*, written in around 1495 before he was excommunicated for his political battle with the papacy, the influential Dominican friar Girolamo Savonarola (1452–98) of Saint Mark's Convent in Florence wrote of two celestial worlds: a flower-strewn heaven for the blessed, filled with white animals, watered by crystal streams, and located behind a high wall of precious stones which encircled the universe, and, beyond this firmament, a paradise for God and His court. The two were linked with the familiar symbol of a ladder.

Signorelli's *Coronation of the Elect*, however, flamboyantly rejected the old view and trumpeted the new. The bottom third of this remarkable scene is dominated by the Adonises and Aphrodites, figures whose loose-limbed grace is in stark contrast to their embattled confrères on the other wall. Almost casually, their reunion with old friends taken for granted, they are gazing upwards as they lovingly receive golden crowns from angels whose colleagues play musical instruments and sing. Two central angels hover, sprinkling spring flowers, showering their blessings like confetti on the whole event.

Given Christianity's poor record on equal rights, I couldn't help noticing the level playing field between the men and women of the elect. All seemed equally favoured, regardless of gender. The only distinction I could discern between the uniformity of their youthful bodies was the presence, centre right, of a monk's tonsure. Heaven was not, then, restricted to clerics, as some boastful preachers were occasionally wont to imply at this time. Men of the cloth achieved it (or not) by the same process as everyone else in Signorelli's authorised version. As if to drive home the point, some of the men and women are holding hands. Marriage would be valued equally with holy orders in the hereafter, a theme the modern Church has now realised it must embrace, though, in my experience, with a notable lack of enthusiasm.

Moreover, earthly marriages would survive death. Unlike the medieval mystics, the humanising Renaissance believed that oneness with God would not suffice for ever. The company of other spirits, and of significant others, would also be desirable. Where once the only other inhabitants of heaven would have been angels, exemplars of a quasi-divine way of being, here these figures acted as guides, entertainers, hosts, a chorus and almost as servants to the souls who entered heaven.

Above and to the right of the *Coronation* is the next stage of the journey – *The Elect Entering Heaven*. Wrapped around the main altar of the chapel, it shows an altogether different landscape. Angels now take over as guides and gently but firmly manhandle the beautiful young people ever upwards through a zone of increased brightness, conveyed by the incandescent gold of the backdrop. Their charges have changed their facial expressions since the *Coronation*, their eyes now fixed on a point above themselves rather than on each other, while their bodies, still naked, are somehow more modest, arms lifted in awe rather than hanging casually at their sides. They have clearly left everything recognisably human behind and have been taken over by some new and higher power which emanates from the court of heaven.

By craning my neck, I could see, in eight triangular vanes linked by vegetal ornamentation, the final point of Signorelli's own journey and the culminating idea of the whole Cappella di San Brizio, located, following the scholastics' logic, high up in the clouds. Against an ever-more golden background, God is joined by saints, prophets, patriarchs, apostles and angels, plus Mary, all in their own captioned sector. There is no impediment here to the beatific vision, no qualification in God's radiance.

These ceiling frescoes, however, contained a catch: they were not by Signorelli. They had been painted fifty years beforehand by Fra Angelico (1400–1455), who had planned to complete the whole chapel but had been called away to Rome before he could complete the task. Signorelli, hurriedly and cheaply commissioned to complete what at the time must have been regarded as the task of providing a suitable but none-too-eye-catching backdrop for the great master's ceiling decoration, had, I realised, effectively gone on to steal the show. It was his innovation and his humanising of heaven and hell that now attracted the admiring gasps, rather than Fra Angelico's stiffer, more God-centred panels. The angels in Fra Angelico's heaven, for instance, are ethereal and asexual in contrast to Signorelli's hearty, full-bodied ones.

Whatever the differences between the two artists – and Fra Angelico, it should be stressed, was, in other works, as much a Renaissance star as was Signorelli, painting one of the first depictions of heaven as a beautiful garden in his *Last Judgement* panel of 1431 (which is now in the Museo di San Marco in Florence) – the concept of a several-stage heaven was all-important. The combination of an earthly outer layer that was tangibly human, a place of reunion with old friends and relatives, with the celestial inner sanctum became common in Renaissance art. The most favoured metaphor to express these two states was the garden and the castle.

My gaze, however, kept returning to the *Coronation of the Elect*, for this was where Signorelli was at his most intriguing, providing not simply a topographical and human outline of heaven, but also what was essentially a psychological portrait. It was the state of mind and being of those in paradise rather than the distracting incidentals of plants, trees or fortresses that provided inspiration. He was fleshing out the Renaissance vision by showing a state of mind where you could be in love with God *and* your wife, spiritual *and* physical, and all without any burden of guilt or gloom. For Signorelli, heaven was a place of liberation, freedom, individuality and licence.

The dramatic impact of such an alluring reinterpretation of paradise is all the greater when considered alongside Signorelli's courage in making such a public statement. For at the start of the sixteenth century, the sort of Renaissance optimism that inspired him was part of an elite movement and was not widely shared by those in the pews who remained hemmed in by a medieval fog. The desire for salvation and the fear of death and of the world beyond the grave meant that life was lived in the terrifying shadow of final judgement, with a constraining sense of the closeness of this world with the next and also of our smallness in the face of an unpredictable God.

The half-millennium in particular – Signorelli completed the frescoes in 1504 – was a time, contemporary records show, of apocalyptic angst when a doom-ridden, end-of-century culture gripped Rome, faced as it was by what seemed at the time to be the relentless advance of Islam, in the form of the Saracens, up through Italy. Indeed, the whole peninsula was the Lebanon of its time – the battleground where Charles VIII of France and his successors slogged it out with the Emperor Charles V for supremacy, leading to the sacking of Rome in 1527. This event dealt a decisive blow to the positive psychological mindset of Renaissance man (as may be seen in the contrast between Michelangelo's *Last Judgement*, painted after the sacking, and the rest of the Sistine Chapel which predated it). In an age of such worries, then, Signorelli was decidedly avant-garde and would have been regarded by some as having his head in the clouds in more ways than one.

While all visions of heaven usually tell us something about the concerns of their age, what I saw at Orvieto included a more prophetic element. Signorelli presents a different version of how life could be lived by portraying, in his *Coronation of the Elect*, an earthly paradise.

This, then, was not only a Renaissance view of the here-after, but an idealised (and in a psychological sense still relevant) vision of what the here and now could be like if people were prepared to cast away their fears.

CHAPTER TEN

If Paradise Was Half as Nice

Signorelli based his vision of heaven and hell in the Cappella di San Brizio on the writings of Dante Alighieri (1265–1321). Below the *Coronation of the Elect*, the artist freely acknowledged his debt to one of the initiators of the Renaissance with a portrait of the poet, pinched in the face and rapt in study. In what was nearly two centuries between Dante's death and Signorelli's commission at Orvieto Cathedral, Dante's *Commedia*, a three-part epic, in the best Greek tradition, through hell (*Inferno*, 1314), purgatory (*Purgatorio*, 1319) and heaven (*Paradiso*, 1321) had achieved such universal acclaim that it was usually called the *Divine Comedy* (not as in the modern sense, but a *comus oda*, or rustic song) because of the perception that God's hand had played a part in creating its powerful imagery of the hereafter.

Written in Italian, rather than Latin, as was still then the norm, it reached a wide audience by the standards of its time who saw in the poet's choice of language a certain distancing of himself from the Church. Yet if Dante showed a Renaissance willingness to look afresh at subjects on which the ecclesiastical authorities had previously pronounced the last word, the work was also deeply reverent. With *Paradiso* in particular, Dante was judged to have pulled off the seemingly impossible task of putting into words what he himself stressed was beyond words.

In this regard, according to Jeffrey Burton Russell, in his *History of Heaven*, Dante remains peerless. His is the influence that still shapes our perceptions. 'Beyond Dante,' Russell writes, 'no merely human word has gone. The *Paradiso* is the most sublime portrait of heaven from the Book of Revelation to the present.'

The eleven panels of purgatory in the Orvieto chapel follow the first eleven cantos of *Purgatorio*. Dante's guide through hell, the Roman poet, Virgil, is present throughout this stage. After their initial journey to the lifeless, dark core of the earth that is hell in *Inferno*, the two return to earth in the southern hemisphere – like many good Renaissance men Dante showed a scientific curiosity with the physical structure of the cosmos – and there discover the Mountain of Purgatory. They climb up through a succession of spheres, witnessing the cleansing of those *anime* or souls (rather than the *ombre* or shades of the *Inferno*) who have failed to make it into heaven because, for example, of their over-interest in earthly success or their improper ideas of love.

Next to the drama of the tortured souls in hell, there is a measured, almost bland, tone to the privations of Dante's purgatory. It is no surprise that this book translated itself into the least interesting section of Signorelli's work. For even though Dante has the lustful purged by flames in purgatory, he makes it clear that they accept their punishment stoically, and occasionally gladly, seeing their suffering as hopeful. You might almost conclude that they are under anaesthetic. Their stiff upper-lip attitude is well-represented by Arnaut Daniel, the Provençal poet mentioned earlier whom Dante encounters on his ascent of the Mountain of Purgatory:

> *I am Arnaut, who weep and sing as I go;*
> *Thoughtful now, I see my past folly,*
> *And I see with joy the day I hope for ahead.* (*Purgatorio*
>   26:142–44)
>   (*The Divine Comedy*, translated by C. H. Sisson)

Then Arnaut dives back into 'the fire which refines them'. Finally, Dante and his guide reach the summit, but Virgil can go no further – the suggestion being that as a non-Christian he is excluded from heaven, though this is later contradicted.

Just as Signorelli's hell attracted the biggest crowds in the Cappella di San Brizio, so it is *Inferno* that has down the ages been the best-read of Dante's three books. For the poet himself it was *Paradiso*, a self-styled 'sacred poem' written in the months leading up to his death and including many of the characters he had known in his life, which he regarded as his greatest achievement. As T. S. Eliot once remarked in a critical study of Dante, 'Purgatory, here and there, might be called dry: the *Paradiso* is never dry, it is either incomprehensible or intensely exciting.'

In *Paradiso*, Dante seems to be claiming to have done what remains beyond the powers of humankind – to have had a sneak preview of heaven, then returned to earth to report back. But to approach the work with such a modern and literal sensibility would be to appreciate only a part of its power. The imagery is certainly informative, but it would have been understood by its original readers as something much more, neither merely an accurate description of heaven nor simply a symbolic treatment of the subject.

What we have developed in Western Europe over the past four hundred years, as a result of vast economic, political, social and intellectual changes, has been an entirely different, scientific and rational concept of the nature of truth. It is a theme that will greatly influence the chapters to come.

What we have lost, and what Dante's audience possessed, is an appreciation of the complementary nature of two approaches which scholars now label *mythos* (myth) and *logos* (reason). Today we may dismiss myth with negative phrases such as 'just a myth', but for Dante's readership, myth, as Karen Armstrong writes in *The Battle for God*, 'was regarded as primary; it was concerned with what was thought to be timeless and constant in our existence. Myth looked back to the origins of life, to the foundations of culture, and to the deepest level of the human mind. Myth was not concerned with practical matters, but with meaning ... The *mythos* of a society provided people with a context that made sense of their day-to-day lives; it directed their attention to the eternal and the universal.'

Myth and *logos* – the rational, pragmatic and scientific – used to be held in balance. Now we are so much in awe of reason and science that we can only view myth through the filter of reason. The mythical qualities of ideas such as heaven, hell, God and the devil are all reduced to the simple question: Can they be proven? And: What precisely do they symbolise? There is no room for notions of what they say about the ultimate value of human existence. This dimension which is now missing is everywhere at play in Dante. He had a strong sense of the semiotic, that imagery could be an intimation of something spiritual and transcendent which was beyond words. It illustrated and gave form to truths that otherwise would be hard to pin down. Modern Christians struggle, for example, with transubstantiation and the Eucharist – water and wine or the body and blood of Christ? – but Dante's readers would effortlessly have taken it in their stride. The concept found in Dionysius of the distinction between what can be known about God and what is ineffable would have been at play in their minds.

Dante's guide, Beatrice Portinari, was a young woman he had met and fallen in love with when both of them were still children. She had married someone else, but died young in 1290, and she remained fixed in Dante's mind and heart as both the one who got away and the epitome of feminine perfection. His hope that one day the two would be reunited in another world caused him first to write of her in *Vita Nuova* (1292) and then to give her, rather than any traditional saint or holy man or woman, the starring role in *Paradiso* where, by virtue of her beauty, she is the medium who draws him, and by association the world, towards God. Yet this is only half the story. We have to make an additional leap of imagination back to an earlier age with its different sensibilities. Beatrice was, for Dante, a theophany, a vision and an epiphany of God in human form, but not God Himself, because God was beyond words and images.

Beatrice appears to Dante at the start of *il paradiso terrestre* – the earthly paradise, the highest point of the Mountain of Purgatory, which is roughly equivalent to the *Coronation of the Elect* panel at Orvieto. At first he does not recognise the figure, described as like the rising sun, her face veiled, wearing white, green and red for faith, hope and charity. When finally he realises who she is – both lost love and epiphany of God – Dante is mesmerised.

Though, together, Dante and Beatrice are being drawn inexorably towards God, they pause to embrace the earthly heaven, with its familiar birds and foliage, soft breezes, fountains, rivers, gentle music and everlasting springtime. The poet bathes first in the River Lethe and then in the Eunoe, where his memory of the virtues is restored. The fountain is a classic Renaissance motif, while the garden that is the ante-room to God's heavenly court is one of its favourite images.

Thomas Aquinas and Bonaventure had both taught that there were neither plants nor animals in heaven, but Dante in this instance ignored them. Scholastic theology could be very severe, and insisted that heaven was an intellectual world of pure light. Medieval legend was much more colourful and attuned to the desires of the populace, and so Dante reached back to borrow from accounts like the *Golden Legend*, compiled in the thirteenth century by Italian archbishop James of Voragine, with its tale of the angel who brought a palm branch from heaven to Mary when he came to tell her of her imminent death. Since the time of Lactantius in the fourth century, the palms of heaven had been the mark of the elect.

Thus cleansed and prepared, the two explorers embark on their journey:

> *If, reader, I had room to write more,*
> *My poem could still not tell you everything*
> *About the sweet drink of which I could never have had*
> *   enough.*

But since all the pages designed for this
Second part of the poem have been filled,
The rules of art stop me at this point.

I came back from that most sacred of streams,
Made afresh as new trees are renewed
With their new foliage, and so I was
Clear and ready to go up to the stars. (Paradiso 33:136–145)
(from *The Divine Comedy*, translated by C. H. Sisson)

It is by looking at Beatrice that he becomes trans-humanised, Dante writes, in the same way as Glaucus in Greek mythology, who was transformed into a sea-god after eating a certain herb. From here on, Dante's tone becomes almost childlike when in Beatrice's quasi-divine presence, that of someone recalling something that he had witnessed but could not truly understand:

What is involved in becoming more than human
Cannot be put into words; so may the example
Suffice for him for whom grace reserves the experience.

Whether I was only what of me was created
Latterly, O love which controls the heavens.
You know, who lifted me up with your light. (1:70–75)

In places his memory is sketchy, in others fulsome. By such a device Dante manages to square the circle of creating an imagery of heaven at the same time as expressing its mystery and ineffableness.

As a map, then, *Paradiso* is generally unreliable, but it has a narrow focus on certain areas. Dante's similes and metaphors draw throughout on different modes of travel – riding, swimming, climbing, sailing, even flying. From the start of *Paradiso* he warns those who are, as he puts it, in small boats, to abandon ship at once for what lies ahead is only for those who have cultivated a love for 'the bread of angels', a reference to spiritual understanding taken from the Book of Psalms.

Just as Dante and Virgil had descended through the various layers of hell, now the writer and Beatrice ascend through the spheres that make up heaven. The key concept throughout is that of light – light that comes from God, light that is God's love, light that some enjoy more than others, light as a defining quality. This theme is reflected in Signorelli's frescoes – the shades of gold that become evermore brilliant on the stairway to heaven, the beatific gazes of the blest who reside there, receiving light from a distant source (presumably God) and projecting it out on to those who look up at them. To see, Dante says, is to understand. No words by comparison are adequate. So when Beatrice looks at him, she sees him as he really is – *vedea me si com'io*. Heaven is a place of looks and glances, gazes and visual spectacles. There is also music, song and dance, but the almost blinding light relegates them all to the backdrop.

The geography of *Inferno* was all Dante's creation, but in *Paradiso* he follows the spirit of the accepted conventions of medieval astronomy, with its debt to such figures as Ptolemy, the second-century Egyptian whose system remained the *vade mecum* of star-gazers until Copernicus in 1543 turned the cosmos on its head.

Dante's first stop is the moon, a solid and pearl-like place where he discerns seven faces that seem eager to speak to him. They appear diaphanous, but Beatrice assures him that they are spirits and urges him to listen. Their bodies, according to the teaching of the time which Dante endorses, will not follow until judgement day.

These are Dante's friends and acquaintances from earth who had died by 1300 (when, in theory, *Paradiso* is set) and won a place at God's right hand.

Piccarda Donati, a relative of Dante's wife on earth, recounts how she is in the lowest sphere of heaven because she, like those around her, broke her vows to God. Piccarda had joined the nuns who followed St Clare, but was seized from the convent against her will by her brother, Corso, and forced into a marriage with Rossellino della Tosa. (Corso Donati had been a political opponent of Dante's and there is an undeniable, though minor, earthbound element in *Paradiso* of a settling of old scores.) So, for Piccarda, heaven performs its classic role – making good a life that was not as she would have chosen.

Dante asks Piccarda if she has any chance of raising herself up to higher spheres in heaven, but she explains that her happiness is complete because this is the place that has been allotted to her by divine love. 'In His will is our peace.' All are equally blest, but some are more blest than others depending on how they have lived their lives. In Piccarda's case, though her 'sinfulness' was not of her own doing, she is being marked down for it (harshly, by modern standards), but again this is to interpret Dante's heaven too narrowly. For all transcend place and therefore inhabit different spheres simultaneously – in the empyrean, or highest level, with God and the saints, and in the sphere which best matches their spiritual qualities. The implication is that some have a greater potential for love, joy and light than others, but all are full to their potential and therefore have no aspirations to further promotion.

Beatrice's gaze then sweeps Dante along to the next sphere, Mercury, where a thousand shining spirits – the

splendori – welcome them. Their spokesman, the sixth-
century Roman Emperor Justinian, explains that this is
the domain of those who were so absorbed in gaining
fame and honour that they neglected their devotion and
service to God. Again, there is no trace of regret in his
voice, merely of description and acceptance. Mercury is
followed by Venus, associated by pagans with love. Here
Dante meets several figures – including Rahab, the harlot
of Jericho rescued by Jesus – who have renounced their
earlier penchant for excesses of the flesh in order to win
eternal life with God.

Dante also discusses with Charles of Naples, son and
brother of the ruler of the southern Italy, the seemingly
random course that earthly life can take. Why should
Charles be a good man and his brother, Robert of Anjou
(King of Naples from 1309) a miserly one? Why should
Esau in the Book of Genesis be so different to his brother
Jacob, planning to kill him, or Romulus be so different
to Remus? It is, Dante is told, down to the influence of
the circling planets, which imprint differing characteristics on humankind. Irregularities in families are down
to Providence, or the stars. If this sounds oddly like
a charter for modern-day astrologers – now so disapproved of by the mainstream Churches – then Dante
quickly brings the argument back round to the Christian
cornerstone of free will, every individual's freedom to
make what he or she will with the inheritance they
receive.

In the next sphere, the Sun, Dante further develops the
idea of heaven as a place which ravishes all the senses.
In describing the twelve lights which he sees there, all
brighter than the Sun itself, he paints a backdrop of rain-
bows, garlands, roses and dancing. The lights 'form a
crown around Him [God], a crown even more beautiful

to hear than to behold'. Residing here are the souls of those who had great wisdom – Solomon, Thomas Aquinas, and the Franciscan St Bonaventure.

Dante is not suggesting wisdom is any lesser of a gift than, say, military prowess, which comes further up in the cycle of spheres. Again, this is too literal a symbolism. He is, instead, following the astronomy of Ptolemy and the medieval association of certain planets with certain callings. Mars, for instance, the next sphere up, was named after the Roman god of war, and so Dante finds it full of soldiers amongst whose number are Charlemagne, Judas Maccabaeus, a Jewish general from the second century BC (heaven is not just for Christians) and Cacciaguida, Dante's own great-great-grandfather. They are, it seems, soldiers of the cross since, on Mars, Dante is transfixed by two beams of light which intersect to form the cross while smaller pinpricks dance around, singing a hymn. This is described as touching his soul and, although he doesn't understand its meaning, he deems it the sweetest pleasure he has yet encountered.

The lights of souls on Jupiter, Dante's next stop, soar and wheel in the sky like a great flock of birds, forming words in the sky like the opening lines of the Book of Wisdom: 'Love justice, you who judge the earth.' Jupiter is the seat of bringers of justice such as David, described as 'the singer of the Holy Ghost', who brought the Ark of the Covenant back to Jerusalem, and, intriguingly, Ripheus the Trojan, a character briefly mentioned in the *Aeneid*. The inclusion of such a pagan figure – though Virgil had earlier been excluded from *Paradiso* – is an ambiguous hint that the state of mind Dante was describing was not only on offer to Christians. If Ripheus was there, and Judas Maccabaeus, baptism may not have been a prerequisite for admission.

Beatrice once more transports Dante, this time to Saturn. This is the sphere of the contemplative, those who in life sought God through prayer, such as the great monastic reformer of the eleventh century, Peter Damian, or the founder of the Benedictines, St Benedict, who, when Dante meets him, has no face and is simply a blazing light. The main feature of Saturn is a golden ladder, on which souls might ascend to contemplate God more closely. It was an image taken from the dream of Jacob in the Book of Genesis and was a standard in the iconography of heaven before and after Dante's time:

> Within the crystal which, circling round the world,
> Carries the name of its beloved leader
> Under whom every malice lay dead,
>
> The colour of gold, with refulgent rays
> I saw a ladder which was erected aloft
> So far, my sight could not follow it.
>
> I saw too, coming down the steps,
> So many splendours, I thought all the stars
> Which shine in heaven were pouring down there. (21:25–33)

Dante follows the souls who are climbing the ladder and finds himself in the stars. At this transitional point Dante looks back to survey the ground he has covered and sees the earth as a tiny dot far beneath him. All worldly ambition, he reflects, is as nothing when seen from here. Our lives are as nothing, save to God. When he swings round to face upwards once more, he has to look away – the light of Christ that greets him is too powerful for one so sinful. However, Mary, Jesus' mother (already regarded, as seen at Chartres, as an intermediary between God and humankind), eases his way, though Dante complains that his vocabulary is insufficient to convey how.

There is a garden, Dante reports, where babies stretch out their arms to Mary, calling, 'Mamma' and where they sing the *Regina Coeli*, Queen of Heaven. Mary is 'the rose in which the Divine Word made himself flesh'. He is ushered before the apostles Peter, James and John – memorably captured by fifteenth-century master, Sandro Botticelli, in his cycle of 92 drawings based on the *Divine Comedy* as flames – who examine him on the three theological virtues of faith, hope and love. These are qualities they tell him, apparently aware of his unique mission, that are surplus to requirements in a heaven bathed in divine love, but which are absent on earth. Dante is instructed to carry this message back.

Faced with such love, Dante goes blind – his losing his sight emphasises the element of mysticism. It is only through Beatrice's ministrations that he discovers a new way of seeing as he enters, in the company of the apostles and saints, who are swept upwards like sparkling snowflakes, the Primum Mobile, the outermost sphere, and what is effectively the skin on the cosmos. This sphere is powered directly by God's love, Beatrice tells Dante, and in its turn powers the other spheres and, by association, the earth. God thus controls time which is likened to a plant, with its roots in the Primum Mobile and its leaves being the planets.

The Primum Mobile is the habitat of angels who circle Dante and Beatrice like sparks. The swiftest and brightest are the seraphim, then, as they spread outwards, come the cherubim, the thrones, the dominations, the virtues, the powers, the principalities, the archangels and the angels. Each acts as one of the nine heavenly spheres, from the Primum Mobile down, and they are the 'intelligence' controlling that sphere.

As the light of the angels fades, just as the stars dim before dawn, Dante finally passes up to the empyrean, the highest heaven. He sees a great river of light, representing divine grace, alive with sparks that are angels and which flows between two flowery banks whose blooms are the souls of the faithful departed:

> And I saw the light in the form of a stream
> Of resplendent brilliance, in between two banks
> Painted with all the marvels of the spring.
>
> From this river there issued live sparks
> Which everywhere settled themselves in the flowers
> Like rubies which have been set in gold.
>
> Then, as if the scents had made them intoxicated,
> They sank once more into the marvellous swirl;
> And as one entered it, another flew out. (30:61–69)

A great snow-white rose whose petals rise to a thousand tiers becomes an amphitheatre filled with the heavenly spirits. The upper sections are for adults, the lower for infants whose salvation has been won by the prayers of others. There are, Dante notes, a few seats still vacant.

At this stage Beatrice takes her seat among the blessed and Dante is left in the company of St Bernard of Clairvaux, the twelfth-century Cistercian monk, mystic and correspondent of Hildegard of Bingen. Bernard will take him on the final, intuitive stage of the journey. Having first addressed the Virgin Mary – now described as a celestial rose and the one closest to God, and seated amid a blaze of golds and yellows – Dante is given her blessing so as to turn his gaze finally to God:

> *And I remember that I was the bolder*
> *To bear the rays, as long as my sight*
> *Had intercourse with the infinite power.*
>
> *O abundant grace, trusting whom I presumed*
> *To fix my gaze through the eternal light*
> *Until I had seen all that I could see!* (33:79–84)

Words fail him, and anyway are, he says, unfit to convey what he sees, but he struggles on to describe the spheres of the universe as fallen leaves gathered up and bound in a book by God. Finally, Dante beholds the incarnation – God taking on human form, amid an ocean of light.

> *In the profundity of the clear substance*
> *Of the deep light, appeared to me three circles*
> *Of three colours and equal circumference;*
>
> *And the first seemed to be reflected by the second,*
> *As a rainbow by a rainbow, and the third*
> *Seemed like a flame breathed equally from both.*
>
> *Oh how my speech falls short, how faint it is*
> *For my conception! And for what I saw*
> *It is not enough to say that I say little.*
>
> *O eternal light, existing in yourself alone,*
> *Alone knowing yourself; and who, known to yourself*
> *And knowing, love and smile upon yourself!*

That circle which, conceived in this manner,
Appeared in you as a reflected light,
When my eyes examined it once more,

Within itself, and in its own colour,
Seemed to be painted with our effigy;
And so absorbed my attention altogether.

Like a geometer who sets himself
To square the circle, and is unable to think
Of the formula he needs to solve the problem,

So was I faced with this new vision:
I wanted to see how the image could fit the circle
And how it could be that that was where it was;

But that was not a flight for my wings;
Except that my mind was struck by a flash
In which what it desired came to it.

At this point high imagination failed;
But already my desire and my will
Were being turned like a wheel, all at one speed,

By the love which moves the sun and the other stars
  (33:127–145)

After the very precise conclusion to *Inferno* – of a piti-ful, weeping Satan encased in ice – there is something unsatisfying for modern tastes about this conclusion to *Paradiso*, but it is only disappointing if there is an expec-tation of a final word or definitive statement about God. The tradition that stretched back through Dionysius, Augustine's vision at Ostia and back to the Greeks, however, allows for no such expectation. Dante instead offers an affirmation of the divine and tackles the question of what God is in a positive way. At the end of *Paradiso* the three circles/colours – the Holy Trinity – give way to a perception of the human contours of the Son of God, while the central mystery of the incarnation, linking God in His heaven with humankind on earth, is revealed to Dante in a mystical flash that he cannot describe or explain. Botticelli, for his part, perhaps offers us the wisest counsel: he left his illustration for canto 33 blank.

Traveller's Tales: 3

In the spring of 1999, Elleke van Kraalingen, a 31-year-old Dutch psychologist, was on holiday in Jamaica with her partner, Hermod, a 45-year-old Norwegian doctor. They were returning home the next day and decided to take a final late-night swim. As they crossed the road, a speeding car knocked Hermod down and killed him instantly.

'We had plans to marry and it had been a wonderful holiday. I knew I had met the love of my life. That day, we had been having a conversation and Hermod had said to me: "These weeks have been so wonderful and timeless, here in this paradisical environment . . . and the way it is between us. This is how it is and it will always be like this. What there is between us now goes beyond time and space . . . You have always been trying to convince me that life can be so beautiful. Now I'm starting to believe you. Never before have I been so close to paradise. And if I were to die right now, I wouldn't mind, for now I know how beautiful life can be."

'There was a radiance about him when he spoke these words. He had reached a stage of surrender. It had been a struggle for him to reach this point. He had always struggled, as many gifted, academic people do, with the sense that this earth was not a good place to be, that humanity did not treat each other well. There had been times when he had longed for death. But all that had now passed. He had told me, with incredible excitement, that he had now found the answer to Shakespeare's question "to be or not to be". The answer was, he said, "to be or not to be touched with love". He was also aware of Buddhist ideas, about transcending this life, moving on to another state of awareness, and we had been discussing that just before we crossed that road. He had always been interested in the idea of an afterlife.

'When the car hit him, I was walking a few feet behind and so was unharmed, but at once I felt a tearing apart. It must have been the moment he lost consciousness. I ran to where he was lying. He was on his side, his legs were broken, there was blood everywhere and his eyes were closed. I began telling him he couldn't leave me. A man came over and said he was a doctor. Together we frantically worked on Hermod's body to start it up again. But as I was doing this, I saw his soul coming out. I was concentrating on his body so much, but I clearly saw his spirit rising as a sort of mist. It's hard to put into words. And then even as I was trying to resuscitate him, I was aware of him standing behind me. At that moment his face, on the body in front of me, became peaceful.

'A crowd had gathered and it was very chaotic. My consciousness was split. Part of me was there, very shocked and devastated. But another part of me felt this light and peace coming over me. We were waiting for the ambulance and I thought I should go to the hotel, which was just over the road, to get our passports. As I started to walk, I was very clear that he was walking next to me, that he was taking my hand, although my physical hand was empty and hanging loosely at my side.

'I wanted to go to the mortuary with him, but the police said no. I was very upset, but it made me realise that I didn't need to be with his body because he was still with me. As soon as I was alone in our hotel room, I saw him, in his physical shape, sitting on the bed. I put my hands up before my eyes. I am a psychologist and I told myself that this was just my imagination, what I expected and hoped to see. But when I took them away he was still there. And then he spoke and challenged me as only he could do: "I'm still here. And our relationship does continue. Everything I've said today remains valid. There is no death, there is no time, there's only reality. Our relationship continues in another reality, in timelessness.''

'I heard his voice in my mind, it sounded like him. It sounded real, it felt real. I asked myself: "am I imagining this?'' It was, of course, what I wanted to hear. He looked at me straight and raised his finger. He sounded clear, insistent but still loving: "You were always the one who was trying to convince me there is another reality we can open up to. Now you shouldn't doubt yourself, you have to believe me. I am there and this is the only way we can be together now.''

'And we talked and talked, and I felt such a peace. There was light all around him and I was aware of other beings there, supporting him. I had so many doubts but deep down inside I knew this was real so I wrote it all down in my diary.

'He remained with me over the next few difficult days, while I was giving statements to the police, meeting the driver who had killed him, watching the autopsy, flying back to Europe to tell my three children who had come to see Hermod as a father, and then going on to his family in Norway for the funeral. It was about four days later when I was finally on my own, in his flat in Oslo, surrounded by the gifts I had given him. It was very quiet and I began to meditate which was something I had learned over the years. I had hardly closed my eyes when suddenly he was standing in front of me, radiant and well, so close that I could touch him. It was as if we were reconnecting beyond the chaos.

'He took my hands. "Come, up we go,'' he said. With a sudden tug, I was being pulled out of my body. Amazed, I looked down. My body was sitting there, relaxed with legs crossed, on the floor. I was standing in my appearance of light in front of him, my hands still in his hands. To make sure, I looked down once more. My physical body was still sitting there, immobile.

'"Do you trust me?'' he asked.

'"Yes."

'And he pulled me further. We put our arms around each other and kissed. It felt so real and as good as in our most intimate embraces when he was still alive, when he still had a physical body. In the end I grew tired and lost my focus and fell back into my body.

'He returned every day and took me out of my body. He did it. If I tried to will it myself I couldn't. I needed him. I felt like Alice in Wonderland. We travelled to a sphere of different colours, of other beings. I saw their shape, but it was not a very physical world. It was like this earth, but with more light, more transparency. One day, he took me to a beautiful garden. On another, I met his mother who had died a few years earlier. On another, we went to a house he had built as a retreat. When I asked him about it, he said he was creating it all by his imagination. In this sphere, he explained, people saw what they expected to see. So, for example, strong Christians saw heaven. Or if they felt so much guilt, they saw hell because that was what they expected to see. Each inhabited his own world.

'He was grateful that I could consciously be with him in this way. Others in his sphere went back to see their loved ones, but they couldn't make contact. Those they visited were not perhaps open in the same way as I was.

'On these trips, I experienced other beings. They had a lighter presence than us, a more elevated consciousness, almost angels, but then that is to think in our earthly terms of shapes, rather than in terms of light, or what energy might look like. What people sometimes describe as long white dresses and wings are light energy fields. I didn't need to talk to these other beings. Words were not necessary. There was a telepathy. There was no time or space. If you thought of Alaska, you were in Alaska. Travel was that easy. If you thought of someone, you were with them, there was an immediate connection.

'These trips went on with this intensity for the first six months after Hermod's death. I think the shock had disrupted my connection with my physical body. My connection to here was getting weaker and weaker and there were times when all I wanted was to be with Hermod in his sphere, to end my life here, but my children were here. I decided to concentrate on the need to be here with them, and develop a will to live.

Over the period, Hermod changed. He became more subtle and I saw him less and less in physical form. I saw less and less his shape. The marks of his accident had gone and he began to look younger. I wondered, again as a psychologist, if this was just how I wanted to see it, but I had loved him as he was. I had never wanted him to be younger in looks.

'He took me through different layers of the other sphere. Since you can create whatever you want there, it is layer upon layer upon layer of illusion. It is good or bad depending on whether you want or expect it to be good or bad. Some souls could not accept death. They stuck closely to their physical bodies and their place on earth. We call them ghosts.

'When Hermod took me beyond that first layer, we were in a less physical place, somewhere less connected to emotions and more to mental thoughts. There was more mutual creativity. Some never get through there, but he took me further, to a layer where beings need no shape, where there is an instinctive communication of the core of your thoughts and so no talking, not even any telepathy. It was somewhere beyond words. And that was where I began to feel my own limitations. My reasoning, my belief-system, and my connection with my body held me back.

'I also experienced the layer of the souls, a very deep, very pure place. I still recognised Hermod in his pure essence, stripped of all personality traits, but there were also deep connections with others there. Even though there were no bodies, that sphere felt more real than life here on earth. There were no longer any illusions, any made-up pictures, but simply a deep love.

'At some point it became so subtle that my being couldn't stand it. I had no thoughts, no feelings, not even any sense of Hermod. All I could sense was light and love. If I could call anything God, and I grew up an atheist, then that would be it. Oneness but consciousness. There was no man on a throne, but what I felt has changed my life for ever. It was so huge that I could only grasp a fraction of it and it is beyond my words. And I still had the feeling that there were more layers, worlds after worlds, but I could go no further.

'Hermod is still with me, but less often now, and it doesn't keep me from being in the here. I am learning to love this life again, to live life to the full, for the sake of my children, for my own sake and to honour life itself.'

CHAPTER ELEVEN

A Delectable Death

The American scholar Jeffrey Burton Russell holds that there were no new developments in thought regarding heaven after Dante. The same old ideas were reworked, reshuffled and fought over time and again until the notion began to fall into decline in the modern era. Certainly, the Renaissance period was a high watermark in terms of conveying the mystery of the hereafter. Henceforth, everything gradually became much more literal and, arguably, in the case of heaven, nonsensical. By the end of the sixteenth century, with the battles of the Reformation directing minds in more strictly scriptural directions, heaven was also slipping down the list of priorities; an also-ran dragged into wider doctrinal disputes. The enquiring, innovative and unbounded spirit of the Renaissance was eclipsed.

The Reformation did, however, concentrate the minds of the faithful on their eternal fate as never before. Whether you stuck with the credo of Rome, or switched to the alternative offered by the Reformers, became a question of crucial, sometimes life-threatening, importance. Wars raged throughout the period because of religious rivalry. Where the narrow scholastic calibration of heaven had once co-existed with the medieval mystics' bridal chamber and the Land of Cockaigne, such differences suddenly became enough to found a new Church upon.

It would be true to say that heaven was never a particular obsession of the Reformers. Theirs was as much a practical and political revolt against Rome as it was a doctrinal one. Martin Luther (1483–1546) did occasionally make fun in his writings of the popular conception of heaven as fulfilment of earthly wishes, and in number 16 of his 95 theses, nailed to the church door in Wittenberg in 1517, he spoke of hell, purgatory and heaven as akin to 'despair, almost despair and the assurance of safety'. Purgatory, in particular, failed to impress the Reformers. They vigorously attacked the notion of it as a fraud and a scandal.

The Reformers' gospel was very God-centred. 'Our very being,' John Calvin (1509–64), Luther's French-born contemporary and fellow-reformer, wrote in his treatise on heaven, *Psychopannychia*, 'is nothing but subsistence in the one God.' This left little room for speculation on the nature, population or landmarks of heaven. In one of his table talks – discussions with his students – Luther said that he often considered what eternal life would be like, but always came up with the same answer, namely that it would unchanging and not punctuated by anything as mundane as eating or drinking. 'We will have enough to do with God. Accordingly [the apostle] Philip put it well when he said, "Lord, show us the Father, and we shall be satisfied." This will be our very dear preoccupation.' (*Martin Luther* by Richard Marius)

For his part, Calvin remarked that the angels would

be so taken up with God that they would 'have nothing better to which they can turn their eyes or direct their desires'. And Luther's close friend and disciple, Philipp Melanchton (1497–1560), who gave the address at his funeral, produced a picture-catechism which, when it came to 'life everlasting' in the last line of the Creed, showed Christ in judgement on the last day. There was no cosiness or incidental friends and furniture in such visions of heaven.

The same might be said of Luther's rejection of the notion of purgatory – the result, he said, of his ordeal on the Scala Sancta. The souls of the departed, he believed, proceeded at the moment of death either to heaven or hell, never to return. Their bodies would join them on Judgement Day. In between the souls would sleep – 'just as a man who falls asleep and sleeps soundly until morning does not know what has happened to him when he wakes up, so shall we suddenly rise on the Last Day' – but that sleep would be in the place of their final destination. Any clouding of the issue of salvation, allowing some a second chance in purgatory to work for eternal rest after death, could not be accommodated. Neither was there any overtly mystical notion of an inner ascent in search of an ineffable God. Both, for Luther, were a distraction and a dilution of the central importance of the Last Judgement and being with God eternally.

Luther's overturning of what had been accepted wisdom on purgatory in the late medieval period prompted Thomas More, then Henry VIII's loyal and clever servant, to pen a riposte – *The Supplication of Souls*. In it he argues that whatever the abuses associated with the sale of prayers and masses for the souls in purgatory, it nevertheless remained a place that met a real need, namely for an abiding relationship between the living and the dead, some of whom have 'long lain and cried so far from you that we seldom broke your sleep'. In allowing for that continuing link, More felt, the Church was wisely buttressing its whole position on afterlife by offering a kind of proof, in its own terms, that time did not come to an end at death, that there was indeed something more, that the promise of salvation could, however obliquely, be verified. It was a position that found little favour with the Reformers.

More made one other contribution which ought, briefly, to be considered here – his 1516 treatise *Utopia*. The title conjures up the sort of dreamlands/earthly paradises exemplified by Cockaigne, but More's intention was less spiritual. His original title for *Utopia* was *The Best Condition of a Society*, and in his portrait of an island state of equality he is less concerned with bringing heaven down to earth than with extolling the worldly wisdom of government based on God's revelation rather than natural law. Utopia is not heaven. It is a mirror of England – its dimensions are the same, it is the same distance from the Equator, the number of its city states is the same as the total of English counties. It is an ironic rather than a laudatory text. More's Utopia, with its equalities, amorality and freedoms, was designed by the author to show the superior qualities of a state run along Godly lines.

Despite differences of opinion on purgatory, however, there was much in Luther's thinking on heaven to connect him in an unbroken chain to the medieval Church. In his insistence on the need for oneness with God in the afterlife, there was a mystical flavour to his theology, but this is to misunderstand his obsession with humankind's fallen nature, as Professor Richard Marius has pointed out in his biography. For Luther, he writes, 'divinity and humanity, holiness and sin are separated by a profound gulf that only Christ can bridge and that we cannot cross over by the emotional and mental discipline that the mystics savoured.' Luther did not believe that humans could transcend their nature (a key concept in Dante, for example, as he accompanies Beatrice to the empyrean) and be with God. There would, therefore, be no intimacy with God in heaven.

It was not heaven itself, but the 'how you got there' and 'if you got there' which concerned the Reformers. Yet, predestination, free will and justification by faith alone, all central points of dispute in the Reformation, were ultimately all concerned with who would enjoy life ever after with God. The Reformers effectively set entry criteria – most of them very rigorous, some almost arbitrary – for heaven, even if they did not waste too much time wondering what it would be like. Any such speculation was couched in terms of negatives. Rome had long sought to teach that there would be a hierarchy in heaven, topped by angels, saints and the Trinity, as a way of buttressing the earthly hierarchy of the clergy, bishops, cardinals and popes. Luther would have none of this – he rejected monasticism, having left an Augustinian priory, before marrying an ex-nun. 'We will be equal,' Luther wrote, in direct contradiction to traditional Christian teaching on the special place of the saints, 'to St Paul, St Peter, our beloved Lady and all the saints in their honour and glory'.

One of the principal points of contention of the Protestant Reformers was that the Church of Rome had corrupted religious life and turned it into a commodity, which could be either sold or bargained for, for temporal advantage. This applied to everything from the sale of indulgences – remission from punishment for sins – through the bloated lifestyles of princely bishops in their palaces to promising the faithful a place in heaven if they followed various devotions. It meant that rich men had been told, in direct contradiction of Christ in the Gospels, that they could buy their place in heaven if they endowed sufficient monasteries or churches. Thus heaven, from this viewpoint, had been as corrupted as anything else in the Pope's armoury.

For both Luther and Calvin, the world of pilgrimages, processions, indulgences and pious works which had been promoted to the laity as their chance to win salvation with God – salvation by good works – was at worst a blasphemy and at best merely a distraction, a way of reducing people's access to God in comparison to a clerical elite whose monastic way of life was judged of superior eternal worth. 'We are beggars, this is true,' were Luther's last words before his death. It was felt that only God in His compassion could save us, whatever we had achieved in life, and so, for Luther, salvation was entirely beyond human manipulation. In 1516, in a lecture on St Paul's Epistle to the Romans, he wrote: 'For in God's presence, man does not become just by doing just works, but by being just, he does just deeds.' There were, he said, no good works 'except the search for grace, because our works do not make us good, but our goodness, or rather the goodness of God makes us and our works good'. What will save us is 'not that which rises from the earth, but that which comes down from heaven'.

Luther's approach – justification by faith – was then a passive one. Only a humbled will, he believed, could lead humankind to the grace that might save them. If we have grace, God controls our intellect and our will, leaving no room for free will which Luther rejected in the strongest terms. He thereby turned his back on the Renaissance's faith in humanity's own power. Because of Adam and Eve, Luther believed, every individual was born a sinner, continued sinning, was judged on the last day, and might then be shown mercy by God.

However, he also rejected the concept of predestination, favoured by Calvin's followers (though not by Calvin himself, who had little interest in such theological speculation and simply dismissed the notion as 'mysterious'). The next generation of Calvinists suggested that God had predestined those who were to go to heaven and those who were to be damned. Since God was part of everything we did on earth, He would guide His elect along the right path. They would necessarily be few in number.

This was not entirely a new idea. St Augustine had written of God's independence in the matter of whom was saved, but he had also allowed for human co-operation, through grace and perseverance, in the business of salvation. Calvinists took this to extremes: they believed that there was only a certain number of free berths in heaven – the total had been predestined since eternity – and that these vacancies all had names attached to them. This conjures up the scene in Dante's *Divine Comedy* where Beatrice takes him into the amphitheatre, full of saints, which has just a few seats left empty.

However, for Luther such an idea turned Christ into a tyrant and removed from him any sense of being a saviour.

The general pessimism that surrounded predestination was an essential part of Luther's new theology. If he spent little time imagining heaven, concentrating his efforts on suggesting why most people would be denied it, then it was perhaps because he was obsessed, like many before and after him, with the other end of the equation – hell and the Devil. In this, Luther was a product of his age. From an early age he was convinced that he had been singled out by Satan, who, at different stages, possessed every area of his life and body – including his small children and his bowels. (He suffered all his life from chronic constipation.) Yet he did not leave us any detailed descriptions of the fires of hell. His focus was on God and salvation, rather than heaven, and, on the other side of the coin, the Devil and damnation, rather than hell itself.

In so far as Luther concentrated on any place, it was the earth which he saw as the least pure of a series of layers leading up to heaven. On Judgement Day, therefore, with one eye on Revelation, he predicted that God would come down through the layers and renew the earth through fire. Everything that was unclean would be burnt and the ashes consigned to hell. The earth would become a suitable place for the saints to explore, moving easily backwards and forwards from the upper echelons of heaven, which would remain their home. What would greet them on earth would be a traditional paradise garden, the antechamber to heaven. 'The flowers, leaves and grass will be as beautiful, pleasant and delightful as an emerald,' he wrote, 'and all creatures most beautiful.' In direct contravention of the scholastics, there would be, he wrote, animals in this paradise, and even the ants, bugs 'and all stinking creatures will be most delightful and have a wonderful fragrance', but this arena of pleasure would be as nothing compared to life in heaven with God who is 'all in all'.

His supremely God-centred vision was no more

thorough-going than that of many who had gone before him. Luther did allow for some fragments of reunion after death. This most austere and self-denying of figures shared the same human weakness that made him yearn to see his loved ones again. Such a loop-hole certainly appears to have gone against his deeply held theological instincts. Yet he hoped he would see again the stern father whom he had always struggled to please. Calvin, by contrast, saw this as sentimentality. He even denied the relevance of such hopes. 'To be in paradise and live with God,' he wrote, 'is not to speak to each other, and to be heard by each other, but is only to enjoy God, to feel His good will and rest in Him.' (*Calvin's Theological Treatises*, J. K. Reid)

Catholicism's response to the Reformers was vigorous, if not innovatory. The message was back to the future – recapturing older traditions to purify the recent literal-minded excesses which had played into the hands of the doubters. For Paul Johnson, in his *History of Christianity*, it is a mistake even to talk about the Counter-Reformation as a distinct movement: 'It had no specific programme other than the negative one of stamping out Protestant "error". It involved no substantial reform of the Church and embodied no change of attitude on the part of the papacy.' Instead, there were new emphases.

The message of the Counter-Reformation with regards to heaven was remarkably similar to that of Luther and Calvin – that God alone suffices and the physical details of paradise are unimportant. So, though the landmark Council of Trent (1545–63) failed in its halfhearted and belated attempts to reunite Christendom, it produced a catechism which defined heaven as 'the vision of God and enjoyment of His beauty who is the source and principle of all goodness and perfection'. Few on either side of the doctrinal divide would have refused to sign up to this proposition.

Yet where the Reformers concentrated on the external journey to God, some Catholic writers harked back to Jewish Throne Mysticism. This is particularly true of one of the keynote figures of the Counter-Reformation Church, St Teresa of Avila (1515–82), who was of Jewish descent. Teresa wrote in *The Interior Castle* of her journey to God that 'the soul is made one with God, being likewise a spirit'. Taking up her chosen metaphor of a spiritual building, the soul, she continued, 'may perhaps be wholly united with Him in the Mansions very near His presence, while thought remains in the outskirts of the castle, suffering the assaults of a thousand wild and venomous creatures and from this suffering winning merit'.

Teresa was not, however, describing a physical heaven, but her own doubts and struggles in this life where she hovered between earthly concerns and her visions of God. The barrier between life and death, she wrote as one who strove to get ever closer to God through self-denial in life, was blurred. The soul progresses in the sort of ascent characteristic of Throne Mysticism through the mansions, achieving various degrees of union with God. In the fifth, it is asleep, totally abandoned to God, in effect 'a delectable death'. She likens this union at the moment of death to silkworms emerging from seeds like tiny peppercorns. Just as the silkworm feeds on leaves until it is fully grown, and eventually emerges as a beautiful white butterfly, so the soul feeds on Christ and is transformed. It is, Teresa said, no longer bound by possessions or earthly relationships. It can fly freely. Finally, in the sixth mansion, God 'confirms betrothal' of the soul with Himself with raptures, ecstasy and trances. Here her debt to medieval mysticism is plain. Once married, there is no chance for divorce. 'It is like rain falling from the heaven into a river or spring; there is nothing but water there and it is impossible to divide or separate the water belonging to the river from that which fell from the heavens.' (*Teresa of Avila: Complete Works*, edited by Allison Peers)

The Council of Trent reiterated the traditional Catholic view that, in contrast to Luther's talk of justification by faith alone, you could play a part in earning your own passage to a happy afterlife. Good works were stressed along with a new enthusiasm for the sacraments. The carrot was being dangled in a new way. Post-Reformation Catholicism was dominated by the Eucharist, by an accompanying upturn in the use of confession as a weekly practice (in the medieval period it had been an annual visit), by the constant exhortation to prayer, and by carefully choreographed acts of piety – adoration of the host, Benediction, perpetual adoration, novenas and so on. There was a strong sense of calibration which chimed easily with congregations. If you hit carefully drawn-up targets in life – the Eucharist on nine first Fridays, for example, was said to be a guarantee of a happy death – you would have saved up enough tokens to get into heaven.

Such a calibration was orchestrated by clerics and drip-fed to the laity. The Counter-Reformers rejected Luther's talk of celestial equality and extolled continued reverence and exaltation of the saints who sat in a privileged position at God's right hand. The traditional subjugation of laity to nuns and priests retained its heavenly stamp of approval. Of the select group of saints up there with God, the women were nearly all virginal (with the exception, perhaps, only of Elizabeth of Hungary, a thirteenth-century princess whose husband died young) and the men largely monks. This, it was believed, was the way God had planned it, and when you got to the next world, you would find the same hierarchy of virtues there.

Heaven was thus a place of chastity, of scholarship, and of separate communities of men and women. In 1575, the Italian Dominican friar Antonino Polti, in his book, *On the Supreme Felicity of Heaven*, listed fifty-eight saints as being specially favoured on high for qualities such as not having sex, not enjoying themselves in life and concentrating on founding religious orders. Whether or not this message sounded attractive, it certainly managed to reinforce the need for continual striving, subjugation to God's representatives and self-abasement.

It was increasingly an imagined puritan heaven which created in its wake a real puritan earth. Driving the construction was intolerance of Protestants. This was the era of the Index of Forbidden Books – a list of texts forbidden by the Inquisition on the grounds of their sedition – and of Daniel of Volterra, the so-called 'trouserer', who was employed to cover the immodesty of the figures in the Sistine Chapel. At Neuberg in Bavaria, the resident community of Jesuits (the order, founded in 1540 by Ignatius Loyola, as the foot-soldiers of this Catholic fight-back) had Peter Rubens's *Last Judgement* painting removed from above the altar of their church because it dared to suggest heaven was a sensual place. The lush women's bodies and the air of love, typical of classic Renaissance, were taken as blasphemous. Heaven was once again being used to instil a moral discipline on earth.

Antonino Polti gave pride of place in his heaven to that paradigm of virtue, Mary, 'the most serene Empress of

Heaven, Queen of the Angels, and Mother of all the Elect'. Radiant in her physical and spiritual beauty, Mary was, he wrote, a 'divine presence' in heaven. This deification of Christ's virginal and selfless mother was not unique to Polti. She had long been thought to wield considerable influence in heaven, but an upturn in her cult was a widespread and distinctive feature of the Counter-Reformation. The celebrated Catechism of the Jesuit Peter Canisus (1521–97), a text which was to run to 130 separate editions, spearheaded the fight-back against Luther on his home turf and earned its author the sobriquet 'the second apostle of the Germans'. In it, Mary is seen in what has since become a familiar stance, floating on a cloud, surrounded by the adoring angels who hitherto had reserved such treatment only for God. Now she had become the queen consort to His king.

While Mary had long been accorded an elevated place – in Dante she ushers the poet into the presence of Saints Peter, James and John and is hailed as Queen of Heaven and 'the rose in which the Divine World made himself flesh' – she was now being further promoted and put on a par with the Trinity. Though any attempt to allot her a special role as mediator between God and humanity went against clear statements in the Bible – 'For there is only one mediator between God and mankind, himself a man, Christ Jesus' (1 Tim 2:5) – the Church of Rome, under attack and anxious to hold on to its supporters, saw elevating Christ's mother as a vote-winner. By locating Mary up there with the Trinity, the Counter-Reformation Catholic Church did not, necessarily, detract from heaven's stated theocentric base. Indeed, they simply denied Mary's humanity and co-opted her as deity so as to use her to reinforce the notion of oneness with God.

To the poor, especially, Mary had since medieval times been the compassionate face of God, but again this idea was given new emphasis. In 1531 Mary was seen in what later became her regular appearances on earth among those living on the margins of society: at Guadalupe in Mexico, she reportedly manifested herself four times to an Indian named Juan Diego and instructed him to tell his bishop to build a church outside Mexico City. Anticipating what was subsequently to become characteristic of such visits, Mary 'proved' herself by performing a 'conjuring trick' – in this case a life-size figure of the Virgin was miraculously imprinted on Diego's mantle. Suitably impressed, the bishop agreed to her request, and the cult of Our Lady of Guadalupe began and thrives to this day. According to the historians Colleen McDannell and Bernhard Lang: 'for the late medieval Catholic, Mary was *advocata nostra*, the supreme intercessor at the hour of death and the Last Judgement. In Last Judgement paintings she was frequently placed near the Christ-judge to mitigate his sentence.' (McDannell and Lang, *Heaven: A History*)

By allotting Mary the role of dispenser of mercy, especially to the poor, Christ's role within heaven was altered. He became less the saviour than the judge, often harsh, while she took on the mantle of the people's champion. She was linked in particular with the souls in purgatory – a point of contention with the Reformers. A popular image of the time had Mary nourishing the suffering souls with her milk. The medieval hymn, *Salve Regina*, came to epitomise her shifting role:

> Hail, Holy Queen, Mother of Mercy, hail our life, our sweetness and our hope.
> To thee do we cry, poor banished children of Eve.

216

To thee do we send up our sighs, mourning and weeping in this valley of tears. Turn then, most gracious advocate, thine eyes of mercy towards us, and after this, our exile, show unto us the blessed fruit of thy womb, Jesus.

The cult of Mary as a travel agent able to get her favourites passes into heaven had a special resonance in what was an age of intense uncertainty. From the 1520s, religious wars were endemic in Western Europe until 1648, with only a brief respite in the first two decades of the seventeenth century. In the long term, this was to prompt a reaction in the form of the Enlightenment, but, at the time, it merely added to widespread anxiety, fear and the destruction of Renaissance confidence in the inevitably of progress and the power of humankind to regulate its own world. Faced by the possibility of random and pointless death at the hands of 'enemies' from the other side of the religious divide, people inevitably fell back on their own mascots – which meant, for Catholics, devotions to Mary and to the promises of heaven.

On both sides of the Reformation divide, a fatalistic view of this world took hold, linked with an ever-greater concentration on the better life that was to come in heaven. Present reality could only be mitigated, it was believed, by the Puritan efforts encouraged by Jansenism within Catholicism or the Pietists and Methodists in Protestantism. This inevitably meant that the God-centric image of the theologians of heaven was diluted, and, once again, writers and artists began to play up to popular yearnings and imagine heaven in a literal, rather than a spiritual way. If you had only a vision of heaven to sustain you in the face of sufferings on earth and the torment of your neighbours, then it helped if it was three-dimensional and contained more than white light and a sense of well-being.

The Pilgrim's Progress, written in 1678, detailed Non-Conformist John Bunyan's dream journey from a land of destruction – earth – to the comfort of heaven, was hugely popular in this regard and remained, until the nineteenth century, the most-read book in English after the Bible. It is Christ himself who shepherds Bunyan's pilgrims through the waters of death and on to the mighty hill that is their final destination.

> The Pilgrims went up that Hill with . . . much agility and speed, though the foundation upon which the City was framed was higher than the Clouds. They therefore went up through the Regions of Air, sweetly talking as they went, being comforted, because they safely got over the River, and had such glorious Companions to attend them. The talk that they had with the Shining Ones was about the glory of the place, who told them that the beauty and glory of it was inexpressible. There, said they, is the Mount Sion, the heavenly Jerusalem, the innumerable company of Angels, and the Spirits of just men made perfect. You are going now, said they, to the Paradise of God, wherein you shall see the Tree of Life, and eat of the never-fading fruits thereof; and when you come there, you shall have white Robes given you, and your walk and talk shall be every day with the King, even all the days of Eternity.
>
> (*The Pilgrim's Progress*, John Bunyan, edited by N. H. Keeble)

Bunyan's heaven is entered through a gate, above which is written in gold 'Blessed are they that do his Commandments, that they may have the right to the Tree of Life and may enter through the Gates into the City'. Beyond the gates are golden streets, palms, harps – in short, all the standard images of the hereafter of the time. Bunyan's was not so much an original contribution to the travel literature of heaven, but one that matched the popular mood. Accepting God's promise involved, certainly at the time it was written, a mental disengagement with the world. For Bunyan, this was just as well, since he was in Bedford Jail on charges of preaching, without a licence, the Non-Conformist message which was no longer welcomed under the restored Charles II. For Bunyan, for his characters, and, hence, his readers, life itself was regarded with suspicion and all earthly pleasure as positively satanic. The only decent joy to be had, future generations of Non-Conformists and Puritans came to believe, was in singing in church, voices raised universally to God on high, in hymns such as 'Jesu, Lover of My Soul' by one of the founding fathers of Methodism, Charles Wesley (1707–88). Its lyrics sum up the dominant picture of heaven as a haven, a place of healing but never of exuberance:

> *Jesu, lover of my soul*
> *Let me to thy bosom fly,*
> *while the nearer waters roll,*
> *while the tempest still is high;*
> *hide me, O my Saviour hide,*
> *till the storm of life is past;*
> *safe into the haven guide,*
> *O receive my soul at last.*

Other refuge have I none;
hangs my helpless soul on thee;
leave, ah! leave me not alone,
still support and comfort me.
All my trust on thee is stayed,
all my help from thee I bring;
cover my defenceless head
with the shadow of thy wing.

Plenteous grace with thee is found,
grace to cover all my sin
let the healing streams abound;
make and keep me pure within.
Thou of life the fountain art,
freely let me take of thee;
spring thou up within my heart,
rise to all eternity.

Though a Non-Conformist like Bunyan, the English poet John Milton (1608–74) produced a much more complex, if similarly enduring, picture of heaven in *Paradise Lost*, first published in 1663; a work which is matched only by Dante for its range, ambition and influence on the subject of afterlife. A Puritan who passionately believed that the work of the Reformation had not been completed, Milton, as a young man, wrote pamphlets against the episcopacy and later acted as a propagandist for Oliver Cromwell. The Restoration of Charles II profoundly affected him, as it did Bunyan, and he grew disillusioned with earthly concerns, a process accelerated by the loss of his eyesight. Yet *Paradise Lost* is anything but a standard Puritan vision of heaven. It combines elements of this, but weaves them into something extraordinary which marks a key transitional point in attitudes to the hereafter, combining, as it does, opinions of the late Renaissance with a romanticism that was well ahead of its time and a still thoroughly modern psychological picture of the principal players.

There are, in effect, two heavens in *Paradise Lost*, on a model that Signorelli would recognise. First, there is Eden, a garden paradise, and then, after the Fall – for the overarching theme of *Paradise Lost* is the exercise of free will, as exemplified by Adam and Eve – there is heaven itself, the domain of angels where they worship God. In Books Four to Eight, it is Eden that is invoked, a place surrounded by:

> *A circling row*
> *Of goodliest Trees loaden with fairest Fruit,*
> *Blossoms and Fruits at once of golden hue*
> *Appear'd with gay enamell'd colours mixt.* (IV:146–9)

In this 'happy rural seat of various view' (IV:247), Adam and Eve go about their lives. They are, in a style later to obsess the Puritans, almost ceaselessly busy, mainly with the gardening, under the direction of the angel Raphael. There is nothing too unusual about the portrait Milton paints up to this point, but there were also other things on Adam's and Eve's minds. At the centre of this Eden is a bower:

> *It was a place*
> *Chos'n by the sovran Planter, when he fram'd*
> *All things to man's delightful use; the roof*
> *Of thickest covert was inwoven shade*
> *Laurel and Myrtle and what higher grew*
> *Of firm and fragrant leaf; on either side*
> *Acanthus, and each odorous bushy shrub*
> *Fenc'd up the verdant wall.* (IV:690–97)

This is where Adam and Eve make love. To misquote
Philip Larkin's remark on the start of the permissive
society, sexual intercourse began in paradise in 1663
between the end of the Reformation and the Enlightenment's first flowering. Milton dealt with the subject in a
fashion much more explicit than any of the medieval
mystics dreaming about their wedding bed with Christ.
Yet his 'fair couple, linkt in happy nuptial League'
(IV:339) were not indulging in any ordinary love-
making. For Milton, their consummation showed how
sex was an enjoyable, natural, unembarrassed, but also
profoundly godly, part of a perfect world before the Fall.
This hymn of praise to wedded bliss worked, as does
the whole of *Paradise Lost*, on several levels. It was not
just detailing what it would be like in the afterlife. It was
also providing a symbol for God's love for humankind,
and the source of all life on earth:

> *Hail wedded Love, mysterious Law, true source*
> *Of human offspring, sole propriety*
> *In Paradise of all things in common else.*
> *By thee adulterous lust was driv'n from men*
> *Among the bestial herds to range* (IV:750–4)

There is, however, an ambiguity about Adam and
Eve's love in Eden. For Satan watches them in the act
and later exploits what he has seen to lead them astray.
Human love then, Milton suggests, is flawed. As a result
of the exercise of free will and hence the ushering in of
original sin, now only God's love, in heaven, can be
perfect, but that love too, *Paradise Lost* makes clear, is
both physical and uninhibited. Adam asks Raphael about
the relationships between the angels on high:

To whom the Angel with a smile that glow'd
Celestial rosy red, Love's proper hue,
Answer'd, 'Let it suffice thee that thou know'st
Us happy, and without Love no happiness.
Whatever pure thou in the body enjoy'st
(And pure thou wert created) we enjoy
In eminence, and obstacle find none
Of membrane, joint, or limb, exclusive bars:
Easier than Air with Air, if Spirits embrace,
Total they mix, Union of Pure with Pure
Desiring; nor restrain'd conveyance need
As Flesh to mix with Flesh, or Soul with Soul.'
   (VIII:618–629)

Romantic love – not what Milton damned as 'casual fruition' – was therefore part of the heavenly landscape as well as the cause of the Fall in Eden. Coming two thirds of the way through *Paradise Lost*, this admission by Raphael radically begins to alter the prevailing picture of heaven. Hitherto, compared to the lush and loving Eden, it has been a cold, impersonal place, where angels fight it out in a great battle between good and evil based on Revelation, and which is dominated by a remote and often cruel God, who has little appeal next to Milton's magnificent but flawed Satan.

Raphael's description of angelic love-making changes the whole tone and thereafter heaven, which we have previously been told is separated by 'worlds and worlds' and 'a vast Ethereal sky' from Eden, is revealed as sustaining a life that has some of the best elements of earthly existence in it. Raphael describes how one day:

As other solemn days, they spent
In song and dance about the sacred Hill,
Mystical dance, which yonder starry Sphere
Of Planets and of fixt in all her Wheels
Resembles nearest, mazes intricate,
Eccentric, intervolv'd, yet regular
Then most, when most irregular they seem;
And in their motions harmony Divine
So smoothes her charming tones, that God's own ear
Listens delighted. (V:618–27)

The angels eat and drink – 'quaff immortality and joy' – rest by streams or under trees and feel the breeze. Heaven has a physical environment. And it is, in line with Milton's hatred of ecclesiastical hierarchies, a meritocracy. Even Christ is, Milton writes (III:309), 'by merit more than Birthright Son of God'. Yet, as with his hell, this heaven is both a place and a psychological state. This was another of Milton's great and distinctive contributions, to use both theocentric and anthropocentric language simultaneously and to push the former to new limits.

He was not the first to use psychological insights. Other late Renaissance figures such as Christopher Marlowe did so in *Doctor Faustus*, but Milton applied them to heaven as well as hell. So if hell is within each of us – 'his troubl'd thoughts, and from the bottom stir/The Hell within him, for within him Hell/He brings' (IV:18–20) – so, too, is heaven: the two are opposite sides of the same coin. Milton is at pains to emphasise the process of inward reformation involved in heaven. This divine garden of heaven, unlike Eden, which by the end of *Paradise Lost* has been washed away beyond our reach by a flood, is sown within the self:

From thy implanted Grace in Man, these Sighs
And Prayers, which in this Golden Censer, mixt
With Incense, I thy Priest before thee bring,
Fruits of more pleasing savour from thy seed
Sown with contrition in his heart. (XI:23–27)

CHAPTER TWELVE

―――――∞∞∞―――――

Reach for the Sky

The denigration of life on earth, when compared with what was to come, remained the stock-in-trade of the Churches in the sixteenth and seventeenth centuries. It was accompanied by an ill-defined but all-embracing sense of awe at the prospect of seeing God in the next life yet still relatively few details as to how, when and where that would take place. It was enough simply to hope and pray that it would.

Slowly, the position changed, influenced largely by the rebirth, in the Enlightenment of the eighteenth century, of a belief, submerged since the Renaissance, in humankind's own powers and potential. The Enlightenment's most distinguished thinkers, many of them buoyed up by new or rediscovered scientific knowledge, sought to concentrate on making earth a better, or at least more comprehensible, place rather than dismissing it as a trial when compared to an ill-defined but glorious future. In this process, heaven all too often fell off the map.

The gradual fading of superstition and fatalism that was a consequence of the Enlightenment resulted in many people no longer feeling so at odds with their environment. They could once again enjoy the here and now. Events that had once passively been accepted as part of God's whim, His 'moving in mysterious ways' as the Churches used to be fond of remarking, were increasingly re-evaluated in the light of a scientific revolution. The physical structure of the cosmos was subjected to scientific principles and not the abstract theorising of the scholastics. Heaven's very location was reassessed.

The roots of this redrawing of the celestial map ran deep. Nicolaus Copernicus (1473–1543) had in *Revolution of the Celestial Orbs* already put the sun, not the earth, at the centre of the solar system in direct contravention of the carefully staged progress from earth via the planets and the sun to heaven as laid out by Aquinas, and followed to the letter by Dante and even Luther. The Dominican Giordano Bruno (1548–1600) had added a philosophical dimension by writing of the sun as the symbol of the living principle that gives life to the earth. He was put to death by the Inquisition for his implied disrespect to God. Galilei Galileo (1564–1642) took up Copernicus's proposition but was another forced by the Inquisition to recant. It did not, though, cost him his life.

The new line of thinking could not be artificially held back for ever by the rack and the pyre. As the Enlightenment gradually saw Europe throw off the mental straitjacket that had been imposed upon it by the alliance of Churches and kings, the science of astrology blossomed and dealt a fatal blow to the academic credibility of a heaven at the top of the staircase leading from earth.

The principal attraction of heaven was, after all, not its physical location, but the mental and emotional succour it offered. Yet, it continued to be asked, if heaven was not in the stars, where else could it be? One solution was to deny it existed in one place at all. This was taken up by anti-clerical groups who thrived on the dislocation in England caused by the overthrow of the monarchy in 1641 and its replacement by a self-avowedly Puritan Commonwealth. Some of these were straight atheists. Gerrard Winstanley, part of a radical workers' sect, known as the Diggers, which embraced an early form of communism, is recorded (quoted in Keith Thomas's *Religion and the Decline of Magic*) as scoffing at the idea of an 'outward heaven, which is a fancy your false teachers put into your heads to please you with while they pick your purses'. Other preferred an Eastern-style pantheism which insisted that God was in all things in this life.

These groups mixed and matched, for they were also millenialist in outlook and took domestic political upheaval and the widespread economic chaos in Europe to be signs that the end was nigh. Yet, rather than anticipating a Second Coming, one such extremist organisation – the Ranters – chose to look inward. The Ranter William Bond wrote in 1656 that 'there was neither heaven nor hell except in a man's conscience, for if he had a good fortune and did live well, that was heaven: and if he lived poor and miserable, that was hell, for then he would die like a cow or a horse'.

It was not an entirely original line of thought, but it was put controversially, and that was what appealed to the Ranters. They may have been influenced by the publication in English in the 1640s of translations of the popular German mystic, Jacob Boehme (1575–1624). Boehme, a cobbler from Upper Lusatia, in Germany, was attacked in his lifetime by Lutherans, though later read with admiration by Carl Jung. He is held to be one of the inspirations for the Quaker sect. He wrote with a modern sensibility that heaven and hell were not places or even anything to do with God, but resided instead in individual souls. Man, he wrote, 'must be at war with himself if he wishes to be a heavenly citizen . . . fighting must be the watchword, not with tongue and sword, but with mind and spirit, and not to give over'. The Devil, Boehme remarked, might go millions of miles to see heaven and not see it because he would be in hell wherever he went. Every spirit, he suggested, was confined within its own principle.

Another possible location for heaven was seen in the Book of Revelation's notion that it would be on earth come Judgement Day. This line was popular with materialists such as the philosopher Thomas Hobbes (1588–1679). He arrived at this traditional conclusion by a daring new route. He dismissed what was in his time the standard position of most thinkers, namely that the soul was an 'incorporeal substance'. If you split body and soul, Hobbes warned in his best-known work *Leviathan*, you create ghosts and necessitate papist paraphernalia like exorcism and purgatory. Hobbes, a classic Enlightenment man in that he was both profoundly religious *and* open to new thought, went back to the scriptures to prove, to his own satisfaction, that 'soul' and 'life' had the same meaning. All talk of a separation between the two was, he held, a result of the malign influence of Greek thinking on the Bible. So, for Hobbes, eternal life could only mean the body coming back to life on Judgement Day. In his view, the dead will literally wake up to enjoy a kingdom of God on earth ruled over by Christ. On that last day, *Leviathan* predicts: 'the faithful shall rise again, with glorious and spiritual bodies and be his subjects in that his kingdom which shall be eternal. They shall neither marry, nor be given in marriage, nor eat or drink, as they did in their natural bodies, but live for ever in their individual persons.'

Later materialists like John Locke (1632–1704) took Hobbes's argument one step further, steadily dismantling many of the tried and trusted connections between heaven and life on earth. His view was that the state had been created by man and not by God in His heaven. At a stroke he therefore cut off the direct line between temporal rulers and paradise. His dismissal of original sin and his suggestion that man was a tabula rasa to be filled by education was revolutionary and necessarily affected views of heaven. It broke with the legacy of Adam and Eve and the consequent loss of a paradise garden.

Immanuel Kant (1724–1804), the German philosopher, was another Enlightenment figure who drew both on theology and science to buttress belief, albeit by reinterpreting it in a modern way. The son of a poor harness-maker and Pietist, Kant went on to teach a wide variety of subjects from physics to cosmology at Konigsberg University, in what was then East Prussia. One of his most challenging ideas was that the world we experience was in part determined by our own cognitive faculties which shape the way the world appears to each individual by contributing its general features – space and time. These features are neither learned nor handed down by God, they are supplied by the mind.

The world then, either in this life or in a future life, was as we imagined it. We would see in heaven what we expected to see.

Kant also developed a sophisticated moral philosophy which was built around an austere ethics of duty. According to this philosophy, the obligations by which all must live were identified not in relation to heaven or belief, but by reason. When he considered the immortality of the soul, Kant argued that it was impossible to prove it, but nevertheless reason demands that we have to assume it to make any sense of morality. So, reason could be used to defend as well as attack the concept of heaven. Reason was, potentially, Rene Descartes (1596–1650) had written in *Discours de la Methode* (1637), God's voice speaking in each of us, a means by which the truth could be sought by each individual without resource to Church or State. Although the Enlightenment then is credited with divesting Christianity of its layers of superfluous miracles, it could also argue in favour of heaven on the grounds of reason.

The Enlightenment was never a mass movement. It encouraged an elite to begin to think freely outside the standard religious confines. There had, after all, long been radical souls at the top end of the social spectrum who dismissed ideas like heaven. Sir Walter Ralegh (1554–1618), the English explorer who attempted to colonise Virginia in honour of his patron, Elizabeth I, was said to have denied the existence of heaven and hell, holding instead that 'we die like beasts and when we are gone there is no more remembrance of us'.

What the Enlightenment did do was to broaden the currency, constituency and context for such scepticism. With the growth of printing presses, newspapers and books, the court, be it monarchical or ecclesiastical, became less important. Writers no longer felt they had to seek the approval of the Church and eventually they were willing to risk its wrath and say what they believed. But, however attractive the Enlightenment seems to us now, it had only a slim social depth. Literacy was still restricted, and many of those who could read chose the

Bible as their text for the day. This period, it is worth remembering, could just as easily be deemed the age of the Wesleys, of the Pietists (like Kant's own family), and of a Catholic revival.

Even these movements, however much they may have set their face against Enlightenment ideas, were inevitably at some level influenced by them. In a world which came to appreciate the material as well as the spiritual, heaven inevitably became more material and thus more literal. The line between the theocentric and the anthropocentric was blurred. One thing that was changing was the notion of oneness with God as 'eternal rest'. Many reformers – including Calvin – had embraced the notion that in death the souls of the faithful departed, while awaiting reunion with their bodies on Judgement Day, would effectively sleep in God's presence. Even Bunyan, who painted such a detailed picture of heaven, believed that day-to-day activity would be simple, joyful and monotonous. But in an Enlightenment era where progress and activity and striving were all, such a passive state seemed anathema. Kant, for instance, was one who combined physics with theology in *Theory of the Heavens* (1755) to argue in favour of the development of the soul once it had reached heaven. Only God, he held, could reasonably claim perfection, so everyone else, even the saints in paradise, had to work eternally and practically to improve themselves.

In the light of such influences, the successors of the initial reformers gradually evolved their stance. By the middle of the eighteenth century, few Protestant thinkers would even countenance the idea that there would be any wait before the dead could actively and vigorously experience God in His heaven. 'Death like a narrow sea divides this heavenly land from our,' wrote the

Non-Conformist preacher Isaac Watts (1674–1748) in his hymn 'A Prospect of Heaven Makes Death Easy'. Crossing from one to the other was no more disruptive than taking a boat across the English Channel.

Watts's 1722 sermon 'Death and Heaven; or the Last Enemy Conquered and Separate Spirits Made Perfect' went into sixteen separate editions as well as German translation. He reflected a wider change in mood when he described a heaven where God was more like the foreman directing His busy crew, than a dormitory monitor. The crew, in their turn, took their cue from the angels: 'When angels are so variously and delightfully employed in service for God, in his several known and unknown worlds, we cannot suppose the spirits of just men shall be eternally confined to a sedentary state of inactive contemplation.' Each would have his or her task – 'perhaps as priests in his temple, and as kings or viceroys in his wide dominions'. Quite what these dominions consisted of, Watts did not specify, but what is clear in this talk of kingdoms and viceroys is that there still could be a hierarchy. Watts believed that everyone would, after death, retain his or her own personality and characteristics, but, depending on what they were, some would be in higher positions than others.

Education would be a particular concern, and the Puritan work ethic and drive to self-improvement crossed the boundary between life and death. 'When a blessed spirit has dwelt in heaven a thousand years,' Watts wrote, 'and conversed with God and Christ, angels and fellow-spirits . . . shall it know nothing more of the nature and wondrous properties of God than it knew the first moment of its arrival there?'

This vision of a heaven as perpetual motion, perpetual learning, perpetual service to God, alongside the angels and other souls, was a standard one in Non-conformism, right through to the twentieth century. David Lloyd George, the First World War British Prime Minister, once recalled as a little boy in a Baptist Sunday School in Manchester that he had found heaven much more frightening than its antithesis, hell, because it would be an everlasting church service with every exit guarded by an angel to stop him escaping.

Watts's concept, however, was not shared by all: others, just as influential and as widely read, clung to a more strictly theocentric view. Richard Baxter (1615–91) belonged to the previous generation to Watts. His book *Saints Everlasting Rest* (1650) was a Puritan classic, written, as he put it, 'with one foot in the grave, by a man that was betwixt living and dead'. It was yet another attempt to use heaven to make good the persecutions of this world. Baxter, who felt that his vocation had been laughed at by others more worldly, conjured up a picture of a laughing God in heaven, amused at the sufferings of the rich and powerful in hell, but it is his strict adherence to the theocentric idea that marks him out from other Puritan writers.

> As all good whatsoever is comprised in God, and all in the creatures are but drops in this ocean; so all the glory of the blessed is comprised in their enjoyment of God: and if there be any mediate joys there, they are but drops from this. If men and angels should study to speak the blessedness of that estate in one word, what can they say beyond this, that it is the nearest to enjoyment of God.

Yet, even with his gaze focused fully on God, Baxter left some room for interplay with the fellowship of angels and saints. He even admitted that he was looking forward to meeting Luther as well as Noah and Moses, but qualified this, and attempted to fit it back into his pattern, by saying that he thought it would happen, if at all, through Christ.

It is possible, even as science was undermining the traditional view of a paradise in the clouds, to draw an ever-upward line from Luther's admission of some degree of heavenly reunion outside the bond with God, through Baxter's fuller (though still qualified) exploration of this, and on to Watts's very human heaven. Luther's had been the orthodox position of his time, but by the time one gets to Watts, he is effectively one of many voices fleshing out the modern and clearly defined heaven. John Dunton, an editor of the *Athenian Gazette*, writing of the death of his wife in 1698 in *An Essay Proving We Shall Know our Friends in Heaven* unashamedly argues that they will be reunited by God in death, though with typical Puritan reserve he adds that there will no longer be a sexual bond between them. Were such a thing to exist on high, he wrote, returning to the stereotype of womankind as daughters of Eve, 'the angels couldn't stand long but would certainly be seduced from their innocence and fall as Adam did'. Aside from this reservation, Dunton's heaven sounds almost ideal. There will be no disabilities, everyone will have the health of a thirty-year-old, and all will look like gods.

A more popular writer was Elizabeth Singer Rowe, whose *Friendship in Death*, first published in 1728 went through fourteen editions between 1733 and 1816. Taking the form of letters written by the dead to the living, the book touched a nerve by promising that a continuation of human love would be part of heaven, which would be a glittering place of 'delectable vales and flowery lawns, the myrtle shades and rosy bowers, the bright cascades and crystal rivulets rolling over orient pearls and sands of gold'.

If theologians and churchmen continually changed their minds on heaven, Singer Rowe's portrait, with its echoes of previous popular depictions of an opulent garden, shows that in the view of churchgoers it had on the surface remained remarkably constant. What had altered was that all the things that were once taken as imagery or signs were now being discussed as if they were literally true.

An added ingredient was that of human love. From a concern to humanise heaven, as the earth was being humanised by the Enlightenment, grew what soon was to become a dominant tendency to romanticise it. An important, but neglected, figure in this transformation, according to Colleen McDannell and Bernhard Lang, was Emanuel Swedenborg (1688–1772), an engineer and scientist of great distinction in his native Sweden, and someone much influenced by key Enlightenment figures such as John Locke and Isaac Newton (1642–1727).

'Swedenborg's popular reputation as a mystic,' write McDannell and Lang, 'underplays his place in the long history of Christian constructions of heaven. It also denies Swedenborgian contributions to the development of the thoroughly anthropocentric view of heaven which flourished in the nineteenth century and is still held by many people today.'

In April 1744 Swedenborg had a vision of Jesus. It changed his life. He turned his back on mineralogy and anatomy, his previous specialist subjects, and turned his attention to heaven. At its simplest, Swedenborg's new vision was that man is a spirit who briefly inhabits a body. After he leaves the body, he once again becomes an incorporeal spirit. The radical mysticism of

Swedenborg's *Arcana Coelestia*, published in eight volumes between 1749 and 1756, fleshed out that initial vision with spirits of the dead who rose from the body and reassumed a perfect physical form in another world. 'It is,' his biographer Peter Ackroyd has written, 'one of Swedenborg's most remarkable doctrines since it suggests that the spiritual form takes human shape and that heaven or hell are extensions of our human desires and capacities.'

Drawing from Christian sources, Swedenborg added quantities of alchemy and ancient pagan beliefs to make what in the late eighteenth and nineteenth centuries proved a crowd-pulling cocktail, though it was later to lose its appeal. At its peak, it stood in marked contrast to the measured, scientific projections of Locke and the Newtonian concepts of space and time.

'I have spoken with many spirits,' Swedenborg wrote in *Arcana Coelestia*. 'It has been my destiny to live for years in company with spirits . . . I have conversed about this with the angels . . . I have often been permitted to see the atmosphere of falsehood which exhales from hell.' In his travels between life and death, Swedenborg claimed to have experienced eternal life as an angel. Consequently, he could report back that after death, the soul enters a spirit-world where it continues to function much as before – thinking, moving, feeling, eating, sleeping. The gap between this world and the next is very small, he wrote, yet heaven itself is not achieved all at once. It slowly unwraps. So it is only when souls have sorted out their psychological and spiritual outlook – and Swedenborg noted in an aside that Luther in particular had struggled with vanity and pride – that they can move on to heaven proper where they become angels. If they fail to make this change, they are condemned to hell.

Once in heaven, Swedenborg continued, the souls have bodies and enjoy an existence that in many ways parallels that of those still on earth:

> Whenever I have talked with angels face-to-face, I have been with them in their abodes. These abodes are precisely like abodes on earth which we call houses, but more beautiful. In them there are chambers, parlours and bedrooms in great number; there are also courts and there are gardens and flower-beds and lawns round about. Where they live together, their houses are near each other, arranged one next to the other in the form of a city, with avenues, streets and public squares, exactly like cities on the earth.

The best bits of real estate – the hills – are populated by the most spiritually developed. Those with some spiritual ground still to make up are confined to the 'ledges of stone'.

> I have also been told that not only the palaces and houses, but all things and each thing, both inside and outside of them, correspond to the interior things which they have from the Lord, the house itself in general corresponding to their good, the particular things inside of a house to the various things of which their good consists, and the things outside to truths derived from good, and also to their perceptions and knowledges; and as these things correspond to the goods and truths they have from the Lord, they correspond to their love, and to their wisdom and intelligence from love, since love belongs to good, wisdom to good and truth together, and intelligence to truth from good.

Swedenborg infused the life of these angels in heaven with a human and earthly ideal of love. Those who thrive there are those, he suggested, who realise that what counts above all is love. Activity, then, was seen in terms of love; showing love for fellow citizens in heaven, forming spiritual bonds of love with others, and even marrying them (rather than your earthly partners) in spiritual weddings.

Alongside these individual bonds was the bond with God – again couched in terms of an ever-deepening love for Him. Yet God is neither the judge, nor even the orchestrater of heaven. Progress is made by one's own efforts, assisted by others. 'God is very man. In all the heavens there is no other idea of God than that of a man; the reason is because heaven in the whole and in part is in form as man. By reason that God is a man, all angels and spirits are men in a perfect form.'

Swedenborg was an Enlightenment man in his belief in the need to strive eternally while God merely watches benignly – and that progress is marked out in stages. After the initial spirit world, there is a first-level 'natural' heaven, very close in its forms to life on earth. Then comes 'spiritual' heaven, an idealised version of earthly life. Finally, there is 'celestial' heaven, the paradise of Eden restored. Angels, Swedenborg said, move between each level, but once at any stage mix only with those at the same point. Each zone, as it were, has its own particular characteristics. In spiritual heaven, there are churches for worship, while in celestial heaven the angels are both sexual and naked – 'because nakedness,' Swedenborg wrote, 'corresponds to innocence'. The highest level of heaven, that closest to God, is a primitive, childlike world which the author, while stressing that much was beyond his capacity to describe, likened to African societies.

There are many recognisable elements in Sweden-borg's vision – from the graded levels of a Renaissance heaven, through a Watts-like insistence on the closeness of heaven and earth and on to a Dantean inability to describe its uppermost levels – but his greatest signifi-cance in the development of the history of paradise is several-fold. First, he provided a systematic, literal map of heaven, far removed from Dante's symbolism. The degree to which his heaven was a cleaned-up, mirror-image of earth stands in stark contrast to the transcen-dent quality of much of what Dante described. Second, he brought into the Christian concept of the hereafter a magical, earthy, erotic influence drawn from pagan beliefs. Third, by doing this, Swedenborg influenced such significant figures as William Blake, the sculptor, John Flaxman, and the writer, Charles Kingsley. Finally, as McDannell and Lang argue convincingly, he ushered in what was to become a very modern view of heaven. 'In his portrayal of heavenly love,' they write, 'we must recognise the beginnings of Romanticism.'

PART THREE

Above Us, Only Sky

CHAPTER THIRTEEN

The Borderlands

Even the most celebrated guides to heaven, such as Dante, preface their descriptions with apologies for their human inability to picture the divine: the portrait they present can only be partial and impressionistic.

Heaven has by its very nature to be beyond the human imagination if it is to be credible. If we could conjure it up at will it would be too earthbound and mundane.

William Blake (1757–1827), for one, would not have agreed, however. For his work as both a poet and as an artist was all about presenting a highly imaginative, highly personal, but immediate portrait of heaven. 'In the visionary imagination of William Blake,' writes Peter Ackroyd, 'there is no birth and no death, no beginning and no end, only the perpetual pilgrimage within time towards eternity.'

Blake's confidence that he could accurately portray life everlasting came from several sources. He possessed an inner belief that he was regularly visited by those in heaven. His beloved younger brother Robert, who died in 1787, was one of those who reported back to Blake from beyond the grave. 'With his spirit I converse daily &

hourly in the Spirit,' he once wrote in a letter of condolence to one of his patrons, '& See him in my remembrance in the regions of my Imagination. I hear his advice & even now write from his Dictate.' On another occasion, Blake said he had been visited by Archangel Gabriel who proved he was not an evil demon by ascending through the roof of Blake's study straight up to heaven where he was received in a blaze of sunlight.

Much of Blake's written work begins with some sort of visitation, as if stressing the divine source of what he created. 'I am under the direction,' he once wrote in a letter, 'of Messengers from Heaven, daily and nightly.' Sometimes it would be the dead who visited him so that he could sketch them. Herod, Socrates, Edward I, Voltaire all dropped in. Blake, arguably more so than any other figure in the recent history of heaven, gave form to its visionary, mystical aspects and, in the process, blurred the boundaries between this world and the next. One might sum up his philosophy with one of his poems:

> *To see a World in a Grain of Sand*
> *And a Heaven in a Wild Flower*
> *Hold Infinity in the palm of your hand*
> *And Eternity in an hour.*
>   *(Auguries of Innocence, c. 1803)*

This is what Blake believed he was doing in his poetry, engravings and paintings. A Non-Conformist by background, and a man for whom an intimate knowledge of the Bible was central to his work, he was driven by a strong sense of divine-ordained mission. This enabled him to draw from external religious and internal spiritual sources and to see this world and heaven as if in one take.

There are elements of Jewish Throne Mysticism in his

work, with its imaginary ascents to the divine. This may have been a tradition he knew for he read widely. Less likely, is that he knew much of the Buddhist nirvana, the place of transcendence in this world, not the next, but in so far as it expresses a hope often found in human-kind there is, nonetheless, some small part correspond-ing to this, too, in Blake's visions.

Life in the here and now for Blake had that added dimension, that other sphere of consciousness, and he struggled throughout his life to convey it. He would evoke standard and indeed popular earthly images of his time – in particular that of the family – but give them a wider, divine significance. Taking this example, he was not confining his vision to one family of mother, father and children being transported to heaven in the same configuration that they had enjoyed on earth, albeit an increasingly popular idea in mainstream nineteenth-century religious thought, but, rather, Blake was attempting to transcend a readily understood symbol to convey the idea of individuals coming together, in God's sight, to create a heavenly family. It was as if he were returning to that earlier and richer tradition of mystical symbolism seen in Dante.

For Blake, humanity itself could become divine. In his painting *Vision of the Last Judgement*, inspired in part by his reading of Milton, he presents a kind of divine theatre where his use of lighting – the dreamy, white light of heaven is a regular feature in his work – and of very formalised and intricate details of gesture and expression combine to give what is at face value an earthly man both the aura and context of divinity. For Blake, unlike so many who had gone before him, there would be no Last Day. Judgement was ongoing and eternal, not a one-off event; continuous assessment rather than an end-of-term exam, and so talk of a Last Judgement was simply 'a Representation of what Eternally Exists, Really & Unchangeably'.

In his illustrated – characteristically, he preferred the word 'illuminated' – poem, *Jerusalem: The Emanation of the Giant Albion* of 1834, this twin-track approach can be seen. It begins with an outline of his approach:

> *Trembling I sit day and night, my friends are astonish'd at me.*
> *Yet they forgive my wanderings, I rest not from my great task!*
> *To open the Eternal Worlds, to open the immortal Eyes*
> *Of Man inwards into the Worlds of Thought: into Eternity.*

He then takes the city of London where he lived, at that time a filthy, miasmic place, and breathtakingly transforms it into the new Jerusalem, which is not so much a heaven on earth, in the terms of the Book of Revelation, but a heaven that daily overlays the earth. 'I behold London; a Human awful wonder of God!' In this 'spiritual Four-fold London eternal', even the beggar 'in his hallowd centre holds the heavens of bright eternity'. And at its heart, Blake wrote, is Golgonooza, a great city of art and science. It is entered by one of four gates, at the far side of 'the land of death eternal', accessible only to those who have acquired the 'Four-fold Vision'. This empyrean is a gilded place of golden looms in which:

> *Every Human Vegetated Form is in its inward recesses.*
> *And all that has existed in the space of six thousand years:*
> *Permanent, & not lost nor lost nor vanishd, & every little act,*
> *Word, work, & wish, that has existed, all remaining still . . .*

For every thing exists & not one sigh nor smile nor tear,
One hair nor particle of dust, not one can pass away.

'It is,' Peter Ackroyd writes, 'the vision of immensity seen in terms of a great city; but this place is also the Incarnation. It is the Divine Humanity that exists within each created being. It is the idealised society, also, and the vivid representation of that moment of creation within the lark song.'

In other works, Blake employed different images of heaven to convey its nature. One of his earliest was the drawings he did at Westminster Abbey, and he revisited these to create a paradise of art and poetry filled with stone arches, steep steps, ancient doorway and cloisters as the signs of a spiritual world. His heaven was also a place, like Swedenborg's, of individual love, though for Blake it was less romanticised and more carnal. 'The treasures of heaven,' he wrote, 'are not negations of passion but realities of intellect from which all passions emanate uncurbed in their eternal glory.'

Swedenborg was an early influence on Blake. Blake read and annotated the Swedish guru's writings after Swedenborg's death. In his first works, Blake, like Swedenborg, combined Christianity with an interest in what might be deemed ancient truths. In his visions he would 'behold our ancient days before this Earth appear'd in its vegetated mortality to my mortal vegetated Eyes'. But Blake was a one-off and cannot be seen as constricted by any one influence.

He singlehandedly and uniquely fashioned his own universe of heaven and earth and created characters – prophets, biblical and mystical figures from the past – who enabled him to unwrap this imagined world. Logically, it follows that one so bound up with heaven should have been detached from this world, and it is certainly true that Blake regarded the world around him with scorn:

> Compell the poor to live upon a Crust of bread by soft mild
>   arts
> Smile when they frown frown when they smile & when a
>   man looks pale
> With labour & abstinence say he looks healthy & happy
> And when his children sicken let them die there are enough
> Born even too many & our Earth will be overrun

It is tempting to think that Blake, like many before him, focused on heaven to make good the deficiencies of life on earth. In his own lifetime he achieved little recognition and lived mostly on the outskirts of artistic society, avoiding poverty only through the good offices of a few long-suffering and far-sighted patrons. Many popular (and now forgotten) artists of the time regarded him as insane. If he was obsessed with death, then perhaps it was because he imagined that only then would he get his just reward for his talents.

Yet such a line of thought, though it fits with his life story, somehow degrades Blake and his vision. He was a man who lived on two planes simultaneously. Seeing heaven was not simply a reaction to earthly lack of success, a calculated move into another universe to avoid the realities of this one. Blake believed absolutely in his visions. There was nothing cynical about them. He saw himself on a par with biblical figures such as Job and occasionally Jesus himself. In his *Christ in the Wilderness*, the figure who has turned his back on the world is the artist himself.

The material world that so eluded Blake was, from his

earliest works when he still harboured hopes of commercial success and the applause of his peers, always characterised as a shadow of some eternal drama elsewhere.
There may have been an element of self-justification
when Blake wrote to his contemporary, the much-lauded
neoclassical sculptor John Flaxman: 'I am more famed in
Heaven for my works than I could well conceive. In my
Brain are studies & Chambers fill'd with books & pictures
of old, which I wrote and painted in ages of Eternity
before my mortal life; & those works are the delight &
Study of Archangels. Why, then, should I be anxious
about the riches or fame of immortality?'

But Blake was only human. Certainly in death, he
showed no fear. 'Just before he died,' a witness wrote
(recorded in *The Letters of William Blake*, edited by Geoffrey Keynes), 'His Countenance became fair. His eyes
Brighten'd and He burst out into Singing of the things
he saw in heaven.'

He was at the start of a journey he had imagined many
times. In his poem, *The Chimney Sweeper*, the subject is
rescued by:

> *An Angel who had a bright key*
> *And he open'd the coffins & set them all free.*
> *Then down a green plain leaping laughing they run*
> *And wash in a river and shine in the Sun*
>
> *Then naked & white, all their bags left behind,*
> *They rise upon clouds, and sport in the wind.*

Blake remained resolutely unfashionable for years after
his death. His greatness was only truly recognised in the
twentieth century, but his reputation had began to grow
under the Pre-Raphaelites. In 1863, the Rossetti brothers

helped Alexander Gilchrist publish the first full-length study of Blake. Dante Gabriel Rossetti even fiddled with some of Blake's verse to make it more palatable to a pre-Raphaelite readership.

There is a superficial case for linking Blake to the Romantic movement. His images of families and lovers in heaven might, if interpreted as encapsulating the dream of eternal reunion with loved ones, mesh with Romantic notions.

The meeting-again motif is seen poignantly in, for example, the work of a key Romantic figure such as Johann Wolfgang von Goethe (1749–1832). In *The Sorrows of Young Werther*, Goethe's young, ill-fated lovers expect an eternal embrace in God's shadow and so Werther commits suicide. Werther's beloved, Charlotte, is married to another as is Pompilia, heroine of *The Ring and the Book* by Robert Browning (1812–89). When her husband discovers that she has borne another man's child, he kills her, but the Romantic poet reassures his readers that earthly marriage will be as nothing in heaven. It is a 'counterfeit/Mere imitation of the inimitable'. True love will triumph there and it will be, if the Revd Charles Kingsley (1819–75) was to be believed, a very physical victory. The author and Anglican priest wrote to his beloved wife of the unbridled passion they would enjoy for ever. 'If I do not love my wife, body and soul, as well there as I do here, then there is neither resurrection of my body or of my soul, but of some other and I shall not be I.'

Throughout the nineteenth century, especially in high-thinking, plain-living, church-going circles, heaven became an extension of people's lives on earth, transported to an idealised countryside setting. It dovetailed neatly with the dominant Victorian ideal of the family. What was promoted as the basic social unit on earth could thus be given a heavenly endorsement. Marriage was not just for life but for life ever after. Against the Romantic poets and Pre-Raphaelite artists, with their erotic speculation about fated love here being blessed by God in paradise, this rather more conventional approach posited heaven as an extension of the home and hearth. In effect, it gave them a halo.

In Catholic and High-Anglican circles in particular, the Holy Family – Mary, Joseph and their boy Jesus – was regularly invoked, surrounded by clouds and angels. It was a perfect motif, for Mary and Joseph were, officially, chaste.

The burgeoning industrial and imperial age provided new impetus for this precise and unimaginative blue-print for heaven. It became yet another thing to be aspired to in an entrepreneurial society. The home and hearth model, as Professor David Chidester writes in *Christianity: A Global History*, conformed 'to the patterns and rhythms of the capitalist world of goods'. The nine-teenth-century historian, Ann Douglas, has documented how between 1830 and 1880 in American Christian ser-mons, hymns and novels, there was a great concentration on the 'eating habits, occupations, lifestyles, methods of childcare and courtship current in heaven'. Not only could one feel reassured that relationships on earth would continue ever after, one might also assume, in keeping with a capitalist, materialist age, that what one had amassed would also be going with you. Moreover, there was, from the pulpit, a constant invocation to people to reform practices in the here and now, especially over personal mortality, in the hope of fitting in more neatly with the prevailing social mores on high if and when they arrived at heaven's gates.

This was not particularly a theological movement – officially, the mainstream Churches remained rooted in ideas about reunion with God, not aunties and uncles – but a popular one. For almost two thousand years, the makers and reformers of doctrine had suggested one heaven, usually to some degree theocentric, while their congregations – often aided and abetted by artists and writers – had mainly stuck out for a more anthropocentric vision. In the nineteenth century, the theologians all but gave up the fight and were superseded, above all, by novelists.

One of the era's most popular books was *The Gates Ajar* by Elizabeth Stuart Phelps (1844–1911), the daughter of a Calvinist minister. Published in 1868, the book sold 180,000 copies, on both sides of the Atlantic; it was a massive and influential bestseller, comparing and contrasting two visions of heaven which were offered to Mary Cabot, a God-fearing woman whose brother John had just died in the American Civil War.

In a diary, she records the reactions of the local Calvinist minister, Dr Bland, who spoke in traditional religious terms of oneness with God, and also those of Aunt Winifred, who trumped him mercilessly in assuaging Mary's grief by the picture she painted of one, long, reunion of relatives: there would be good home-cooking, pianos in the parlour for sing-songs, and sweets galore. In short, life on earth would carry on in heaven, but with icing on the cake:

> 'Heaven? Eye hath not seen, but I have my fancies [Winifred tells Mary]. I think I want some mountains, and very many trees.'
> 'Mountains and trees?'
> 'Yes, mountains as we see them at sunset and sunrise,

or when the maples are on fire and there are clouds enough to make great purple shadows chase each other into lakes of light, over the tops and down the sides – the ideal of mountains which we catch in rare glimpses, as we catch the ideal of everything.'

Later, Winifred gives her own interpretation of the scriptures:

'In the Father's house are many mansions. Sometimes I fancy that those words have a literal meaning which the simple men who heard them may have understood better than we, and that Christ is truly "preparing" my home for me. He must be there, too, you see – I mean John.'

Phelps – who, in allowing Winifred to carry the day against the male minister by the nature of her own happy death at the end of the book, might be credited as an early pioneer in feminising heaven – was the undisputed queen of Victorian consolation literature. But she wasn't without her detractors. The theologians may largely have let this democratisation of heaven go unchecked, but other writers, with more ambition than simply pandering to what their readers wanted to hear, felt moved to raise their voices in protest. The American Romantic poet, Emily Dickinson (1830–86), had been brought up in the Calvinist tradition, but came to regard suggestions of this well-ordered paradise – somewhere, as she memorably put it, where it is Sunday all the time – with contempt. For one thing, she pointed out, it would be very crowded.

Mark Twain (1835–1910) had a very particular aversion to *The Gates Ajar*. It was, he said, 'a book which had imagined a mean little ten-cent heaven about the size of

Rhode Island – a heaven large enough to accommodate about a tenth of one per cent of the Christian billions who have died in the past nineteen centuries.' Accordingly, he sent it up something rotten in *Extract from Captain Stormfield's Visit*, his last book, published in 1909. The Captain, dead already for thirty years, flies around space on the lookout for flashing lights. When he finally spots them he finds himself at heaven's gate. He enters and immediately is given the paraphernalia predicted by Aunt Winifred:

> 'I had been having considerable trouble with my wings. The day after I helped the choir, I made a dash or two with them, but was not lucky. First off, I flew thirty yards, and then fouled an Irishman and brought him down – brought us both down, in fact. Next, I had a collision with a Bishop – and bowled him down, of course. We had some sharp words, and I felt pretty cheap, to come banging into a grave old person like that, with a million strangers looking on and smiling to themselves.'

Later, in conversation with another long-term resident, Stormfield hears that the image of heaven as a contented, egalitarian world, fashioned in the image of America, but under God's benign gaze, is far from the reality:

> 'You have got the same mixed-up idea about these things that everybody has down there [he is told]. I had it once, but I got over it. Down there they talk of the heavenly King – and that is right – but then they go right on speaking as if this was a republic and everybody was on a dead level with everybody else, and privileged to fling his arms around anybody he comes across and be hail-fellow-well-met with all the elect, from the highest down.

How tangled up and absurd that is! How are you going to have a republic under a king? How are you going to have a republic at all, when the head of government is absolute, holds his place for ever and has no parliament, no councils to meddle or make in his affairs, nobody voted for, nobody elected to take a hand in its matters, and nobody allowed to do it? Fine republic, ain't it?'

This heaven, Stormfield's host tells him, is more like Russia under the Romanovs. The extent to which heaven had become a wish-list of potentially conflicting ideas in the hands of writers like Elizabeth Stuart Phelps was not lost on Twain, himself the son of a devout Presbyterian mother and a freethinking father. You couldn't mix an all-powerful God, presiding in His kingdom, with an endless chain of family reunions in a pseudo-backwoods American fifty-third state without so much confusion that it could render the whole idea of a celestial after-life redundant.

The popularity of *The Gates Ajar* vision of a self-contradictory heaven shamelessly shaped in the light of present needs prompted others, too, to satire. One popular Victorian work, often heard at funerals and occasionally still seen on old gravestones, was the poem, 'Where Is No More Sea', published in 1863 in a compilation of *Hymns to Heaven* under the pseudonym 'Fysh':

> *My little bark has suffered much*
> *From adverse storms; nor is she such*
> *As once she seemed to be;*
> *But I shall shortly be at home,*
> *Nor more a mariner to roam;*
> *When once I to port am come,*
> *There will be no more sea.*

Rupert Brooke (1887–1915) so disliked the mawkish sentiments and hackneyed imagery of this that he responded with his parody poem *Heaven* which has a fish speculating that 'somewhere, beyond Space and Time/Is wetter water, slimier slime'.

In using humour to debunk heaven, Twain and Brooke stood in a long tradition, stretching back to encompass such figures as Henry Fielding (1707–1754) (whose *A Journey from This World to the Next* (1743) presented a picture of paradise where angels had no use for their wings because they hopped everywhere) and Lord Byron (1788–1824).

Byron had a good laugh at the expense of pompous pictures of heaven, but his lampooning was more political and personal than theological. His target was *A Vision of Judgement*, written by the Poet Laureate, Robert Southey, on the occasion of George III's death in 1820. It suggested that the late (and, for Byron, unlamented) monarch was newly installed on high:

> *O'er the adamantine gates an Angel stood on the summit.*
> *'Ho!' he exclaimed, 'King George of England cometh to judgement! Hear, Heaven! Ye Angels, hear! Souls of the Good and the Wicked, Whom it concerns, attend! Thou, Hell bring forth his accusers!'*

The vote of confidence George III wins from the heavenly choir may have been the basis for Byron's dislike of Southey's work. In his 1822 *The Vision of Judgement*, he sends the king to hell.

There was also a personal grudge between the two poets. Southey, as celebrated in his day as his Lakeland neighbour William Wordsworth, represented the Establishment and was thus anathema to Byron who refers to him in the last line as 'Bob Southey raving'. Perhaps he had in mind Southey's description of Byron as belonging to the 'satanic school of literature', but, whatever the source of animosity, what were for many the cherished details of heaven are sent up in Byron's poem:

> *Saint Peter sat by the celestial gate:*
> *His keys were rusty, and the lock was dull,*
> *So little trouble had been given of late;*
> *Not that the place by any means was full.*

Later, he continues:

> *The angels were singing out of tune,*
> *And hoarse with having little else to do,*
> *Expecting to wind up the sun and moon,*
> *Or curb a runaway young star or two.*

Such escapes into humour were as yet rare. Heaven was for most people a serious business indeed but ultimately a rather banal one. As the nineteenth-century drew to a close their very seriousness brought a new whiff of excitement, if not insight. In their determination to draw ever nearer to their loved ones on the other side by every means available to them, including the new 'god', technology, they ushered in the spiritualist movement.

Traveller's Tales: 4

Brian Moore was seventeen when he died on 27 May 1997. His car left the road in Pickaway County in the United States and hit an electricity pole. He got out unhurt but stepped on a fallen power line and was electrocuted.

Brian was a devout Christian in the evangelical tradition and a keen scholar. He was due to take up a four-year scholarship at Capital University in Columbus that autumn. Among his possessions, his parents found an essay, written in the style of a confession, that he had prepared days before his death for a meeting of a group called Christian Athletes which he attended regularly. Its theme was a dream he had had about heaven. He wrote of finding himself in a room. One wall was covered as far as the eye could see with small index card files, as in a library:

'As I drew near the wall of files, the first to catch my attention was one that read, "Girls I have Liked". I opened it and began flipping through the cards. I quickly shut it, shocked to realise that I recognised the names written on each one. And then, without being told, I knew exactly where I was. This lifeless room with its small files was a crude catalogue system for my life.'

He wades through all the details of his life.

'Often there were many more cards than I expected. Sometimes fewer than I hoped. I was overwhelmed by the sheer volume of the life I had lived. Could it be possible that I had had the time to write each of these thousands or even millions of cards? But each card confirmed this truth. Each was written in my own handwriting. Each signed with my signature.

'When I came to a file marked "Lustful Thoughts", I felt a chill run through my body. I pulled the file out only an inch, not willing to test its size, and drew out a card. I shuddered at its detailed content. I felt sick to think that such a moment had been recorded. An almost animal rage broke on me. One thought dominated my mind: "No one must ever see these cards! No one must ever seen this room! I have to destroy them." In an insane frenzy, I yanked the file out. Its size didn't matter now. I had to empty it and burn the cards. But as I took it at one end and began pounding it on the floor, I could not dislodge a single card. I became desperate and pulled out a card, only to find it as strong as steel when I tried to tear it.

'Defeated and utterly helpless, I returned the file to its slot. Leaning my forehead against the wall, I let out a long, self-pitying sigh. And then I saw it. The title bore: "People I Have Shared the Gospel With". The handle was brighter than those around it, newer, almost unused. I pulled its handle and a small box, not more than three inches long, fell into my hands. I could count the cards it contained on one hand. And then the tears came. I began to weep. Sobs so deep that they hurt. But then, as I pushed away the tears, I saw Him. No, please not Him. Not here. Oh, anyone but Jesus. I watched helplessly as He began to open the files and read the cards. I couldn't bear to watch His response. And in the moments I could bring myself to look at His face, I saw a sorrow deeper than my own. He seemed intuitively to go to the worst boxes.

'Finally, He turned and looked at me across the room. He looked at me with pity in His eyes. But this was a pity that didn't anger me. I dropped my head, covered my face with my hands and began to cry again. He walked over and put His arm around me. He could have said so many things. But

He didn't say a word. He just cried with me. Then He got up and walked back to the wall of files.

'Starting at one end of the room, He took out a file and, one by one, began to sign His name over mine on each card. The name of Jesus covered mine. It was written in His blood. The next instant I heard Him close the last file and walk back to my side. He placed His hand on my shoulder and said, "It is finished." I stood up, and He led me out of the room.'

Brian's parents, Beth and Bruce Moore, both devout evangelical Christians like their son, have a copy of the essay framed on a wall in their home. They have also made it available to a wider audience via the Internet. 'I think God used him to make a point,' says Beth Moore. 'I think we were meant to find it and make something of it. I know I'll see him again someday.'

———— ∞∞∞ ————

CHAPTER FOURTEEN

I Hear You Knocking

K atie and Maggie Fox were twelve and fourteen years old respectively when, on the evening of 31 March 1848, they decided to play a childish prank on their devoutly Methodist parents at their home in Hydesville in New York State. The family had moved in only the week before, and the previous tenant, Michael Weekman, had left because he said the place was haunted. It probably began with the girls dropping an apple on the floor of their bedroom to frighten the rest of the family into thinking that Weekman had been telling the truth. When their father anxiously rushed to check out the source of the noise, the girls noticed that the house contained a strange echo. Snapping and cracking their fingers and toes, they could set off strange, knocking noises at will.

Their mother Margaret later wrote (quoted in Ruth Brandon's *The Spiritualists*) of her reaction:

'I then thought I could put a test that no one in the place could answer. I asked the noise to rap my different children's ages, successively. Instantly, each one of my children's ages was given correctly, pausing between them sufficiently long to individualise them until the seventh [child], at which a longer pause was made, and then three more emphatic little raps were given, corresponding to the age of the little one that died . . .'

She was convinced that a spirit was speaking from beyond the grave through her daughters. Katie and Maggie were, the Foxes believed, mediums, bridges between the living and the dead. The two sisters, delighted by their parents' reaction, soon trained themselves to make the knocking noise by clicking their toe joints inside their shoes so as to remain to all observers quite still. The movement required to make the sound was so slight that no-one guessed their secret. Instead, they were hailed by all who saw them in action as establishing direct contact with heaven for the first time in history.

It was the end of a long journey, begun in post-Reformation times, towards a physical and verifiable heaven. Neither the Fox sisters nor their supporters, who soon turned them into a spectator sport in Rochester and then New York, had plucked the idea of communicating with the dead out of nowhere.

The direct source of the Foxes' belief is still debated. One suggestion is *The Night Side of Nature*, a bestselling collection of ghost stories by Edinburgh-born Catherine Crowe, published in 1847. It contained a story with direct parallels to the Fox sisters' claims.

Audiences embraced the Foxes' promise of an open channel to heaven as a logical extension of the parallel belief among churchgoers, later exemplified by *The Gates Ajar*, that heaven and their dear, departed loved ones were near at hand. The more humanised heaven became in the popular imagination as somewhere that could be accessed, as Victorian gravestones put it, simply by 'falling asleep', the more there developed an exaggerated openness to such reports as those which emerged from the Fox household. As the gap between heaven and earth narrowed, it was inevitable that efforts to bridge it would become more common.

On 21 October 1888, at the New York Academy of Music, the Foxes confessed that they had been lying, Maggie even demonstrating her ever-so-flexible big toe to convince her one-time supporters that she had taken them in. Such a fall from grace did little to affect the popularity of spiritualism. The message had become greater than the messenger. Many had fallen for the Foxes, including, in 1854, the wife of US President Franklin Pierce who invited them to the White House to perform a seance in an effort to contact her son who had been killed in a railway accident. It was an official seal of approval for this new approach to heaven.

Others who made claims similar to the Foxes also gained the same mainstream endorsements, but they were never shown up as fraudsters. Some, like Daniel Dunglas Home, who made his debut in Greeneville, Connecticut in 1850 at the age of seventeen, built a career on his rapping seances, but added extras like floating in the air and lifting tables to win an international following that included the Empress Eugenie of France and Elizabeth Barrett Browning. (Elizabeth's husband, Robert Browning, regarded D. D. Home as a con-man and sent him up in 1864 as 'Mr Sludge the Medium'.) Home's biographer, Jean Burton, describes (as quoted in Colin Wilson's *Afterlife*) a typical Home show in January 1863 in Paris. Princess Metternich and her husband, the Austrian ambassador, were among the fifteen guests sitting around the table, while Home sat in an armchair to one side. First, a knocking was heard, then the chandeliers swung and, finally, an empty chair began to move. A vase of violets on a nearby piano apparently floated through the air and landed in the princess's lap. She became a disciple on the spot, though her husband dismissed Home as a magician.

In New York, Madame Blavatsky used her acclaimed skills as a medium to found the Theosophical Society in 1881 – a cocktail of Eastern esotericism and spiritualism. 'These experts were no more than a logical extension of the American ideal,' Ruth Brandon, a historian of the spiritualist movement, has written. 'If a man could engage in constructing a new country and a new society, why should he not equally devise his own form of religion?' And, indeed, a new heaven?

It was not just an American phenomenon, however, though the States remained the powerhouse of the spiritualist movement. In London in the 1870s, Florence Cook would disappear into a cupboard of her East End home and re-emerge as one of her audience's dead relatives. The bandwagon remorselessly gathered speed and it infuriated the philosopher Ralph Waldo Emerson. It was, he said, 'a rat-hole revelation', but his voice was drowned out in what, despite its high-born devotees, was at heart a popular, working-class movement which successfully catered for the appetite for blurring the line between life and death. This taste also found sustenance in the popular Gothic novels that appeared from the 1830s onwards, written by authors such as Edgar Allan Poe.

The spiritualists' attempt to contact paradise was distinctive in two ways. First, there was their uneasy relationship with mainstream Christianity: spiritualism undeniably grew out of Christian belief. Its supporters were nearly all God-fearing folk. As a movement, it fed off religious naivete and piety, but it was akin to a one-issue pressure group that develops within a political party. It had only one agenda – contact with the dead. It had next to no interest in God and only the most passing and banal curiosity in the nature of eternal life. It was all about ascertaining the fact of immortality. In seances, little was said of God Himself beside platitudes about how loving He was. Awkward Christian doctrines such as the Last Judgement were avoided since they would involve the possibility that those attending seances might find their loved ones had gone to hell. Spiritualism did not want to bite the hand that fed it by offering anything other than comforting messages.

Yet the mainstream churches could never quite shake off the impression that spiritualists somehow came under their umbrella. They may deride spiritualism as a blasphemy – the Catholic Cardinal, John Vaughan (1853–1925), described it as 'illusive drivel and profane trifling' – but the spiritualists presented themselves as simply offering an added extra, something that mitigated one of Christianity's hardest demands – having faith in, but no proof of, an afterlife.

Though the idea of communicating with your ancestors was, in one sense, profoundly pagan, this did not appear to faze the spiritualists who would go to church on a Sunday and then fit in a couple of seances during the week. For them, the two happily co-existed. Indeed, when the spiritualists did get round to sketching the heavenly landscape, they did so in a way that no Protestant reader of Elizabeth Stuart Phelps could fail to recognise.

Second, there was the age's newfound confidence in

technology. There was no problem, it was believed, which couldn't be addressed and solved with a little technical assistance. Spiritualism flirted with this to establish its own pseudo-scientific credentials as opposed to mainstream religion's insistence in what was effectively blind faith. So, when considering the claims of the Foxes and D. D. Home, for example, much credence was given to the theories of the Austrian physician Antoine Mesmer, developed at the end of the eighteenth century, about the strange state of trance which he said could be achieved because of the mysterious magnetic fluid within the body. One of the leading American apostles of Mesmer and of hypnotism was one-time shoemaker Andrew Jackson Davis, author of another spiritualist bestseller, *The Principles of Nature: Her Divine Revelations* (1847), and also a prominent supporter of the Foxes.

This, in its turn, led some spiritualists to attempt to validate their claims by 'manifestations' – producing out of their various orifices a stream of what they called ectoplasm, a 'bound ether' which was, they said, the spiritual substance of the body and something which survived death. Doctors may have scoffed (and often the ectoplasm was shown to be a sheet of muslin which had to be either swallowed or hidden inside their bodies by mediums, many of whom had backgrounds as circus performers), but without today's X-ray machines or resonance scanners they could not easily prove their point. Spiritualism was a very physical credo and the soul was, in keeping with the spirit of the age, taking on a literal form, though that form was seldom scrutinised carefully. In part, this had to do with Victorian reticence at thoroughly investigating the bodies of what were largely female mediums to check out how they might have been producing ectoplasm. No self-respecting doubter wanted to prod around too much in search of the source of the bound ether under a layer of dresses, corsets, stockings and petticoats.

An additional fillip of respectability for the spiritualists came with the invention of photography. William Mumler from Boston is credited with being the first 'spirit photographer', after producing in 1861 a picture of himself with a shadow alongside which he claimed was his soul. Thereafter, a rush of photographs appeared of mediums with what looks like a stream of thick milk flowing out from their noses, mouths and groins. These were greeted as conclusive proof by many who were unaware of the possibilities for manipulating photographic plates.

Spirit photography was soon discredited, but an insight into the sort of credulity that greeted these first photographic pieces of 'evidence' comes from the life story of Guglielmo Marconi (1874–1937), inventor of the radio. When first he managed to transmit signals, Marconi, a brilliant man of science, believed that what he was hearing was not a result of his own technical work, but of voices from beyond – possibly from other planets. In the last years of his life, he devoted much energy to the possibility of establishing a channel of communication with the dead.

One early ardent spiritualist was the distinguished American chemist, Robert Hare (1781–1858). The inventor of the oxyhydrogen blowpipe sacrificed his energies and his reputation to proving the key tenet of the spiritualists – namely that there was a scientific basis for their claims. In *Experimental Investigation of the Spirit Manifestations: Demonstrating the Existence of Spirits and Their Communion with Mortals*, published in the last year of his life, Hare wrote at length of his consultations, via a medium, with a panel of the great and good of the past – including George Washington, Isaac Newton and Lord Byron. In a series of often one-word replies, this group 'confirmed' a Dantean picture of concentric spheres reaching up to the heavens. By the third sphere, they agreed, the scenery was a definite improvement on earth. At other stages, however, they became a little more responsive to Hare's questioning, offering up pseudo-scientific insights:

(Q) What designates the boundaries of the spheres, so as to make spirits perceive when they are passing through the partition between one and another?

(A) Diversity of impression made upon the spirit.

(Q) What confines a spirit to his proper level, so that none can mount above it into a sphere to which he does not belong?

(A) A moral specific gravity, in which the weight is inversely as the merit, prevents the spirit from rising above his proper level.

Only briefly, towards the end of the interview, do they turn to moral matters and to God:

(Q) As in the spiritual world there is no necessity, desire or passion which spirits can gratify by violence or fraud, on what is virtue founded?

(A) In the spheres, vice is displayed by the endurance of bad passions; virtue is manifested by love, purity and the aspiration for improvement.

(Q) When a being virtuously constituted is murdered by one of the opposite character, who is most an object of commiseration? Which is most favoured as a creature of God?

(A) The victim is most favoured.

Not all of the mediums were out-and-out charlatans. They may have been mistaken or deluded, but some were, it seems, sincere. And, for many, dabbling in spiritualism was little more than a parlour game. Even Queen Victoria and Prince Albert tried it at Osborne. The Fox sisters' admission that they had been lying may have marked a gradual downturn in spiritualist beliefs from the high point of the late 1860s, when there were an estimated eleven million spiritualists in America alone, but, well into the twentieth century, this democratisation of heaven retained substantial popular appeal.

The roots of its pull, as always in any effort to bring heaven to earth, lay in what was happening in the real world. The very technology that played a part in giving a pseudo-scientific aura to mediums, magicians and seances was also changing the world at a frightening pace as industrialisation grew evermore widespread. It was not only the physical landscape that was altering. In 1859, Charles Darwin's *On the Origin of Species*, with its theory of 'natural selection', definitively damned previous accommodations between religion and science which allowed that the earth was a machine, but insisted God was the chief engineer.

Darwin effectively 'did God out of a job' and presented a huge challenge to what had previously been taken as read – that life was somehow guided by a divinity and that individuals were not wholly responsible for their fate. For some, such a theory was a great liberation, but for many others, suddenly to be asked to take responsibility for themselves was a challenge they could not quite contemplate.

The theory of evolution may have continued the Enlightenment's work in freeing hearts and minds from the control of the Churches, but it also so polarised opinion as to throw many back by way of a defensive reaction on their religious beliefs, which they upheld in a gesture of defiance against the spirit of the age. 'Men find,' wrote Charles Kingsley, 'that now they have got rid of an interfering God – a master-magician as I call it – they have to choose between the absolute empire of accident, and a living, immanent, ever-working God.'

Faced with Darwin's logic, many, including eminent scientists such as Hare, preferred to retreat into the myths that organised religion offered. Within that spectrum, spiritualism was a form of fundamentalism, but definitely on the Christian side of the equation, offering the most immediately satisfying 'proof' that Darwin had got it wrong by means of the messages it relayed back from on high.

The First World War unleashed the second great spiritualist wave. The war left many mothers, fathers, husbands, wives, brothers and sisters in mourning, anxious for reassurance that their lost loved one was enjoying eternal rest. Mediums reacted to market forces. They produced consoling messages – to parents, that their son did not die alone; to widows, that their husband was waiting chastely for them; to sisters, that their brothers were happy but missing them.

It was a finely tuned service and attracted some unlikely figures. Sir Oliver Lodge (1851–1940) was a leading British physicist and pioneer in the field of tele-communications and electromagnetism who had pre-viously flirted with spiritualism. The loss of his son Raymond in 1916 tipped him over the edge and prompted him to contact a medium who relayed mes-sages back from a place called 'Summer Land'. Lodge subsequently published these in book form as *Raymond, or Life and Death* (1917). Gaining weight from Lodge's academic reputation and, in particular, his expertise in the technology of communication, it quickly ran to twelve editions:

> My body's very similar to the one I had before. I pinch myself sometimes to see if it's real, and it is, but it doesn't seem to hurt as much as when I pinched the flesh body . . . I know a man who had lost an arm, but he got another one . . . When any body's blown to pieces, it takes some time for the spirit body to complete itself . . . There are laboratories over here and they manufacture all sorts of things in them. Not like you do, out of solid matter, but out of essences, and ether and gases. It's not the same as on the earth plane, but they were able to manage what looked like a cigar.

This heaven was so precise as to be absurd. Raymond had the home comforts, as well as the language of the spiritualists and a positively Victorian love of manufac-turing. What is missing from his picture is any mention of God in Summer Land. Lodge even avoided the word heaven. So geared towards its listeners had spiritualism become that a divinity seemed almost too confusing to mention. Heaven was all about earth.

When the distinguished Edwardian social campaigner and journalist, W. T. Stead (1849–1912), one-time editor of the *Pall Mall Gazette*, became interested in spiritualism, it was only in so far as it enabled him, as he reported in the *Daily Chronicle*, to locate long-dead figures such as Catherine the Great, whose advice he sought on the growing crisis in Russia under the Romanovs in 1908, or Gladstone, whose input he sought on the 1909 People's Budget. The very fact that the *Chronicle* splashed Gladstone's utterances from beyond the grave over its front page under the banner 'Amazing Spirit Interview: The Late Mr Gladstone on the Budget' shows just how seriously such matters were taken.

Another recruit to spiritualism at this time was the eminent writer and creator of Sherlock Holmes, Sir Arthur Conan Doyle (1859–1930). His son, Kingsley, had died in 1914 and his brother-in-law, Malcolm, perished at Mons in 1916. Conan Doyle consulted mediums and first made contact with his son through a medium in South Wales.

The location is in itself revealing: a poor, pious area, its people were dislocated and disorientated, having within that generation left rural areas to work in often appalling conditions in the new mines and iron foundries. Faced with such a bleak life, invocations from the pulpit each Sunday to have faith in God's promise of a better hereafter could easily be found wanting; turning to mediums for proof that there was indeed something better offered a surer guarantee.

Once convinced, Conan Doyle, a literary celebrity on both sides of the Atlantic, used his fame to promote spiritualism on many a public platform, defending the Foxes even after they had been disgraced, endorsing ectoplasm and even, in May 1920, proclaiming his belief in fairies on the basis of a photographic plate that was later shown to have been tampered with. A Jesuiteducated lapsed Catholic, he remained like many spiritualists a convinced Christian. For him, the point of spiritualism was its power to prove in a literal way God's promise that you don't die. In the process, he felt there was a pleasing knock-on effect in this life, namely, 'to prepare ourselves for an afterlife by refining away our grosser animal feelings and cultivating higher, nobler impulses'. In 1918, on the basis of his many sessions with mediums, Conan Doyle was authoritatively able to set out in his book, *The New Revelation*, chapter and verse on dying:

> All agree that passing is usually both easy and painless and followed by an enormous reaction of peace and ease. The individual finds himself in a spirit body which is the exact counterpart of his old one, save that all disease, weakness or deformity has passed from it. This body stands or floats beside the old body and is conscious both of it and the surrounding people. At this moment the dead man is nearer to matter than he will ever be again.

Certainly the ideal way to die, Conan Doyle's description cannot be faulted. Death without pain, eternal youth, gently floating along ... 'No woman need mourn her lost beauty,' he once remarked, 'no man his lost strength or weak brain.' Dead children will grow into perfect adults in a landscape of gardens, lakes and woods. People will even have pets. And best of all, there was proof. It was, Conan Doyle said, 'fully discernible in messages of pioneering travellers who have got news back to those who loiter in old, dingy homes'.

Under close questioning from an American audience when he was on a lecture tour in 1922, he fleshed out his own personal heaven as somewhere which sounded rather like a Surrey golf club, with tobacco and drinks on tap and a constant supply of congenial souls.

'There are many weak and foolish people in this world and the next,' he remarked. 'One chooses one's companions.' Pesky bodily functions such as going to the toilet would be a thing of the past because spirits eat 'anything of a light and delicate order' and thereby avoid the need to empty bowels or bladder. In terms of sex, he preferred the concept of 'soul affinity' to actual heavenly reunion of spouses. (This may have been a neat formula to get over the problems posed by the fact that he had had two wives.)

Despite Conan Doyle's evangelising on its behalf, spiritualism regularly found itself attacked from all sides. Most scientists, buoyed up by Darwin, derided it. The magician, Harry Houdini, devoted a great deal of his energy to disproving it by revealing the tricks the mediums were using. And the Churches objected in ever louder tones to its marginalisation of God – the beatific vision that so had once so obsessed the scholastics.

However, thinking in both Catholic and Protestant Churches on heaven was changing, in order to meet the challenge not only of the spiritualists but also of the vision offered by books like *The Gates Ajar*. Some Catholic writers, such as the nineteenth-century French Jesuit, François-René Blot, read the popular mood and moved away from the stark theocentric heaven towards something resembling the Elizabeth Stuart Phelps version. His *In Heaven We Know Our Own* (1863) became a piety stall rival to Phelps with its account of families reunited on high under God's benign gaze. 'If enjoying the society of your relations is a consolation,' Blot told his readers, extolling the Holy Family and drawing eccentrically on

Sing, choirs of angels: Dante's *Paradiso* (1321) is for many the most complete attempt to map heaven. Among those to have illustrated his vision was Sandro Botticelli, the fifteenth-century Renaissance master, in a cycle of 92 drawings. Here Dante and his guide, Beatrice, are surrounded by angels in the penultimate level of heaven as they gaze, for the first time, at the point of intense light that is God.

EMANUEL SWEDENBOR

Romance lives on: Emmanuel Swedenborg (1688–1772) in his eight-volume *Arcana Coelestia* ushers in a modern and Romantic vision of heaven, where earthly human love would be reproduced but refined. He illustrated his account of his own journey to the other side in his *Spiritual Diary* (*below*).

As a new heaven is begun, and it is now thir-
ree years since its advent: the Eternal Hell
revives. And lo! Swedenborg is the Angel sitting
at the tomb; his writings are the linen clothes folded
up. Now is the dominion of Edom, & the return of
Adam into Paradise; see Isaiah XXXIII & XXXV Chap:
Without Contraries is no progression Attraction
and Repulsion, Reason and Energy. Love and
Hate, are necessary to Human existence.
From these contraries spring what the religious call
Good & Evil. Good is the passive that obeys Reason
Evil is the active springing from Energy.
Good is Heaven. Evil is Hell.

Eternal pilgrim: 'In the visionary imagination of William Blake,' writes his
biographer, Peter Ackroyd, 'there is no birth and no death, no beginning
and no end, only the perpetual pilgrimage within time towards eternity.'
His *Marriage of Heaven and Hell* (1790) is a work of poetry, proverbs,
observations and parodies (of Swedenborg).

The Last Day: Blake's 1808 *Vision of the Last Judgement* celebrates the 'new Jerusalem' that 'is ready to descend upon Earth'.

THE GATES AJAR

BY ELIZABETH STUART PHELPS
EDITED BY HELEN SOOTIN SMITH

Soaring sales: *The Gates Ajar*, written by Calvanist minister's daughter, Elizabeth Stuart Phelps, and published in 1868, was the most influential book on heaven in the nineteenth century. With sales of 180,000, it promoted the idea that heaven would be a cleaned-up version of earth.

The bridge: the writer Sir
Arthur Conan Doyle
(1859–1930) staked his
reputation on the authenticity
of claims by mediums to be able
to communicate with the dead.
Peaking twice, first in the 1860s
and later during the First World
War, Spiritualism appeared to
offer proof that heaven existed.
Mediums would regurgitate for
'spirit photographers' ectoplasm,
supposedly the spiritual
substance in their body (*left*).
Many were subsequently
shown to be frauds using
muslin and their skills those of
circus performers out to trick
audiences. A leading sceptic
was Harry Houdini
(1874–1926), pictured above
right with Conan Doyle.

'Angels and dirt': Stanley Spencer rarely strayed far beyond his home village of Cookham in his efforts to paint the transcendent in everyday life or, as he preferred to put it, 'angels and dirt'. His *Resurrection: Cookham* (1927) showed the living and dead joyously reunited.

Indian summer: heaven may now be little mentioned by the mainstream Churches, but continued in the twentieth century to fascinate writers such as C.S. Lewis.

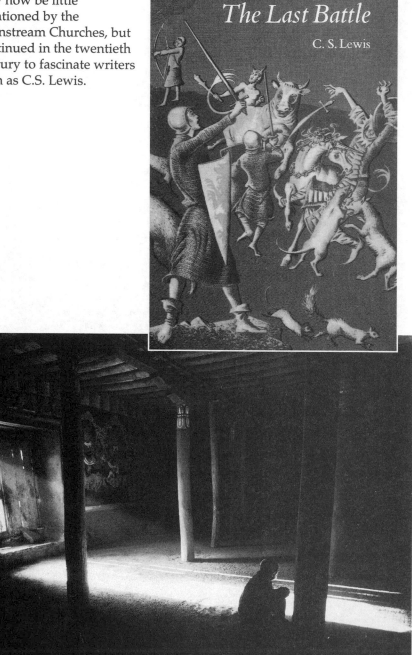

The Last Battle

C. S. Lewis

Nirvana: Buddhism teaches that nirvana is not some external heaven, reached after death, but rather individual and internal enlightenment in this life. Buddha, writes his biographer Karen Armstrong, 'believed that he could find the freedom he sought right in the midst of this imperfect world'.

the lives of saints, 'then you may indulge [in it] without fear, without scruple and without imperfection.'

More theologically-inclined Catholic thinkers shied away from such a pat sentiment as Blot's mantra that Christ met his mother again in heaven, so everyone else can expect to meet theirs in similar fashion. They were also less keen than Blot on being modern. They clung, unfashionably, to the suggestion that heaven might be something imaginative rather than literal, mystical rather than architectural. Yet they needed a mascot, so, like the Counter-Reformation, they hit upon invoking the Mother of God as both the Queen of Heaven and the bridge between the sufferings of this world and the reward waiting in heaven. 'He is the Wisdom of God,' wrote Cardinal John Henry Newman (1801–1890), the leading Anglican Tractarian who converted to Catholicism in 1845, 'she therefore is the Seat of Wisdom; His Presence is Heaven, she therefore is the Gate of Heaven; He is infinite Mercy, she then is the Mother of Mercy. She is the Mother of fair love and fear, and knowledge and holy hope.' Mary's popularity was again increasing, and there was another round of apparitions to peasant children, exclusively in the rural areas of devoutly Catholic countries, including that reported by Bernadette Soubirous in 1858 at Lourdes. But Newman was using Christ's mother as window-dressing for what remained at heart a thoroughly theocentric idea of heaven. In his best-known work, the autobiographical *Apologia Pro Vita Sua* of 1864, he wrote:

> God alone is in heaven; God is all in all. Eternal Lord, I acknowledge this truth ... There is One God and He fills Heaven; and all blessed creatures, though they ever remain in their individuality, are, as the very means of

their blessedness absorbed and drowned in the fullness of Him. If ever, through Thy grace, I attain to see Thee in Heaven, I shall see nothing else but Thee, because I shall see all whom I see in Thee, and seeing them I shall see Thee ... And so I might begin again, after this material universe, and find a world of knowledge, higher and more wonderful, in Thy intellectual creations, Thy angels and other spirits and men.

Newman's view was very much in tune with that of one of the giants of Protestant theology, the German Friedrich Schleiermacher (1768–1834), who rejected the cosy, modern heaven in no less defiant terms. In his textbook, *The Christian Faith* (1827), Schleiermacher argued for heaven, but as somewhere beyond imagination. 'We cannot really make a picture of it. To such a task our sensuous imagination is unequal.'

These two thinkers were rare examples of a willingness in the Churches to engage in a debate as to the nature of heaven. Most of their colleagues were happy to keep their heads down and, when pressed, to fudge. Thus, even though the official Catholic line remained defined in terms of being with God in heaven, Pope Leo XIII, in an encyclical letter of 1878, was writing to extol each family to 'present a likeness of the heavenly home'. The pressure to be literal was just too powerful, it seems, for even Saint Peter's successor to resist.

CHAPTER FIFTEEN

Speaking Words of Wisdom?

S ir Arthur Conan Doyle stares out reassuringly from his portrait above the fireplace. The tilt of his head is slightly defiant, no doubt the product of enduring years of ridicule for his spiritualist beliefs, but his rabbit-in-the-headlights eyes, almost comical handlebar moustache and tweeds, all standard in pre-Second World War British films, make me smile. Which is a good deal more than I can say of the other twelve people in the Conan Doyle Room at the British Spiritualist Association headquarters in Belgrave Square, central London.

They are a disconcerting group, busy fidgeting in their seats and doing everything possible to avoid meeting anyone else's gaze. When I break the taboo and stare back at the man in the row in front, he bolts for the door. I play it safe and look at my knees. There is a palpable embarrassment in the air. We might all be sitting in the waiting room of a sexually transmitted diseases clinic but, instead, we've paid our £4 and are expecting the duty medium – there's one on offer every day at 3.30 p.m. and again at 7.30 p.m. – to appear. Not literally. At least I hope not.

I have been feeling oddly uncomfortable about the prospect of going to a seance. It will be my first, and I had planned to keep myself chaste for ever. Once, for a newspaper, I interviewed a psychic who claimed to be able to read your past, present and future by holding something you wore every day. I duly handed over my watch and, in return, she predicted an imminent trip to Table Mountain in South Africa. I'm still waiting, six years on, though she did later ring me to ask if I'd write her biography.

I took the trouble of looking up the *Universal Catechism* on the subject of mediums just before I set off for Belgrave Square. Despite – or probably as a result of – my Catholic upbringing, I'm not a great one for rule books, but somehow John Paul II's compilation of guidance on every subject under the sun has ended up on my bookshelves and just occasionally it can put into words a buried anxiety. 'Spiritism,' he counsels, 'often implies divination or magical practices; the Church for her part warns the faithful against it.' This just about summed up my mood. If he'd said it was bunkum, worthless reassurance that had been shown time after time to make false claims, I'd be sitting more comfortably now, but there was that disturbing note of menace in his words: tamper with this at your peril.

The exit door is close to my seat and looking very inviting. But a fearless traveller in search of heaven, I have to tell myself, should road test every route. So I stay. Despite my unusually clammy palms, linked defensively in front of my body, I am only here for the research. I then leaf through a copy of *Psychic News* which I'd picked up in the rather grand foyer. Its front page splash harks back to another age of spirit photography. 'Is This the Spirit Manifestation of Abby's Grandfather

Caught by the Camera?' it asks, alongside a grainy photograph that looks like it's covered in thumb prints after having being handed round at a coffee morning.

I snort. Quietly. But it doesn't quite reassure me or disguise my own mixed motives. I haven't, for instance, brought a notebook (just in case I find myself being guided by a spirit into automatic writing or jotting down in perfect order the notes of the Hallelujah Chorus). The rational, twenty-first century part of me tells me it is stuff and nonsense, but I am terrified of putting it to the test lest it be proved to have some value. Logically, then, I must, at some level, believe in the claims.

My reaction is a good metaphor for contemporary attitudes to heaven. History, science and psychology point to it being a collective delusion, designed to take the edge off mortality and to soften the random blows of fate in this life. On one level, most of us sign up to this randomness, and treat heaven as some quaint medieval antique, nice to look at in paintings in art galleries, but utterly irrelevant to our lives. Yet, when push comes to shove, and the specialist tells us the test results are bad – in other words, when the heaven that we have scorned suddenly becomes our best hope – then we often find we have some core belief in a greater power and the trappings that go with it.

Heaven offers consolation by the bucket-load and so, potentially, does spiritualism, but at least heaven requires some investment by way of imagination and faith. Spiritualism, it seems, only requires £4.

I recall Mark Twain's line about a mean little ten-cent heaven. Allowing for inflation, this may be what I'm about to get. But equally, I could be so surprised by what happens in the next hour that I'd end up like Conan Doyle, hopelessly hooked, and the despair of erstwhile friends: 'Poor Peter, he was doing fine until he stumbled into that seance!' What if my dead mother is about to speak to me? Am I ready for that? Isn't it what I have listened for almost everyday since her death? I am, after all, no different from Oliver Lodge or any other bereaved individual who hopes against hope.

Thankfully, before I can carry that particular thought any further, and begin to replan my future, Joan Davies sweeps in. In my mind, of course, I am expecting Madame Arcati, as played by Margaret Rutherford for Noël Coward. Instead, I get a Welsh housewife in her mid-50s, in a plain, blue dress and neat, white jacket. She might be about to do a cookery demonstration, except that her bottle black bob would need tying back to stop it getting in her eyes. She takes her place at what looks disconcertingly like an altar at the front of the room. The dull, blue cloth hanging over the lectern is embroidered with a yellow lighthouse, sending out signals into empty space.

The fidgeters are suddenly caught in its beam and they fall silent as the old man who has been innocuously collecting tickets at the door comes up to the front and introduces himself as Wally, a retired teacher and writer of education textbooks. He could be Conan Doyle back in spirit. He welcomes us all on behalf of the British Spiritualist Association, one of a plethora of bodies that sprang up at the high point of the spiritualist vogue at the turn of the last century, and invested its reserves in this massive house in Belgravia which now, like the organisation, is slowly fraying at the edges through neglect – along with Wally's hair, hearing and ability to hold an audience.

I can only hope he was a better textbook writer in his day than he is a speaker now, for within minutes he has lost the gaggle in front of him as they all start jiffling in their seats once again. They need the smack of firm government and so up steps Joan, eyes fixed in a glazed expression on the back wall, looking like every fortune-teller you've ever seen pictured at the back of a magazine at the dentist's.

She launches into a brief and understandably partisan introduction to spiritualism. What catches my attention is not so much her bald statement that its claims have been scientifically proven, since I know they haven't, as her effort to place spiritualism firmly within the Christian tradition. Hers is a sanitised version of the long and uneasy relationship between the two. She even rounds off by leading us into a group prayer to God to encourage us all to be open.

While she does not use the word heaven, preferring to talk of 'those who live in the spirit' inhabiting 'the astral plane', she nevertheless conjures up a heady cocktail of all the best audience-pleasing-details of heaven's history – the promise of reunion with loved ones, the hum of constant activity ('you can even learn new skills there,' she chimes, like an employment counsellor), the physical beauty both of the landscape and of the inhabitants who are all at their physical and mental peak. What she doesn't borrow from Christianity, however, is any idea of judgement in death – i.e. that some of those her audience may be searching for may not have made it into heaven. We are all going to be satisfied in the next hour, it seems.

Joan explains that her own spirit guide has arrived at her shoulder. She even starts a little as if he or she has just goosed her. At this point I half expect Wally, who has crept to the back of the room, to turn down the lights, but he appears to be asleep. Joan is transfixed by that beige wall, and her eyes are now spinning like a roulette wheel. Someone's lucky number is about to come up. We all go tense. I sink down into my chair and curse being so tall. 'I want to come to the lady sitting at the back, wearing the beautiful necklace.' Joan is pointing elsewhere. The rest of the room breathes a collective sigh of relief.

'I have a tall African gentleman here for you. Can you accept him?' The woman looks around confused, as if the said gentleman is about to appear through the curtains behind the makeshift altar like a guest on *This is Your Life*. 'He has a special concern for you.'

The woman is still straining to see him. Joan doesn't hang about waiting for her to catch up. 'Can you hold on to that, think about it later, ask others?' The woman nods, utterly disorientated. Joan effortlessly changes tack and begins to talk of trips coming up in the future – Germany, Australia, America. This is fantasy travel agent land, but again there is no sign of her hitting the jackpot. So another switch, this time accompanied by a theatrical turn behind her to take an imaginary birthday cake from her spirit guide. 'You've a birthday coming up.' The woman has at last cottoned on. It's her granddaughter's birthday next month, she tells us all. It's a result. Let's hope the cake will last.

It hasn't been an auspicious start, but Joan now lights on much more receptive raw material, a well-scrubbed young blonde woman sitting eagerly in the front row.

'I'm seeing the word healer above your head.' The woman nods eagerly, apparently unafraid of jumbling up the letters. 'I could do with some healing myself,' Joan confides in a camp aside, as if chatting to her next-door neighbour over the garden fence. It could be a rare moment of insight, poacher-turned-gamekeeper, but instead, she scratches her freckly arm as if in search of a fix, and adds, 'but this is about you, dear.' There follows much talk of alternative remedies, health foods, tai-chi, yoga and a long-lost grandfather who is playing the role of guardian angel. The blonde head is nodding enthusiastically at every take and Joan understandably seems reluctant to move on.

It is the high point of the session. She scores very few more hits as she darts around the room, often falling victim to her own stereotypes. Two Afro-Caribbean women are told there is a spirit from the West Indies calling them, but they insist that they have lived in Birmingham for generations. An Indian-looking man is being contacted by a man sitting in a restaurant. By the time Joan gets to me, I am more intrigued than frightened. There is a father figure calling me from New England. My father only got his passport two years ago at the age of eighty, so she is way off there. Then she tries to read the words above my head, and after toying with 'technology' – I've a big head – then 'teacher' she plumps for 'actor'. In a narrow sense, she is right. I suppose I am acting a part in the seance, but her reassurances that my audition next week will go well and that I will get the part that will make my name give the game away.

There is something in the way she gives me my 'messages' that means I find myself, instead of saying 'Actually, completely wrong', muttering 'Well, yes, sort of'. In part, it is because this doesn't seem the forum for an argument, and since I'm not sure how the others feel about Joan, I don't want the rest of the room to turn on me as the non-believer in their midst. Yet it is also that I would be easy game for any second-hand car dealer and Joan's technique is, I recognise, classic salesmanship that is trading on my embarrassment. Never take no for an answer. Roll on relentlessly until you force your hearer to say yes.

But what, exactly, is Joan selling, and to what profit? The second question is easier. A dozen people at £4 a head is £48 an hour. Then there is her final pitch; after having given us all a taster, she offers individual, in-depth sessions. The blonde woman has her cheque book out once. That will be another £50.

Yet it is still such a small-scale fraud that I cannot quite believe it is worth the effort unless the motivations are more complex. Transparent as Joan's deception is, there is no obvious malice in her, and I am quite happy to believe that her play-acting is born out of a genuine desire to help the walking wounded who turn up each day. With a touch of the frustrated actress thrown in. She may even delude herself that she really is hearing messages. The only damage done comes in terms of unfulfilled expectations, but in terms of life after death in this life, all hopes are pipe dreams.

I'm just wondering whether Conan Doyle would have defended Joan with the same gusto that he showed for the Foxes when the only satisfied customer in the room walks past my chair. She is smiling, no doubt looking forward to the one-to-one trip to heaven she has just booked. Swinging from her hand is a white plastic bag – which was no doubt at her feet in the front row of the room – emblazoned with the logo of an alternative medicine shop.

CHAPTER SIXTEEN

Man is What He Eats

Behind the conflicts and heated debate of nineteenth-century religiosity, a change had taken place. For the first time, thanks to the advancement of science, atheism had become socially and intellectually respectable. The discovery, for example, by geologist Sir Charles Lyell in the 1830s that the world is millions of years older than had previously been thought, undermined the creation account in Genesis. Charles Darwin, inspired, among others, by Lyell, took this one giant step further by providing in *The Origin of Species* an entirely new version of the birth of humankind. At the same time, biblical scholars had begun to look at the provenance of the sacred texts and found that many were not quite what they had been made out to be. Religion found itself under the spotlight of science and scrutinised as never before. Many predicted its imminent demise, or, in the case of the Victorian poet and essayist, Matthew Arnold (1822–88), the 'melancholy long, withdrawing roar' and retreat of the 'Sea of Faith'.

In such a climate of scepticism, in an age where the head increasingly ruled the heart, life after death inevitably lost some of its appeal. Philosophers lined up to attack religion and to damn, inter alia, the notion that there was some celestial reward awaiting us on the other side. Reason no longer needed heaven, as Kant had once argued, while Sigmund Freud (1856–1939), the originator of psychoanalysis, dismissed it as wishful thinking, encouraged by controlling clergymen, to divert attention from earthly matters. Karl Marx (1818–83) put it more bluntly when he memorably decried religion as 'the opium of the people'. Marx was deeply influenced by the radical German theologian, Ludwig Feuerbach (1804–72) who, in his *Essence of Religion*, translated into English by George Eliot, had argued that God is an outward projection of man's inner self and is therefore a dangerous delusion. The real challenge, he said, is to live in the present. Hankering after immortality in heaven by contrast is both selfish and stupid. Feuerbach's views led to him being sacked from his theological teaching post. *Den Mensch ist was er isst*, he wrote in *Essence of Religion* – man is what he eats.

This remains, very largely, the response of modern scientists when questioned about heaven. Confronted with individual testimonies of visions of the hereafter, they point to the hallucinatory qualities of some drugs used to treat standard medical conditions. Among the Indians of the Amazon rain forest, it has been reported, the habit of downing a particularly potent mix of the ayahuasca vine and the leaf of another plant has been a common practice among those wanting to communicate with ancestors on a higher plane for generations.

In those without recourse to such remedies, the belief in heaven is ascribed by some scientists to brain damage: 'hyper religiosity' is equated with temporal lobe epilepsy, and it is true to say that the powers of the brain defy understanding. A neurophysicist can describe what happens inside the brain without getting one whit closer to its internal mystery. Within that 'mystery', it is argued, lies the root of humankind's attachment to ideas like heaven. What they are adamant about, however, is that there can be no scientifically valid separation of brain and what is called the soul, so that when we die, our brains die and that, as they say, is that.

Not all, however, have accepted science as a new religion in place of the old. Some eminent scientists have laboured long and hard to reconcile the two. Much of this effort was initially orchestrated by those sympathetic to spiritualism – the Society for Psychical Research, for instance, founded in Britain in 1882 and soon afterwards in the States. Yet even from within such subjective ranks, some theories arose which commanded a wider audience. One of the key figures in the Society, Frederick Myers, the son of a clergyman, wrote *Human Personality and Its Survival of Bodily Death* which was posthumously published in 1903. From a series of case studies, he argued that there were two sides to the brain: the left, more practical, and the right, the key to the 'subliminal mind', which had both the potential to live on after death and to receive messages by telepathy.

Amongst those impressed by such controversial marshalling of scientific argument to create a space for an afterlife was the author of *Brave New World*, Aldous Huxley (1894–1963). In his preface to the US edition of Myers's book, he praised it for raising once again the question of whether 'the house of the soul is a mere bungalow with a cellar or does it have an upstairs above the ground floor of consciousness as well as a garbage-littered basement beneath?'

Myers (and, indeed, telepathy) was very much on the

margins of mainstream science. A much more potent name linked with the American branch of the Society for Psychical Research was that of William James (1842– 1910), the brother of the author Henry James. He was not only a Harvard professor, but one of America's most distinguished psychologists. James felt a great attraction to religion, and though it fitted neatly with his own pragmatic philosophy – he once wrote, 'we have the right to believe at our own risk any hypothesis that is enough to tempt our will' – he was also tormented by doubt. He became intrigued by spiritualism after having attended a seance at the behest of his mother-in-law, and in *Varieties of Religious Experience* (1932), highly influential in its time, he all but sidelined heaven as an irrelevant question when placed alongside the much more important issue of immortality.

This was a distinctly early twentieth-century habit. By employing philosophical arguments, rather than traditional Christian imagery and theology, James tried to buttress Kant's position, that reason demanded that we believe in life after death, against the post-Darwinian onslaught. 'For my own part,' he once remarked, 'so far as logic goes, I am willing that every leaf that ever grew in this world's forests and rustled in the breeze should become immortal.'

A different and more enduring approach was taken by Sigmund Freud's most influential disciple, Carl Jung (1875–1961), the Swiss founder of analytical psychology. Unlike Freud, with whom he parted company in 1913, Jung rejected his master's line that all religion was neurosis. 'About God himself,' he wrote in 1941 (quoted in Ronald Hayman's biography), 'I have asserted nothing because according to my premise nothing whatsoever can be asserted about God Himself. All such assertions refer to the psychology of the God-image.' He was neither for nor against God, but instead he preferred to speak of an identifiable force, the human subconscious, which is repressed within each of us and which is beyond the bounds of conventional or imposed morality. It could be applied to individuals, groups and whole movements and trends in history.

Within the unconscious he also saw a collective element that transcends the individual and embraces all of human history. In particular, Jung studied symbols and found that ancient cultures with no links to each other had developed remarkably similar myths and stories on a whole range of subjects, including afterlife and heaven. In the East, Taoism, for instance, as we have seen, spoke of layers leading up to a heavenly centre. Two thousand years later, in the West, so did Dante. Jung argued that the structure of the brain had evolved in the same way throughout humankind, whatever the geographical location, and in the unconscious were various archetypes.

The collective unconscious was for Jung 'a receptacle of all lost memories and of all contents that are still too weak to become conscious'. And from it were drawn by religious searching ideas or archetypes which fell into 'specifically human patterns'. It was, he argued, 'in the great religions of the world that we see the perfection of those images and at the same time their progressive encrustation with rational forms'.

In other words, humans wanted to live after death, had always done so, and so fashioned an afterlife out of the ideas in their collective unconscious about afterlife, compiled and refined down the ages. In modern times, though, either for their own pleasure or under attack from science, people had turned those archetypes into facts that could be investigated as if they really existed. In an interview in 1959, he tried to explain the process by which various images had been passed down through the history of humankind. He had, he said, been treating a schizophrenic who pointed at the sun and told Jung that it had a penis, which could be spotted if you moved your head around when you looked at it, and which caused the wind. Later, Jung came across an account of Mithraism, an ancient Persian creed based on sun worship. It believed the source of the wind to be tubular-shaped growths on the surface of the sun which could be seen if you looked from East to West. His patient, Jung concluded, knew nothing of Mithraism and so had got his delusion about the sun from the collective unconscious. Within this great storehouse of ideas resided all the features of heaven.

Jung refused to take any aspects of the Christian story at face value or to fall into the trap of testing out archetypes against the claims of science, which would render heaven an unnecessary obstacle – unnecessary in the sense that belief in God should not rest on its existence. Jung could understand and even sympathise with the idea of heaven in so far as it expressed a yearning in the unconscious for something after death, a desire to express something inexpressible. Yet one of his first pieces of advice to Christians was to read from the sayings of Buddha, in particular about the search for the transcendent in this life.

Jung was a complex character, especially when it came to religion, and there is confusion in his writings about afterlife. He chronicled, at great length, his own dreams and visions and even recorded a near-death experience after he suffered a heart attack in 1944. He floated a thousand miles above an earth bathed in light. While he was looking down, he was approached by a dark block of stone, like a meteorite. There was an entrance, with a Hindu next to it in a white gown, sitting in the lotus position. He ushered Jung in:

> As I approached the steps leading us up to the entrance into the rock, a strange thing happened: I had the feeling that everything was being sloughed away; everything I aimed at or wished for or thought, the whole phantasma- goria of earthly existence, fell away or was stripped from me – an extremely painful process. Nevertheless, some- thing remained; it was as if I now carried along with me everything I had ever experienced or done, everything that had happened around me. I might also say: it was with me, and I was it. I consisted of all that, so to speak. I consisted of my own history, and I felt with great cer- tainty: this is what I am. 'I am this bundle of what has been, and what has been accomplished.'
>
> This experience gave me a feeling of extreme poverty, but at the same time great fullness. There was no longer anything I wanted or desired. I existed in an objective form; I was what I had been and lived. At first the sense of annihilation predominated, of having been stripped or pillaged; but suddenly that became of no consequence. Everything seemed to be past; what remained was a fait accompli, without any reference back to what had been. There was no longer any regret that something had dropped away or been taken away. On the contrary: I had everything that I was, and that was everything.
>
> Something else engaged my attention: as I approached the temple I had the certainty that I was about to enter an illuminated room and would meet there all those people to whom I belong in reality. There I would at last

understand – this too was a certainty – what historical nexus I or my life fitted into.

At this point, Jung was interrupted by his doctor, who floated up and brought him back to earth. While he was convalescing, he had other visions of beauty and intensity culminating in a joyous final revelation:

> I walked up a wide valley to the end, where a gentle chain of hills began. The valley ended in a classical amphitheatre. It was magnificently situated in the green landscape. And there, in this theatre, the hierosgamos was being celebrated. Men and women dancers came onstage, and upon a flower-decked couch All-father Zeus and Hera consummated the mystic marriage, as it is described in the *Iliad*.

Jung tried subsequently to explain what he had glimpsed in terms of his own theory of archetypes – images from his collective unconscious which he had brought into his conscious through the journey he made while on the border of death. Yet he as good as admitted that such an approach could only go part of the way. 'It was not a product of imagination,' he wrote. 'The visions and experiences were utterly real; there was nothing subjective about them; they all had a quality of absolute objectivity.'

Finally, Jung found a formula to categorise them. 'We shy away from the word "eternal", but I can describe the experience only as the ecstasy of a non-temporal state in which present, past and future are one.' Jung never quite went so far as to state his own belief in afterlife, but the survival of the psyche is implicit in the visions he recorded.

CHAPTER SEVENTEEN

The Sound of Silence

In the face of this sustained and insistent onslaught from science, heaven faded from the map in the twentieth century as a trees-and-meadows-and-ambrosia continent beyond the clouds. Like hell, limbo, and any number of other once-popular devotions, it was increasingly seen as anachronistic and even straight superstitious. The more information that was given about it – though it might please a minority – the more the majority dispensed with it altogether as if discarding a medieval left-over.

As a result, the mainstream Churches, once its greatest champions, are now wary of providing any directions for, or details of, landmarks in the afterlife. Like the explicit promise in the Gospels of a Second Coming, heaven is simply no longer mentioned. This risks making the resurrection and salvation parts of their creeds taboo as well, so, when pressed, the Churches talk simply and without enthusiasm of experiencing God's love in a more perfect way than on earth and treat heaven as a metaphor that has a confused past and which has now all but passed its sell-by date.

Is this a sensible strategy? The co-ordinates of heaven have, certainly, continually changed over the centuries, swinging from the literal to the mystical and back again via a series of gardens, castles and ladders, usually in an effort to maintain a lever on the behaviour of the congregations of this world. Its study, then, has never been a pure science, but an applied one. It may simply be that in our own age we are seeing another turn in this process of evolution. It could plausibly be argued that it is the language and imagery that are changing, often being found wanting, not the core idea of living on after death which, nevertheless, still retains a great fascination. Witness the 71 per cent of those questioned in a Gallup Poll in the United States in 1982 who spoke of their belief in living on after death, a percentage little changed from the 1950s, though this time round, many fewer could be specific as to what form that afterlife would take. The challenge on this evidence would seem to be for the Churches to find a new language with which to speak of afterlife. Our language of the imagination in all spheres is, after all, constantly being revised. We grow out of one vocabulary as we grow out of school uniform. We discard one, then another, and even retrieve what we have previously discarded, as fashions change.

Officially, of course, the mainstream Churches haven't changed their positions on heaven much in the past two centuries. The subtleties lie in how enthusiastically they promote the message.

In the nineteenth century, while the faithful were getting excited about *The Gates Ajar* and spiritualism, and the Victorian obsession with death was at its height, churchmen spoke up loud and clear with a theocentric message that rejected literal interpretations of the promise of heaven and stressed that afterlife was all about meeting and fully experiencing God. This is essentially still what they say today, though in an age of disbelief and logic, they have become rather keener, when they do occasionally get drawn on the subject, to say what heaven isn't, than what it is. This new angle on an old story, it is judged, gives them the best chance of exploiting the universal interest in afterlife. St Augustine, if he's watching, would approve.

In July 1999, Pope John Paul II publicly declared that heaven is not a place above the clouds where angels play harps, but simply 'a state of being' after death. 'The heaven in which we will find ourselves is neither an abstraction nor a physical place among the clouds,' he told pilgrims in St Peter's Square in a message carefully weighed to appeal to their anxiety for immortality without demanding too much faith in the incidentals. It was, he went on in more positive terms, 'a living and personal relationship with the Holy Trinity'. Just as hell was separation from God, the Pope said, heaven was the reverse – 'close communion and full intimacy with God ... Heaven is a blessed community of those who remained faithful to Jesus Christ in their lifetimes, and are now at one with His glory'.

And that was the sum of it. In the previous twenty-one years of his pontificate, John Paul II had not deigned to mention heaven publicly at all. Here was a single morsel to satisfy hungers on a subject which, seven hundred years earlier, came close to bringing down the papacy of John XXII. To be fair, there had been one other intervention since John Paul II took office. In 1979, the old Holy Office which orchestrated the Inquisition, now renamed the Congregation for the Doctrine of the Faith, had set the style for purging any unnecessary ornament from pictures of heaven. 'When dealing with the human situation after death,' it warned, 'one must especially be aware of arbitrary imaginative representations: excess of this kind is a major cause of difficulties that Christian faith often encounters.' Desmond Tutu, when Anglican Archbishop of Johannesburg, was once asked if he believed that the architects of apartheid, or even Hitler, would get into heaven. A lesser man might have stumbled, or muttered something about heaven not being as we imagined it, but Tutu elegantly affirmed his belief that all would be there, wherever 'there' was, because God was so forgiving.

If one is in doubt about the status of any particular item of doctrine in Catholicism, there is an easy way of judging its current importance: see how many pages are devoted to it in the *Catechism of the Catholic Church*, published in 1994 as a replacement rule-book for the Penny Catechism of my youth. It encapsulates every aspect of belief in one volume and spends chapter after chapter plotting the minutiae of sexual relationships. By contrast, it is brief and terse on the subject of paradise, but at least, unlike the Congregation for the Doctrine of the Faith, it is prepared to use the h-word: 'Heaven is the ultimate end and fulfilment of the deepest human longings, the state of supreme, definitive happiness.' The 'who art in heaven' line in the Our Father 'does not refer to a place but to God's majesty'. Purgatory too merits a brief name-check, as the 'final purification of the elect' rather than as a place. Even the Second Coming, so imminent according to St Paul, now only gets three pages. The sum total of these pointers comes to hardly more than half a dozen out of almost eight hundred in the latest English edition.

The same spirit of keep-quiet-and-hope-people-will-stop-asking is true of Anglicanism. In a poll carried out by the BBC at Christmas in 1999, 40 per cent of Anglican clergymen said they did not believe in heaven as a physical place. Questioned about the findings, an embarrassed Bishop of Oxford, Richard Harries, tried to put a good gloss on what was being presented as yet more evidence of a Church that scarcely believed in God. He spoke of a 'symbolic realism' that was neither literal truth nor poetic myth, but something in between about which he was less than precise. To be fair, his position sounded remarkably similar to that of Pope John Paul II.

Even the leading progressive thinker in Anglican circles, David Jenkins, the retired Bishop of Durham, is for once uncontroversial, in theological terms, on the subject. The man who denied the Virgin Birth and questioned Christ's bodily resurrection so publicly as to prompt calls for his resignation says simply that 'Heaven is God, and God is heaven. He is the beginning, the middle and the end and so to concentrate on heaven is a failure to raise our eyes and realise that God is beyond our imagining.'

We have, he adds illuminatingly, become confused over the distinctive Christian ideal of the resurrection of individual persons through the power and life of God and the resurrection of Jesus. This is, he claims, not the survival of individual souls, as has been the line of the Churches down the ages, 'but a reconstitution of personality in relation to the fulfilment of all persons in God'.

In a Western context, where every pressure is geared towards greater individualism, such collectivism might be deemed brave talk, designed to appeal only in North Korea. When questioned as to what exactly life after death will consist of, David Jenkins, like most modern churchmen and women, is naturally unwilling to start creating castles in the sky in any shape or form. 'I don't believe [he told me] that death is the end of our potentialities. I prefer to see it as being taken up into a woven fabric of life which is the fulfilment of all in all by the love and reality of God. I have no clue what that individually or collectively will mean or be like.' He does, however, see 'a powerful clue in the Trinity' as an icon of the unity of all in each other. 'Thus we can look forward to being ourselves in better ways than we have so far experienced. God's web of life is Himself.'

When, on a BBC Radio programme, he outlined his view of the dead as being somehow part of the ether of life, Jenkins prompted a sympathetic response from his listeners. There is still, it would seem, an appetite for challenging talk on heaven. Most senior Anglicans, by contrast, are extremely cautious in their reaffirmations of a theocentric line. In a 1999 TV documentary on the subject of heaven, chaired by the novelist Melvyn Bragg, Professor Keith Ward, the Regius Professor of Divinity at Oxford University, was pitted against a prominent scientist and Gore Vidal. He spoke only of living in relation to God now and for ever. 'God is the supreme object of human desire, so there has to be a way to come to know him. We can't do it in this world, so it has to be elsewhere . . . The motivation for belief is then belief in God, not the desire to live for ever.'

There is, arguably, a common thread in all these positions, which might be seen as the modern position among churchmen, though it has ancient roots – namely, the stressing of a sense of a unity between this life and the next that is more profound than traditional formulations of good behaviour here followed (or not) by reward there.

In their concentration on knowing God, however imperfectly, in this life, and how this is effectively the beginning of heaven, modern theologians in the Christian tradition might be seen to be moving closer to Eastern positions on transcendence in the here and now. In his July 1999 address, Pope John Paul II for instance, told those who wanted a sneak preview of heaven that they should follow 'the sacramental life, of which the Eucharist is the centre' and devote themselves 'to fraternal love for fellow human beings'. In this sense, the interior and the exterior journey are one.

If a Buddhist-like focus on this life, implicit in the lack of interest taken by today's clergy in the next, was a distinct trend in Christian theology in the twentieth century, it often went hand-in-hand with a commitment to a social gospel which echoes Muhammad's concerns, stated in the Qur'an. Thus theological writers from the American Protestant scholar Walter Ruschenbusch (1861–1918) to the present-day Catholic feminist Rosemary Radford Ruether have argued persuasively that the Christian imperative is to work for a just and fair world today, the new Jerusalem here on earth, rather than for something in the future. Many contemporary clerics and theologians similarly talk of afterlife simply as continuing a pilgrimage and a commitment to justice begun in life. One progressive English Catholic priest inspired me with the thought: 'If we empty ourselves, share our life with others, share our good fortune, we create an inner vacuum for God to fill. The more we give, the more we receive. So we take into the afterlife only what we have given away. Shrouds have no pockets. We go naked out of life.'

In linking the social gospel of the Church with

heavenly reward, he was combining both modern and ancient thought. Heaven as a place of reward is the oldest attraction in Christianity's travel brochure. Setting this reward in the context, not of an individual's persona and sexual morality nor in acts of piety, as has been the recent Christian tradition, but in relation to the social gospel and how we act in relation to our world, is on the one hand to take a leaf out of the teachings of the radical liberation theologians of Latin America, and on the other to follow Jesus in his remarks about Lazarus, and heaven's preference for the poor rather than the rich.

A parallel, though much more individualistic, approach in theological circles has been to embrace modernism (though in the early years of the twentieth century, the very word was decreed a blasphemy by Rome). This theory of religion, aiming to reconcile theology with science, emphasised that heaven could best be seen as a myth, metaphor or symbol of extraordinary psychological potency. If not literally true, such symbols did answer a human craving, the modernists held, and delineated a pathway to a God who could only be known on a one-to-one basis.

This was not a new idea. In pre-Reformation times, as we have seen already, myths were much better understood and appreciated as something beyond reason but not compromised by it. Only since the Enlightenment have they been poked, prodded and found wanting by the new empirical standards of science. Modernism tried to adapt to that science and so brought psychological insights to bear on how the mind worked. As a result, it argued for religion as a subjective and highly individual experience, rather than something set in stone by Church officials and handed down to people en masse.

With heaven, this process was not as marked as it was

elsewhere – for instance, in the downgrading of hell and the Devil – but two theological writers stand out as exploring the symbolism of heaven in this modernist context – Reinhold Niebuhr (1892–1970) and Paul Tillich (1886–1965). Niebuhr, reviewing the history of heaven, decided that the symbols were just too confusing to make any sort of guess as to what lay behind them, though he remained sceptical of individual immortality. Tillich too found the traditional symbols 'dangerously inadequate' and was dismissive of what he deemed the 'neurotic consequences of the literalistic distortion', seen especially in popular religion of the nineteenth century, but he was nonetheless prepared to speak of eternal life. The danger in trying to brush older images of heaven under the carpet, he warned, was that you might throw the baby out with the bath water. If heaven was a confusing symbol, it did not mean that eternal life was impossible to contemplate. For Tillich, afterlife was a state that combined group and individual fulfilment, this world and eternity in God's presence. Beyond that he did not go.

A third writer should also be considered in this context of reviving an appreciation of the profound and complex symbolism of heaven, though her approach concentrated much less on the individual and her insights were wholly negative. More publicly, perhaps, than any person in the twentieth century, Simone Weil (1909–1943) struggled to reconcile the attraction she felt for God with her distaste for the promise of heaven as usually formulated. In her writing she belittled the promise of resurrection as a distraction. Born a Jew, and an atheist in her youth, she spent much of her adult life on the threshold of religious belief, or, as she put it, as 'a Christian outside the Church'. The appeal for her was both intensely physical

– she had a strong sense of the world's beauty and saw it as the manifestation of God – and political.

Christianity, or the social gospel of Catholicism, came the closest of any system to her own utopian left-wing beliefs. As she confided to her friend, the almost-blind Hebrew scholar, Father Joseph-Marie Perrin, Christianity was 'opening up the earth' to her. He replied by asking when could he open up heaven, but even on her deathbed, she resisted the lure of paradise.

The ideas of personal salvation and eternal life were alien to Weil. A mystic, she stressed the impersonal quality of a God 'who loves not as I love but as an emerald is green'. If you maintain the idea of a personal God, and of life ever after with Him in heaven, she argued, you can only reach a certain halfway point of the path of perfection. 'To go further it is necessary, by force of desire, to make oneself resemble an impersonal perfection.'

Such a conviction was grounded in the Gospels. Though she never formally joined the Church, she wrote in her final statement: 'through love, I hold on to the perfect, unseizable truth which these mysteries contain, and I try to open my soul to it so that its light may penetrate me'. This focus on striving after a potentially unobtainable enlightenment in this world, at the expense of expectations of the next, was one of the major obstacles for her in being received into the Church. 'If the Gospel omitted all mention of Christ's resurrection,' she wrote to Father Perrin, 'faith would be easier for me.' Weil formulated a highly personal position which dispensed not only with heaven but with all idea of finding God as opposed to being found by Him, as she outlined in *Science, Necessity and Love of God*:

It is not for man to seek, or even to believe in God. He has only to refuse his love to everything which is not God. This refusal does not presuppose any belief. It is enough to recognise what is obvious to any mind, that all the goods of this world, past, present or future, real or imaginary, are finite and limited and radically incapable of satisfying the desire which burns perpetually within us for an infinite and perfect good. All men know this and more than once in their lives they recognise it for a moment, but then they immediately begin deceiving themselves again so as not to know it any longer, because they feel that if they knew it they could not go on living. And that feeling is true, for that knowledge kills. But it inflicts a death which leads to a resurrection.

That mystical moment of transcendence, she described, has as many obvious parallels in Eastern religions, about which Weil had read widely, as it does in the experience of medieval nuns such as Mechthild of Magdeburg. Moreover, Weil appeared to be arguing, like Tillich and Niebuhr, that all efforts to describe a heaven, to interpret the imagery and myths and symbols that surround it, were doomed to inadequacy. Where Weil went further, and where she was potentially more influenced by the East than they, was in her dismissing heaven as an irrelevance.

This overall process of blurring the divide between the once-distinctive positions of the faiths on heaven can only be taken so far. What continues to distinguish most Eastern religions from Judaism, Christianity and Islam is the latter group's belief in resurrection after death, and thus a setting in which it can take place, be it called heaven, djanna or paradise. Consequently, the current crop of Church leaders cannot remain silent on heaven and expunge it from their catechisms.

There has emerged the middle line, made up of equal measures of silence and vague talk of God. For some, this is a controversial and mistaken gospel. They believe that more plain-talking on heaven might buttress the faith rather than destroy it, and so they oppose the relegation of paradise to the Churches' equivalent of a doctrinal retirement home.

In 1961, for instance, an official Vatican spokesman, beguiled by all the public interest surrounding US and Soviet missions into space, sounded positively medieval when he speculated that the astronauts might encounter angels on other planets. Today's generation of clerics at the Vatican are rather more guarded, but Father Gino Concetti, a chief theologian at the official newspaper, *l'Osservatore Romano*, did suggest, in August 1999, in the wake of Pope John Paul II's remarks on heaven, that there could be ship-to-shore messages from heaven to earth: 'Communication is possible,' he wrote, 'between those who live on this earth and those who live in a state of eternal repose ... It may even be that God lets our loved ones send us messages to guide us at certain moments in our life.' Father Concetti quoted the dying Saint Dominic, who said in 1221: 'Do not weep for I shall be more useful to you after my death and I shall help you more effectively than during my life.' Catholicism has long taught of the power of intercessions to and by the Virgin Mary, but by extending this influence to all other souls on high, Father Concetti was stepping on the outer limits of the current belief.

One larger-than-life character who would have approved of such brinkmanship was Fulton Sheen (1895–1979), the American Catholic leader who, during his fifteen years as a bishop in New York and three as head of the diocese of Rochester, spoke candidly and often of a heaven peopled by angels.

Sheen, a prolific author and that rarity, a Catholic cleric who was comfortable being a star-turn on radio and television, spoke not in theological niceties, but in terms that he knew his audiences would understand. And so he painted heaven with broad and clear brush strokes, enthusing about seeing God face-to-face in a setting of incomparable grandeur. The extent of his impact can be judged by the plethora of websites set up to his memory and current moves to have him canonised.

Sheen did not quite break ranks with the official theo-centric Church position, but he stretched it as far as it could go in an effort to appeal to those floating voters who, while rejecting organised religion, retained a hankering for a glorious afterlife. He recognised that the 71 per cent approval rating for heaven quoted earlier represents a much larger constituency than merely those who are currently paid-up members of the Churches.

There are apparently many who believe in heaven without signing up for any other part of the package, yet if this offers an opportunity for evangelism by the mainstream Churches at a time when many are drifting away from their embrace, then it is one that they are ill-equipped to exploit because of their own doubts about paradise. In short, any message they would feel easy putting over about afterlife would be so mealy-mouthed as to have little appeal to the target audience. In this Gallup Poll, for instance, half of those questioned expected to see their relatives again. This is not the official position of any of the mainstream Churches.

They do not seem to practise what they preach, for they manage to accommodate such talk in their cemeteries. The messages on the smaller modern tomb-stones are much the same as those underneath the angels' wings on their Victorian neighbours: 'Rest in peace, we will meet again'; 'Parted temporarily'; 'Until we meet again'. These may be more of a wish than a theological sentiment – which priest or vicar is going to tell a griev-ing family that they have to change the wording they have chosen? – but it eloquently makes the point that, save on stonemasonry, such wishes currently have rela-tively few outlets for expression. Many fundamentalists, however, with their love of paying greater heed to the literal sense of the Bible, continue to preach unashamedly of a place called heaven.

They are unabashed in employing the old home and hearth model of paradise, but they have given it a modern twist, for it is amongst such groups that the idea of rapture is popular. Based, as mentioned earlier, on a passage in St Paul, and often to be heard on the lips of such fundamentalist leaders as the bestselling writer, Hal Lindsey, and evangelical Christian leaders, Jerry Falwell and Pat Robertson, 'the Rapture' (which emerged as a doctrine in the late 1960s) offers those who have been born-again in Christ a seven-year trip to heaven during which time the rest of us will slog it out in some almighty Armageddon. When Christ has sorted out the surviving combatants, the raptured will return to earth to assist him in his millennium of direct rule, predicted in the Book of Revelation. Rapture was outlined with character-istic colour by the Revd Jerry Falwell: 'You'll be riding along in an automobile,' he predicted, 'and when the trumpet sounds you and the other born-again believers in that automobile will be instantly caught away – you will disappear, leaving behind only your clothes . . . That unsaved person or persons in the automobile will suddenly be startled to find the car moving along without a driver, and the car suddenly somewhere crashes.'

Rapture is intimately linked with a fundamentalist school of thought, known as Dispensationalism, which teaches that the establishment of the state of Israel in 1948 was the first stage in the build-up to the end of the world, again as predicted in the Book of Revelation. Indeed, the Dispensationalists say that the whole recent history of the Middle East is contained in Revelation and that we are moving towards a third and final world war, starting in that region. So appealing to some did the prospect of getting a peek at heaven seem, that they were determined to hurry along the conflict there. The year 2000, which these fundamentalists mixed up with the millennium mentioned in Revelation, seemed to be their best chance, so groups headed off for Jerusalem through-out 1999, with the aim of getting the Jews and Moslems in that troubled city at each others' throats. Once they had started the conflict, they believed, they would be raptured up to heaven while all hell broke loose beneath them. They were fearless in risking their own lives because they were so certain that God was watching over them, ready to beam them up when the going got tough. The authorities in Jerusalem became so concerned about the potential threat of these groups that in the summer and autumn of 1999 they deported large numbers of them back to the States.

If trouble was averted in Jerusalem by such timely action, elsewhere, the short step from Bible belt to twi-light zone has cost lives. In March 1997, thirty-nine members of the Heaven's Gate religious group, led by Marshall Applewhite, committed suicide at their head-quarters near San Diego in southern California. They had embraced ideas of rapture, but mixed them into their own science-fiction fantasy. They believed that a space-ship from the 'Kingdom Level Above Human', which lurked behind the Hale-Bopp comet, was coming to take them to eternal life, and so they overdosed on barbiturates to achieve rapture. Applewhite's group had a clear view of what this afterlife was going to entail and, like many extremists in the past, they had begun to prepare for it in advance. They had all given up alcohol and sex, and six of the men had even undergone surgery to have their testicles removed in the sure and certain knowledge that they would be of no use to them in eternity.

Next to such excesses, self-mutilation and tragedy, the afterlife beliefs of the Church of Jesus Christ of Latter-Day Saints, otherwise known as the Mormons, are tame, but, like other fundamentalists, their beliefs have won an ever-expanding audience by placing the highest premium on an active and literal heaven.

Nine million or so Mormons worldwide follow the teachings of Joseph Smith (1805–44), a New Yorker who believed he had been chosen by God to restore Jesus's original church to its rightful standing. He dispensed with original sin and taught instead that before birth all are 'spirit children' who live with their heavenly mother or father. The period on earth is by way of a testing of that parent–child bond. Depending on how it stands up, each spirit after death awaits final resurrection either in the company of the virtuous or among the wrongdoers.

These two places are neither heaven nor hell. The righteous will have a paradise along traditional lines, with gardens, trees and stunning architecture, where families are reunited. The wicked are not damned, but if they have undergone a Mormon 'baptism of death', a feature unique to the Church, they will have the opportunity in the spirit realm to redeem themselves, recognise the worth of Joseph Smith's insights and join the 'A' team before the final resurrection. The barrier in the next world between the domain of the good and the world of the wicked is a thin one, because all those who have heard the Mormon gospel are encouraged in death to continue their missionary work by trying to educate those who do not know of it and so enable them to save themselves.

The Mormons do not rule out contact between the dead and the living. In her book *Angel Children*, published in 1975, Mormon Mary Hill told of the death of her infant son, Stephen. When she was giving birth to her next child, Stephen came to her in a vision, fully grown and 'dressed in softly draped white clothes', to tell her that all was well and that they would be together come the final resurrection.

Mormons, like born-again Christians, follow the Book of Revelation to the letter and anticipate a thousand years of direct rule by Christ on earth when he will clean up all of its faults and punish the sinners. At the end of this time, Satan will be allowed 'a little season' before final judgement. All will then be reunited with their bodies and will take their place in one of three levels of heaven, or in hell (mainstream Christianity recognises no such distinctions in heaven after Judgement Day). The *crème de la crème* will be raised to the status of gods in a world of glass mingled with fire. This is accessible only to those who are married for eternity, in line with a heavy Mormon emphasis on the family and wedded bliss. Those married women who have been childless on earth will find that they can have children in this top-notch heaven. The best you can hope for if you are single, though, is to be an angel, not a god.

Smith's vision, developed in the nineteenth century,

was shaped by the times in which he lived. He could easily have been a disciple of Swedenborg. And if Elizabeth Stuart Phelps had tried to start a new Church based on the image of heaven she presented in *The Gates Ajar*, it would have differed very little from what Mormons continue to preach. The illustrations used today in textbooks of Smith's teachings still show a rural Arcadia of long flowery dresses and buttercups and daisies where every family is happy, every father strong and masterful, every mother a domestic manager, and every child loved and healthy. The continuing appeal of the Mormons, and their slow but steady growth around the globe, is evidence that preaching of a heaven that belongs to a mythical golden age on earth, however dated such a practice seems to many, retains, if not the overwhelming enthusiasm it once generated amongst believers in the nineteenth century, then a strong and enduring attraction for a minority.

CHAPTER EIGHTEEN

Through the Keyhole

One doesn't have to be a born-again Christian, waiting for the Rapture to get a peep at heaven. One
doesn't even have to be conventionally religious. All that
is required is a brush with death.

The number of Americans who have had near-death
experiences (NDEs) is said by one survey to be 5 per
cent, or eight million people.* The International Association for Near-Death Studies (IANDS), founded in 1981,
claims to speak for a constituency of thirteen million
individuals in the States alone. The systematic study of
the reports of those having undergone a seemingly
supernatural experience while hovering near to death is
a recent phenomenon, though its advocates hold that
such near-misses with the hereafter have been experienced and been unquantified for centuries. Accounts of
the soldier, Er, who returns from the dead in Plato's
Republic, or even Lazarus rising from his tomb in the
New Testament, are often drawn into the debate. One
could also add to the list every mystic and saint who

---

* Quoted in *Adventures in Immortality*, George Gallup.

ever went on a journey to heaven in his or her dreams. They may well have been describing a Near-Death Experience, but using different vocabulary. One saint, Christina (1150–1224), is recorded as having been declared dead, put in her coffin and taken to her funeral. Halfway through the service, she sat up and, her legend tells, promptly flew up to the ceiling. Once tempted down, she spoke movingly and at length of the physical torments of hell and purgatory and of her final redeeming experience of the beatific vision.

Those who claim to have had an NDE today no longer sit up in coffins, but the effect is much the same. What has sparked off the present interest has been – as with the spiritualists – scientific developments. Medicine today has opened a window of opportunity for a glimpse of the hereafter, by often making it possible to resuscitate a person when the heart has stopped beating. This is the moment when, in layman's terms, it requires only a small leap of the imagination to believe that we start the journey to death only to be called back at the last minute.

Two figures in particular are associated with promoting NDEs – the American psychologist Raymond Moody and the Swiss physician, Elisabeth Kubler-Ross. Kubler-Ross based her observations on her work, since 1965, with terminally ill patients. While her greatest emphasis is on coping with the process of dying – she commendably challenged America to abandon its head-in-the-sand stance as a 'death-denying society' and face up to physical mortality – she did draw part of her information, in the various books she wrote from 1974 onwards, from the testimonies of those who had had NDEs.

In 1975, Moody produced *Life After Life*, cataloguing around fifty cases of NDEs. It quickly became a bestseller in America and worldwide. Moody set out a series of key identification factors for NDEs, including a buzzing or ringing noise which marks the onset of death, peace and painlessness thereafter, often accompanied by an out-of-body experience, then a journey up through a tunnel towards a light, followed by an experience of a divine/ mystical aura of light, which in turn prompts an overview of all that has gone before in that individual's life and, finally, a reluctant return to their body and life on earth.

His formulation was, he stated, anecdotal and non-scientific, but many have taken issue with the nature of the revelations he detailed: they bring little that is new to the imagery of God or heaven, and therefore may simply be a projection of what the individual has been conditioned by a religious upbringing, or by religious iconography, to expect to see. For example, the following is pasted on IANDS's website by a correspondent who, at the time of his experience, had been suffering from low blood pressure and a low pulse rate.

> My experience occurred in the spring of 1964 in State College, Pennsylvania ... It occurred in the afternoon after I had returned to my dormitory room from a class. I was feeling very tired and decided to listen to some classical music on my transistor radio. I lay down and drifted easily into a deep sleep. I became aware of myself drifting out of my body; I was moving toward the upper left part of the dorm room window. As this was taking place I experienced no fear and accepted things as they came. While I was in the room I did not see the bed where I was sleeping; nor did I see my physical body. I did see the window at the far end of the room. I passed through the window and moved rapidly outward into space. I found myself in a relatively dark, empty region

of space; there were no planets or stars in this area. In front of me, I saw a small light in the vast distance. The light started to get larger. It became more brilliant and it stopped in front of me. I felt an intense love, which came from the Light. I know without a doubt that this beautiful, intense, loving Light was God. The Light started to communicate with me; but the communication was telepathic, it was not verbal. The Light asked me if I wanted to come with it. At this point I completely understood the nature of the question and the consequences of my answer. If I chose to continue with the Light I knew that I would die and never return to earth. I thought about this and replied that I thought that I still had important things to do back there (on earth). At that point the Light began to recede. I found myself waking up on the bed of my dorm room. The feeling that I had was of extreme contentment and love. It was so strong that I wanted to return to the Light; I tried but could not. I was very disappointed but not angry because the choice to return was mine. The experience was very real and I can clearly remember it.

This is, in a crude form, a modern take on what an earlier generation of theologians might have called the beatific vision. The traditional context for such a vision, a garden, is just as popular. Jennine Wolff of Troy, New York, recounts in a collection of NDE stories by P. M. H. Atwater called *Beyond the Light* what happened to her in the spring of 1987. During emergency surgery, this thirty-year-old floated out of her body and entered another realm of existence:

Suddenly I was aware of being in the most beautiful garden I've ever seen. I felt whole and loved. My sense of well-being was complete. I heard celestial music clearly and saw vivid, coloured flowers, like nothing seen on earth, gorgeous greenery and trees. As I looked around, I saw at a distance, on a hill, Jesus Christ. All he said to me was that it was up to me whether to come back to earth or not. I chose to come back to finish my work. That is when I was born again.

Both chroniclers saw, or imagined they saw, what they had been programmed by a standard Western education to see. The same observation may also be made of the parallel movement which collects and collates After-Death Communications (ADCs), or messages from beyond the grave. In 1987, *American Health* magazine published a poll, overseen by the Catholic priest, novelist and sociologist, Andrew Greeley, where 42 per cent of those questioned believed they had had contact with someone who had died. In an anthology of messages received from beyond the grave, God and heaven come across in stereotypical terms. Rachael, an office manager from Minnesota, had an ADC vision some four months after her seventeen-year-old daughter, Dawn, had been murdered:

She was barefoot and doing a liturgical dance to this song. It was like she was floating. Her hair was blowing, and she moved her arms with the music. She had on a long, white robe that came down to her ankles, with a sash of braided rope. Everything was very bright, very light. She was very happy, with a beautiful smile like she always had. Dawn was expressing spiritual joy through dancing. At the end of the song, she vanished. I was grateful and began to cry.

(from *Hello from Heaven*)

These communications from beyond come in many forms. One increasingly popular format is electronic voice phenomenon (EVP), imprints of the voices of the dead which are either left on tapes or which emerge through static on a radio. EVP has been promoted by the Latvian parapsychologist Konstantin Raudive, and has been taken up by enthusiastic groups of individuals around the globe (see Judith Chisholm's *Voices from Paradise*).

Often present in such messages, and in other ADCs and NDEs, is an account of the tunnel which links heaven to earth. Again, this idea is a familiar one in Christian history. In his celebrated *Ascent into the Empyrean*, Hieronymus Bosch (1450–1516) shows the newly departed floating upwards through a dark tunnel towards the light.

However, it should be noted that within the NDE movement the focus is not only on updated variations on Christian ideas of afterlife. In his 1977 follow-up to *Life After Life*, Raymond Moody writes of the recurrence in the stories he gathered of what he calls 'the vision of knowledge', a flash of mystical insight into the nature of the universe which would sit neatly with Buddhist ideas of striving for enlightenment. It is echoed by Margot Grey, founder of IANDS in Britain, whose own NDE happened in India. She interpreted it as a 'mental rebirth . . . refined by a new consciousness'.

More challenging than the link between these visions and basic religious iconography of heaven is the question of why they are so popular and attract so many devotees. An immediate answer would be to challenge the assumption that there need be anything new to say about heaven, and to assert that one should not therefore decry the repetition of standard imagery, albeit in a new context. It simply shows an ongoing, unchanging human fascination with death. The fact that the answers are so similar to those that have been proffered before, enthusiasts say, merely adds weight to the pictures they conjure up. It is part of the case for the defence of heaven. If so many people have seen a garden or a white light, the theory goes, that must be what's there. Perhaps not quite. People used to believe they regularly saw the Devil in epileptics, and in medieval times it was taken as read that this was the case, but now we know better.

A more thoughtful approach to the NDE movement would see it as just another manifestation of a trend, running through all religions down the ages, which, when confronted with death, has sought to try and reach beyond it by whatever means are to hand. In the pre-modern world this was done by myths and rituals of faith which helped people accept their own limits, but now we are encouraged to think that we have no limits, that myths are 'just' myths, and that rationalism and science will have the answer to everything. And so, as well as providing the evidence to damn them, science, (more precisely, a splinter group of scientists) is enlisted to support NDEs. In formulating the case for the defence – again, in the manner of the spiritualists – the defenders of NDEs have to some extent attempted to steal the scientists' clothes. So, for example, they point to their own scientific work to show that small children, who have not had any religious instruction or exposure to the paraphernalia of heaven, and who have never even read Hans Christian Andersen's original *Little Mermaid*, report back on afterlife in exactly the same terms as adults.

Set against these studies, however, is a formidable block of scientific opinion which says, unequivocally, that what is being reported by individuals are hallucinations, induced by a combination of psychological, physiological, neurological and pharmacological factors. The dying brain is starved of oxygen, which, in its turn, causes neurons or brain cells to rush about to try and make good the deficiency. All this last-gasp activity creates a sensation of light at the centre of our visual field. This, scientists say, is the white tunnel to heaven or the aura of God that many report having seen.

Oxygen deprivation also has a profound effect on the brain, and hence on memory and emotion. This may explain the sensation common in NDEs of a lifetime flashing before people's eyes. Furthermore, as the brain begins to close down, it releases an opiate-like substance that creates a feeling of euphoria – the well-being that is described by those who recall a NDE as washing over them. The sensation of floating, the scientists continue, can be put down to the loss of control in the dying process of our limbs and internal organs. The brain is no longer receiving feedback and so feels detached from the physical body.

It is a powerful array of arguments to counter, but the NDE movement remains undaunted. It has produced a study by James Lewis which says NDEs have regularly been experienced by people who register flat EEGs (electroencephalograms) – i.e. people in whom all brain activity has stopped. If the visions were just hallucinations brought on by morphine, for example, then they would show up as brain-wave activity.

The truth about science, however, is that those who want to believe in NDEs will always 'cherry pick' it to their advantage, rather as politicians will always find a grain of encouragement, however bad, in their electoral defeat. The parapsychologists' courting of science and logic has certainly had a direct effect on the manner of the debate:

they have adopted a one-dimensional attack with the ultimate goal of proving the veracity of NDEs. The existence of heaven, then, stands or falls on the purely empirical. It is the modern-day equivalent of medieval astronomers who, having read the scholastics' formulations of what went on where above the clouds, pointed their telescopes upwards so as to see the angels and saints at play.

If anything is keeping eschatology alive in our age, it is precisely this fact-based approach. It is not enough to say, 'Here are some people's experiences which might tell us something, or give us something on to which we can attach ourselves emotionally and psychologically.' No, what is reported has to be seen as literally true. The result is a polarised debate. Heaven is either warmly embraced or scornfully dismissed as a place, but never examined in any imaginative way.

There is a basic fundamentalism that links those who believe in NDES, those who embrace the Rapture and all those who take the promise of heaven literally. It is a clinging to something tangible, whether it be paradise or God or enlightenment, rather than accepting that it can only ever be mythical, symbolic or imagined. Running alongside this is a determination to find an answer to the question of the existence of life after death which is, history has taught us, unanswerable in any tangible form. The attraction of such fundamentalism is not hard to see in a world which is becoming evermore secular.

The twentieth century was one of genocidal horrors, of a removal of rules, regulations, sacred doctrines and barriers which had the power to both empower and frighten people. A retreat into religion in such circumstances is a natural recoiling from the modern world. The hankering after a heaven that can be touched and felt is an equally natural response from those who feel confused and embattled, who fear being washed away on a tide that says there is nothing more than this world, nothing more than humanity, that we are like robots, or the ants in the animated film *A Bug's Life*, going round and round in circles at our meaningless tasks. For some, a world with a giant spiritual void at its heart, where once they had assumed was a greater meaning, is a terrifying prospect. In seeking to fill Sartre's 'god-shaped hole', NDEs have an understandable part to play.

CHAPTER NINETEEN

An Indian Summer

In 1999, a religious research group called Cesnur interviewed one thousand people for a survey which showed that two out of three Italians said they believed in angels. Massimo Introvigne, Cesnur's director, noted that his findings showed that such a belief was rooted not in traditional Catholicism, as might be imagined, but in cinema and television. 'These are post-modern angels,' he said, 'and not necessarily Christian ones.'

For those who find the NDE movement or Christian fundamentalism rather too extreme for their tastes, popular culture provides another outlet for the age-old, and still attractive, dream of heaven. A world without extremes of good and evil would be, Milton suggested, bland and meaningless, and certainly, for novelists, film-makers, artists, song-writers and even advertising executives, heaven remains an attractive, instantly recognisable, elastic metaphor, the symbol of the ultimate happy ending or wish-fulfilment.

The most powerful impression heaven has made down the ages has been a visual one, whether it be in Blake or Signorelli, Bosch or Fra Angelico, or in the imaginations of individuals, so it should be no surprise that the primary visual medium of our age – the film industry – has taken to it with gusto as a subject. Areas explored have ranged from the relatively trivial matter of the eternal fate of animals in the two cartoon films *All Dogs Go to Heaven* (the first made in 1989 and the remake appearing in 1996, with Burt Reynolds and Charlie Sheen respectively voicing the main character) to the search for enlightenment in *Jacob's Ladder* (1990). Starring Tim Robbins as a paranoid Vietnam-war veteran who goes over his life trying to make sense of it until, in his confused state, he begins to see a pattern and so arrives in another world, *Jacob's Ladder* was one of a trio of films written by Bruce Joel Rubin. The others, the box-office hit *Ghost* (1990) with Patrick Swayze and Demi Moore, and the earlier *Brainstorming* (1983), showed something of an obsession on his part with the hereafter, though there was little attempt in any of the three films to involve the character of God.

This followed a familiar pattern in Hollywood, which was to steer clear of something potentially sensitive. Thus, from James Stewart's 1946 classic *It's a Wonderful Life* to Timothy Hutton's *Made in Heaven* (1987), the angels on high have been judged only by what is palatable for cinema audiences. *Bill & Ted's Bogus Journey* (1991), starring Keanu Reeves, has plenty of saints playing charades in heaven, but God remains off-camera, even when He speaks.

Heaven has traditionally been exploited as a consolation to those mourning lost ones, especially during periods of international conflict, and during the Second World War the cinema rediscovered this appetite. There was white light aplenty and a celestial reunion of brave brothers killed on the battlefield in *The Fighting Sullivans*

(1944), time out for dead fighter pilot Spencer Tracy to console his grieving fiancée in *A Guy Named Joe* (1943), and a similar can't-quite-bear-to-leave-you-this-way storyline, with added stiff upper lip, in David Niven's *Stairway to Heaven* (1946). The journey between earth and heaven, and back again, has been a much-covered one. Robert Montgomery in *Here Comes Mr Jordan* (1941) and Warren Beatty as a hapless quarterback in *Heaven Can Wait* (1978) both played the same part – that of a sportsman at the height of his powers mistakenly claimed by an over-zealous angel and taken to paradise. When the error is discovered, it is too late because the body has been cremated.

More profound – albeit at the cost of later being much satirised, not least by *Bill & Ted's Bogus Journey* – was Ingmar Bergman's 1956 art-house classic, *The Seventh Seal*. Taking its title from a familiar source, the Book of Revelation, *The Seventh Seal* famously opens with Max von Sydow as a knight who returns from the Crusades and who is drawn into a game of chess with Death. The film's primary concern is death, not heaven, but Bergman brings into a medieval allegory a sense of the potential for both joy in the hereafter – the dance of death towards the end of the film is a celebration of eternal rest, not a grisly performance of raging reapers – and for an all-embracing love. As cruelty and indignity unfold around them a 'holy family' escape the apocalypse in their wagon, protected by an invincible but unidentified shield.

In much the same vein as Bergman is Jean Cocteau's classically inspired 1949 *Orphee*, or *Orpheus*. Both films provided little by way of simplistic answers, but much dense and often contradictory imagery. *Orphee*, a 1940s poet, believed to be based on Cocteau himself, travels to the place of the dead to rescue his beloved wife, guided by messages which (as fans of EVP will no doubt recall) are broadcast over car radios. Cocteau portrays the next world as separated from this one by a mirror. To heighten the effect, he shot his actors walking backwards, then reversed the film, and so produced an effect where they appear to be moving underwater.

In terms of satirising standard images of heaven, as once Mark Twain and Lord Byron did, the contemporary prize must go to *Monty Python's The Meaning of Life* (1983) which takes the team by spirit cars to a heaven that is a luxury hotel in the clouds where a choir sings 'Every Day is Christmas' and the Queen Mother does a cabaret turn in the ballroom to reveal the purpose of existence. Some religious groups were outraged, but the Python team were as astute and provocative as ever in picking their targets from the inner sanctum of the religious canon.

There has been humour and satire too in written explorations of a celestial hereafter. English novelist Julian Barnes ends his *History of the World in 10½ Chapters* in heaven. After satisfying himself with the endless room service and the waitress, not to mention a whole range of exotic outdoor pursuits, he asks his guardian angel if he can see God:

'Heaven is democratic these days,' she said. Then added, 'Or at least it is if you want it to be.'

'What do you mean, democratic?'

'We don't impose Heaven on people any more,' she said. 'We listen to their needs. If they want it, they can have it; if not, not. And then of course they get the sort of Heaven they want.'

'And what sort do they want on the whole?'

'Well, they want a continuation of life, that's what we find. But . . . better, needless to say.'

'Sex, golf, shopping, dinner, meeting famous people and not feeling bad?' I asked, a bit defensively.

'It varies. But if I were being honest, I'd say that it doesn't vary all that much.'

'Not like the old days.'

'Ah, the old days.' She smiled. 'That was before my time, of course, but yes, dreams of Heaven used to be a lot more ambitious.'

Barnes writes from no public position on religion. C. S. Lewis (1898–1963), however, was for some of his admirers the greatest Christian writer of the twentieth century. An Oxford academic, a children's writer and a convert who, through his writings and broadcasts, became known as the 'apostle to the sceptics', he had a lifelong interest in afterlife, prompted by the death of his mother when he was ten years old (see R. L. Green's and W. Hooper's biography). He was unfashionably fascinated by eschatology and spoke up in defence of purgatory. 'I hope,' he writes in *Letter to Malcolm*, 'that when the tooth of life is drawn and I am coming round, a voice will say, "Rinse your mouth out with this". This will be purgatory'. Lewis tackled head-on the subject of heaven and gave it its fullest airing in *The Last Battle* (written in 1956), the final instalment of his celebrated Narnia sequence of children's books. These are both a complex description of an entire moral universe and an allegory, with Aslan the lion a Christ-like figure and the land of Narnia a supernatural place.

In *The Last Battle* Lewis portrays the Last Days, with ample reference to the Book of Revelation, when a clever ape (the anti-Christ) fashions a false Aslan and plunges

Narnia into chaos. The children, who first met Aslan when they walked through the back of a cupboard in *The Lion, The Witch and The Wardrobe*, are killed in England in a railway accident, and, though they don't realise what has happened to them, find themselves propelled through another door – this time that of a stable – landing 'on grass, the deep blue was overhead, and the air which blew gently on their faces was that of a day in early summer'. This idealised place is the new Narnia, or heaven, where 'the inside is larger than the outside' and where they are reunited with old friends.

If Lewis, at face-value, appeared to be endorsing a literal heaven, such an impression should be tempered by the fact that he was writing for the young. Once in heaven, for example, the children are told that it goes 'further up and further in' to glorious adventures too beautiful to describe.

Lewis, moreover, had an outstanding understanding of the use of myth, especially in the medieval period. His academic reputation has been built on *The Allegory of Love*, written in 1936, which revolutionised literary understanding of the function of myth in medieval literature. He was certainly not, as some of his critics have suggested, a fundamentalist Christian giving sustenance to adults who were emotional children, and in other books he demonstrated the subtle appeal, in an age of science and reason, of a religion based on ideas and symbols with great resonance.

In relation to heaven, he presented in *The Screwtape Letters* (1942) an imaginary correspondence between a senior figure in hell and his nephew, Wormwood, a young demon with a soul to capture. When that soul escapes and is swept up to heaven, Lewis described the experience thus:

When he saw them he knew he had always known them and realised what part each one of them had played at many an hour in his life when he had supposed himself alone, so that now he could say to them, one by one, not 'Who are you?' but 'So it was you all the time.' All that they were and said at this meeting woke memories. The dim consciousness of friends about him which had haunted his solitudes from infancy was now at last explained; that central music in every pure experience which had always just evaded memory was now at last recovered. Recognition made him free of their company almost before the limbs of his corpse became quiet.'

Half a century separates Lewis's writings from Philip Pullman's *His Dark Materials* trilogy. The two share common ground in being eschatological allegories, directed primarily at children, but also to a wider audience. Aside from this, however, they are poles apart. Pullman's universe has been created in an age where science's triumph has spawned a thriving market in science fiction, and so he turns the world on its head, with God the force of repression, authority and evil and Satan that of curiosity, enlightenment and wisdom. Pullman, an atheist, is concerned with dismantling religious beliefs, including the notions of heaven and hell. The Republic of Heaven, setting for the final instalment, *The Amber Spyglass* remains close to earth – reached by wielding a 'subtle knife' to link the two.

There is nothing sentimental about Pullman's fiction. In the hands of others, however, in our secular-age heaven has become something of a by-word for a widespread sense of powerlessness and bemusement when faced with death, a word and a metaphor stripped of any directly denominational religious significance but retaining the dream of a place that is both 'other' and full of consolation. In 1991, for example, the four-year-old son of guitarist, Eric Clapton, fell to his death from the fifty-third floor of an apartment block. As a result, Clapton wrote 'Tears in Heaven', hoping for some reunion after death with his son in a place where there would be no tragedy or suffering. It was an enormously popular song, touching a chord and going on to win a string of Grammies in 1992. If Christianity has given up talking about heaven, others are still using the bank of imagery it built up to good effect.

Clapton's theme was based loosely on a line in Revelation – 'here God lives among men. He will make His home among them . . . He will wipe away all tears from their eyes; there will be no more death, and no more mourning or sadness' (Rev 21:3–4). Others too continue to promote scriptural details in new and unlikely settings. There is, for example, a computer game called Afterlife: The Last Word in Sins, which allows players who get through the celestial gates to build celestial cities. And, on Interstate 85, near the town of Gaffney on the border of North and South Carolina, country-music promoter Howard Knight Jr is planning a theme park to rival Disneyland and Legoland with all the paraphernalia of heaven. God's Wonderful World, announced in 1997 and to be based on the site of an old nuclear power station, will feature the 'many mansions' spoken of in the Gospels, harps, clouds, golden streets and even a large statue of God, lit from behind so as to approximate to the beatific vision.

CHAPTER TWENTY

A Village in Heaven

W hen he was a student at London's Slade School of Art for four years up until 1912, Stanley Spencer (1891–1959) would travel back every night on the Great Western Railway to his family home at Cookham, nestling twenty-eight miles upstream in a crook of the River Thames as it ambles through Berkshire. His fellow students nicknamed him 'Cookham' on account of this trek, and the number of times he referred to the village in conversation. They seem to have regarded him as something of a country bumpkin, yet Spencer went on to become one of the greatest explorers of religious ideas and imagery in the twentieth century. Cookham remained his home for much of his life; the eternal backdrop to his work and somewhere, with an intensity not seen since William Blake, he explored the transcendent in everyday life – or, as he preferred to put it, 'angels and dirt'. Cookham was, Spencer claimed, 'a village in heaven'.

Some critics have marginalised Spencer as merely another English painter of idealised Arcadian landscapes, though he is currently undergoing something of a revival. The Cookham where he and his seven older siblings were brought up by eccentric, musical but godly parents no longer exists. But it had disappeared long before his death. From the 1930s onwards, suburbia and the world of machinery were embracing the countryside around London like the tentacles of a man-made octopus. Many of Spencer's images of Cookham mixed what he saw with what he remembered and what he imagined. He was always harking back on a literal level to an ideal childhood, and beyond that, to a place of innocence in which every detail of life, however ordinary, was encoded with spiritual meaning.

Today Cookham is an unlikely place for any sort of pilgrimage beyond mere homage to Spencer. There is hardly a break in the remorseless sprawl of greater London or an uninterrupted vista of fields and sky before I am sitting in a traffic jam, waiting to cross the narrow metal bridge, a feature of several of Spencer's paintings, which spans the Thames and leads on to Cookham High Street.

Any isolation and physical separateness that this place once enjoyed has been sacrificed on the altar of the motorcar. Spencer recalled bakers, butchers and greengrocers in an introspective and self-sufficient society, but they have now been exorcised by out-of-town supermarkets. The High Street isn't exactly dead, but it is certainly struggling for breath, the chi-chi children's clothes' boutique and estate agents the standard fare of a suburban tourniquet.

Spencer once likened this parade of shops to the nave of a church. It was where he located *Christ Carrying His Cross*, which he painted in 1920. The Son of God hosted the Last Supper at the Malthouse at its western end, and, round the corner, he preached to the crowds at the Cookham Regatta from the terrace of the Ferry Hotel. This had now become a Harvester chain restaurant, I noted, as I crossed the bridge. Heaven in a Harvester?

I park near a shop teaching the art of Japanese flower arrangement. Opposite, is the Spencer home, Fernlea, a semi-detached Victorian villa built by his grandfather. In Spencer's childhood it looked out on to the meadows and the river, but now it is protected from the cars by a well-trimmed privet hedge.

In his depiction of the Via Dolorosa, Spencer gave the house a soft brick colour, with angelic figures bursting out of every window. Today it is painted the sort of bright yellow popular with owners of modern open-topped sports cars as a way of ensuring they get noticed.

If Spencer would have regretted the destruction of his past, he might not, perhaps, have disapproved too heartily: 'I really feel that everything in one that is not vision is mainly vulgarity,' he once wrote. It was the tension between the two that he captured; the divine in the mundane.

Taking with me a small, illustrated book of Spencer's works, I walk down past the Malthouse to where an unadopted road, Berries Lane, leads down to the riverside. It marks the edge of the village proper. In the middle and later periods of his life when many critics had written him off, Spencer would earn money by taking landscape commissions. One of his better results, *The Magnolia Tree* of 1938, was executed here in the garden of Westward House, an outsized Edwardian family home. The tree is still there, to the right of the main entrance, and is in full bloom, its white petals, with pink bases, pointing up like candle holders, just as in Spencer's picture. Magnolias were my mother's passion, our garden at home was littered with them, and today, by pure coincidence, would have been her eightieth birthday.

Behind the houses is a cordon of fields and commons opening on to the green-and-white chalk down, no doubt now carefully preserved by planning legislation, but nonetheless unchanged. It was here that Spencer set the first painting to win him acclaim. In 1912, Roger Fry, then an all-powerful critic, included *John Donne Arriving in Heaven* in the much-heralded Second Post-Impressionist Exhibition in London. The reception it received established Spencer's reputation. An avid reader of the Bible, the young Spencer had been inspired by Donne's sermons to visualise paradise. Soon afterwards, he would retreat from such a direct approach, but when he was twenty-one he placed the poet walking amid simplified, almost dehumanised figures in an austere, flattened landscape. Clad in white vestments, wrapped up in prayer, and facing in all directions, these characters were part of a world out of time, a garden paradise cloaked in grace.

The years before the First World War were Spencer's first flowering, and in his visionary imagination heaven quickly became not somewhere remote, but rather the world on his doorstep. He had only to reach out to touch it. His *Zacharias and Elizabeth* of 1914, even more celebrated when it was first shown than *John Donne*, told how when Mary's cousin, the aged and childless Elizabeth, learned from the Angel Gabriel that she was to have a child, she did so in the garden behind Spencer's studio at Fernlea. Again, there was a trance-like, timeless, almost mystical quality about the canvas, but its characters were more flesh and blood than the shadows in *John Donne*. Spencer even included a Christ-like gardener dragging an ivy branch, traditionally the emblem of everlasting life. 'I wanted,' he later wrote, 'to absorb and finally express the atmosphere and meaning the place had for me . . . It was to be a painting characterising and exactly expressing the life I was living and seeing around me . . . to raise that life round me to what I felt was its true status, meaning and purpose.' Every day, every action, contained the seeds of heaven.

As I emerge from the lane on to the towpath, the Thames on one side and Bellrope Meadow, a favourite Spencer location, on the other, this idea quickly takes on a life of its own. For it is not hard, once you start to think yourself inside Spencer's mind-set, to see in the commonplace all around the potential for some more profound insight into the human condition. Dotted around in front of me are just the sort of ordinary vig- nettes that Spencer could have invested with that greater meaning – the elderly couple, care-worn but intimate over lunch on their boat, the two young women sharing confidences as they lap up the spring sunshine, the child feeding the ducks, oblivious to his mother's growing impatience. All are images that can be seen anywhere. They are not particular to Cookham.

After his war-time experiences had clouded his early metaphysical vision, Spencer wrote to his first wife, Hilda Carline, 'I know it was not Cookham that gave me ideas, but just the degree of consciousness that God has brought me to. I must hope for this consciousness to return & not in the meantime fill up the emptiness with Cookham "padding".'

Spencer's search to wring a measure of ecstasy out of the everyday clearly had its roots in his own deep Christianity, but it was a particularly idiosyncratic form of Christianity. Some of the principal ideas the Spencer credo encapsulated might fit more neatly into the mind of a medieval mystic, or even be deemed Buddhist. It could reasonably be argued that what Spencer saw in daily life in Cookham was not only a kind of Eden, but also nirvana, a commune of enlightenment, glimpsed through a glass darkly.

There is indeed much evidence that Spencer was influenced by Eastern religious thought. As early as 1911, he was admiring reproductions of Eastern art and, later, his letters to Hilda contained repeated references to Buddha, Lao-tzu, Confucius and Muhammad. After their marriage in 1925, he admitted to Hilda, 'A good two thirds of what I love in vital religious expression comes from periods & times when Buddhism or Mohammedanism was the religion.'

There is much in his writings – and Spencer, like Blake, was an inspiring writer – to confirm the expression that, at his best and most inspired, he had an instinct to see beyond the literal. In a letter from Macedonia, where he saw front-line service in the First World War, he recaptured a typical day in Cookham:

Everything is so dull . . . so unhappening, uncircumstantial and ordinary. I go home to breakfast thinking as I go of the beautiful wholeness of the day. During the morning I am visited and walk about being in that visitation. How at this time everything seems more definite and to put on a new meaning and freshness you have never before noticed. In the afternoon I set my work out and begin the picture. I leave off at dusk feeling delighted with the spiritual labour I have done.

'Unhappening, uncircumstantial and ordinary' – it is an apt description of what I see on the towpath and in the garden of the modern civil service retirement home that now borders it. How Spencer went about transforming this into something more is best seen at the parish church, which lies further along the towpath – it is set back from the river and approached by a lane with bowing walls, overhanging trees and partially glimpsed Georgian windows that exude timelessness.

The neat and unremarkable graveyard is both Spencer's final resting place, marked by a simple stone, and Hilda's. This was also the setting for one of his greatest critical triumphs, *Resurrection, Cookham*, first exhibited in 1927. *The Times* called it 'the most important picture painted by an English artist in the present century', and it was purchased straightaway by the Tate Gallery. In it, the dead rise bodily from their tombs in the graveyard – a place Donne once called (a description which Spencer borrowed) 'the holy suburb of heaven'. God the Father sits under the rose-entwined porch of the church, a row of prophets, including Moses, line up along the outside wall of the nave, and a group of African tribespeople gather together, two of whom appear to be making love.

Spencer painted this work while living away from Cookham, in London, and there is a strong sense of exile in it, both physical and historical. He drew from memory and so presented an idealised version of the church and graveyard. The tower that dominates the church, for instance, is missing.

More important than this, though, is his quest for some lost wholeness, a harking back to pre-war days and a rising again of that almost childlike vision of life moving on different planes that had been compromised by his war-time experiences. That trajectory is there in the picture – in particular, in the depiction of a steamer on the

Thames in the top left-hand corner, just down the path I have walked. Hence Spencer was giving something routine a greater meaning:

> This is supposed to be people going to heaven [he subsequently explained] . . . This is not so far fetched as it sounds. When I was at Cookham, I used to watch these big boats go by on the river. I had never been in one and had a feeling that somehow they were different from me. The river was a sort of holy of holies & people who went on it had as a result a kind of magicle [sic] feeling about them . . . Then of course in the case of these steamers, they did not stop at Cookham; they came from a world I did not know & disappeared into an unknown.

Resurrection, Cookham brought a new and highly significant element to Spencer's vision of heaven in the here and now. While many of the figures seen rising from the dead were Spencer's friends and family, part of a previous and now distant life, several were also based on himself and Hilda. In his search for religious enlightenment, Spencer had discovered, through his marriage to Hilda, sexuality – albeit here in a primitive and pure form. He once told a critic that the painting showed a specific moment – 2.45 p.m. on a Tuesday in May – and this may have been the moment Spencer lost his virginity. His physical love for Hilda was, for Spencer, a resurrection into a new life of bliss that was to be found on earth.

Inspired by Spencer's belief that heaven is so palpable, I make a detour into the parish church to say a prayer and light a candle to mark my mother's birthday. It is something I do in a mechanical way every Sunday at church with my children, but now I'm hoping that some of the barriers in my own mind may have been lifted by Spencer.

I try to convince myself that it is not so much a question of getting beyond my physical surroundings, as of seeing them in another light, catching sight of that other dimension. But it's to no avail. Maybe it's the stiff formality and self-conscious sacredness of the church, as against the more profane settings Spencer preferred. Or perhaps it's just that some have that vision and some don't, as Dionysius had remarked rather imperiously. Whatever it is, I end up like a tone-deaf member of the audience at an opera: I know what it is that I'm meant to hear, I've read the reviews and can imagine the sublime, but I can't get beyond the fact that what I hear is everyday noise in order to experience it properly.

On the other side of the churchyard is the Spencer Gallery, housed in what was once the local Methodist church, where he attended Sunday school. It contains a selection of his paintings and letters. If anything puts its most famous son in context in modern-day Cookham, it is this unassuming building on the bland High Street. For the power of Spencer's work, its poignant capacity to turn the world on its head, comes over so much more forcibly in this gentle, unremarkable setting than in any of the bigger, more formal galleries where normally his pictures hang. But I want to see one more location, that of the painting which Spencer called *A Village in Heaven* (now in the Tate collection), completed in 1937 as part of his Last Days sequence and destined for his never-realised Church-House project, a shrine to his work, his belief, his loves and himself, what Spencer once called 'a cathedral of me'.

The War Memorial, which stands beyond my car at the west end of the High Street, is unremarkable: a stone cross set in rough boulders, a list of names inscribed on it, including that of Spencer's brother Sydney, who died in the First World War. However, in his *A Village in Heaven* Spencer lopped off the top of the cross and so turned it into a phallus, while the base was transformed into a makeshift altar. On and around it older villagers were wrapped up in love-making, youngsters had their first fumble and even schoolchildren began to undress each other. Spencer's first title for the work had been *The Celebration of Love in Heaven* and what he was seeking to convey was the redemptive nature of physical love in heaven as on earth.

The idea of finding heaven or, to be more accurate, that transcendent dimension, through uninhibited sexual love, a kind of village orgy, had two sources. Once again, Spencer was influenced by the East. At around this time, he had been greatly struck by photographs of the temples of Khajuraho in India, encrusted with hundreds of figures making love or, in Spencer's own phrase, 'assembled in sexuality'. And then there was also Spencer's increasing self-absorption – his interior spiritual journey – as he broke up with Hilda and made a brief, disastrous second marriage to Patricia Preece, a painter who had acted as his nude model, had wooed him and then dumped him once he had made her his wife, taking with her much of his money to support her menage with her long-time lover, Dorothy Hepworth. The figures in *A Village in Heaven* were thus grotesques, humanity in pursuit of the divine but falling short of it, but that was the point. All, for Spencer (himself included), were failures, redeemed only by God's love.

It was a position he came to through bitter experience. Hilda was never to take him back, and she died in 1950 of cancer. Spencer spent his last years writing letters to her in his notebooks. She was not, for him, somewhere other, but close at hand. In 1957 he wrote to her in a characteristic jumble of words whose meaning is nonetheless clear:

> What I mean is that the flowing and hardenings of our love makes the bases shape over which our succeeding love will flow. And this new flow, having no regard for what it flows over other than it loves, it forms yet another 'us' surface which again will be loved by us & flowed over.

Of heaven itself, of life after death, he remained convinced that the nearest we could get to it was through having another vision of this life. 'One might never be able to conceive what Heaven is like,' he wrote in his notebook towards the end of his life, 'but nevertheless the contemplation of it is, I think, the greatest thing of all for the creative artist.'

Traveller's Tales: 5

A couple of months before she died of cancer, my mother had a minor operation to bypass a blocked bile duct. Given her poor state of health, there were fears about how she would weather the trauma of an anaesthetic. Though she seemed to come round very well, thereafter she went into a steep decline. It wasn't so much her physical condition, precarious as it was, which was giving cause for concern: her mental state was deteriorating. Twenty-four hours after the operation, she was moved into a side ward. The nurses began to shake their heads and talk of waiting for the inevitable. Though my mother was conscious and she half knew who we were, she was somewhere else in her mind as she stared up at the ceiling and started singing.

As a girl, she had been in the church choir and each Sunday at Mass with us she would join in with the hymns. But no-one could say she was blessed with much of a voice. It was weak and rather shrill. Even in the more conducive atmosphere of family parties, with her seven extrovert siblings, when she would do her 'turn' – usually a rendition of 'Second-Hand Rose' or 'Little Old Lady' – she struggled to get the notes and make herself heard.

Yet in that hospital room her singing was transformed. It was powerful, determined and had a tone and range that none of us had ever heard in her before. Her sister Rita, two years her junior, was amazed. It was almost, she remarked, as if my mother imagined she was part of a choir and was singing her part with rather too much brio.

It is often said that as you approach death you leave the

present and start to explore the past. So my mother's reversion to chorister was not so inexplicable, even if her hitherto unsuspected vocal talents were a revelation. What was so strange though, because it was entirely outside any knowledge that she had, was her choice of music: it was unmistakably ecclesiastical, more Gregorian chant than recognisable lyrics, and certainly entirely foreign to the dreadful happy-clappy 'Walk in the Light' dirges that were pumped out in our parish church each Sunday at three quarters their intended speed.

Rita now remembers only the broad grin on my mother's face and the sense of contentment she radiated. At the time, I found it all profoundly disturbing, but was in such a stew about the failure of the medical staff to attempt to address what was causing this behaviour that I couldn't think it through. Eventually, I insisted on seeing the senior physician on duty who quickly realised that the sudden withdrawal of the powerful cocktail of drugs my mother had been taking for years for her multiple sclerosis might have triggered this period of madness. He put her back on them and within hours she was herself again.

But I never forgot that singing. When Rita later asked her about it, my mother looked unflustered. 'Did I?' she said, and left it at that. It may very well have been simply a chemical reaction set off by the withdrawal of her drugs, but if drugs could affect one's singing voice, we'd all be vying for a place on the stage at La Scala. And where had that Gregorian chant come from? 'She was with the angels,' Rita now says with a certainty I find hard to dismiss. The same thought has crossed my mind. Certainly, when the end came a few weeks later, it was utterly peaceful. She exhibited no fear and left this world as if she were just popping out to somewhere familiar.

CHAPTER TWENTY-ONE

But I've Never Been to Me

As human beings we are the only animals who have to live with the knowledge that one day we will die. It is something we have struggled to cope with since the start of time. We seem to prefer to ignore mortality but that can only work for so long, as I have discovered. I count myself privileged to have put it off for almost forty years, but one can only get so far in life keeping death out of sight, out of mind, switching off whenever we see a hearse, immersing ourselves in the rituals of relatives' and neighbours' funerals to avoid thinking about what it is they are marking, casting our minds no further forward than the other side of that crematorium curtain, and keeping our fingers crossed that the doctor will tell us that the ache or pain we've been having for the past six months is nothing serious. We crave youth, and some of us go to great lengths to arrest and reverse the signs of ageing. Preparing for our declining years is now all about taking out personal pension plans. It is the ultimate triumph of hope over experience.

It is best if we first try to look death in the eye through the loss of someone close to us rather than waiting until our own end is imminent. When a valued colleague recently died of bowel cancer, she went out unable to admit openly, even at the bitter end, to those closest to her, what was actually happening. A mutual friend, who visited her on her penultimate day when she was so drugged up that she could no longer speak or make sense, recalled later that her blue eyes looked utterly confused and terrified.

I now realise that if this journey has been anything for me, it has been a kind of trial run. It's not so much that I have been wandering about dressed in black, humming 'The Lord is My Shepherd' and putting my affairs in order, but rather that I have found a sense of my own mortality inescapable. I am dying. There, I can say it. It may not have quite the impact on me that it might have if a doctor had just told me I had six months to live, but it's a start. We should all try saying it as an exercise in confronting reality. We may not be at the Dennis Potter stage of rhapsodising over cherry blossom and life's unbearable beauty while we swig liquid morphine, nor share Dylan Thomas's 'rage, rage against the dying of the light', and, hopefully, most of us can manage something a little brighter than Philip Larkin's pessimism when he remarked that if we were really conscious of our mortality we wouldn't be able to get out of bed in the morning.

Yet the reason Potter and Thomas and Larkin made such an impact with their remarks is because they were publicly breaking a taboo about dying. As a society, we have become ever more naked in our avoidance of death. It is an odd, modern affectation. Death has been central to the development of our culture, if only because it establishes a tyranny of time, where trial and loss and dissatisfaction can thrive within flexible but ultimately finite boundaries. Today, we try to ignore this and, from the rebranding of funeral directors as 'morticians' to the publisher who renamed Martin Amis's novel *Dead Babies* as *Dark Secrets* for fear of alienating readers (and hence losing the irony intended by the author), we treat death as if it should never be mentioned.

Though it was introduced in the death-soaked Victorian 1880s as a way of relieving pressure on overcrowded cemeteries, cremation is now preferred to burial by three quarters of Britons (or their grieving relatives). It anaesthetises death: after a cremation, few people go back to the crematorium's tidy, well-fertilised garden to put flowers in a vase, whereas a churchyard grave contains an actual corpse and is a permanent invitation to mourn.

While I am unashamed to mourn, I feel no more comfortable with the reality of death at the end of this trip than I did at the outset of it. Which, of course, makes me no different from the vast majority of humankind. 'It's not that I'm afraid to die,' Woody Allen once wrote, 'I just don't want to be there when it happens.' But he will be. And so will we all. Impossible as it is to contemplate it, our demise one day is inevitable. Such thoughts are uncomfortable, and so we don't usually entertain them for very long, which may perhaps explain why so much of the thinking about afterlife has been confused, not thought out, simplistically earthbound and, often, plain banal.

The advantage of this journey has been that I have been forced, over a long period of time, to think about death and life after death and, moreover, to do so in the company of the relatively exclusive club of writers, artists and thinkers who have directed their considerable powers to contemplating eternity. As a result, I can't say that I yet feel the peace that I saw, for example, in my mother in her last days, and in the calm of the late Cardinal Basil Hume, when he revealed publicly in 1999 that he was about to meet his maker. Both had some vital ingredient of an unshakeable faith which I feel I must lack.

With regard to life after death, we are faced with a stark choice: namely, 'nothing' or 'something'. Nothing is increasingly popular and removes any sense of expectation and, therefore, of worry. But it is so bleak. The historically preferred option is that there is something after death and this is still, according to most polls, our heart's desire, coming in several shapes and forms: a shadow life, with some essence of us floating in the ether; an immortal soul; an immortal body and soul in a place resembling earth (what is called the anthropocentric option); an immortal body and soul with God existing somewhere beyond description (the theocentric option); or a series of reincarnations in pursuit of enlightenment and transcendence in this life (nirvana) leading to eternal rest. Inevitably, there is a good deal of overlap. Christianity, for one, has long mixed up the anthropocentric and theocentric, and most religions, save their most fundamental elements, have slowly drifted towards the central ground of placing an increased value on the search for transcendence in this life.

The general consensus seems to me to be the most obviously appealing. It gives us something very definite to do in this life beyond simply following rules and regulations, laid down by ecclesiastical bigwigs, which often bear little relation to the realities of our circumstances. It is empowering and individualistic, which appeals to the zeitgeist and, essentially, it suggests an imperative to fight to make this a better and more equal world. It also chimes easily with the trend in Western culture for rediscovering a mystical and spiritual dimension to life, something beyond (though not divorced from) the capitalism, globalisation and the various all-too-tangible forces that rule our planet.

In the manner of most seekers after heaven, I am creating it in the image of my own reaction to the world around me. The history of heaven, touching so directly on a universal experience (death), tells us the history of humankind, and is a more reliable barometer of our collective past than such currently fashionable fads such as the history of what we have eaten. It reveals how we have coped with the lot we have been dealt in life, and how we have dreamed of making it better or achieving some form of redress for injustices suffered. Our reactions come in all shapes and sizes. At one end of the spectrum lies the fundamentalist option, 'turning one's back on this awful world', a 'placing one's hope in the future' scenario, be it Christian fundamentalists with their expectation of imminent 'Rapture', which will beam them up to heaven from the backseat of their Cadillac, or the suicide bombers who targetted the World Trade Center and the Pentagon on 11 September, 2001 in the firm belief that by dying to kill others they would achieve the sensual djanna with its Valkyrie-like virgins just waiting to fête them. There is no tolerance for suicide in the Qur'an, but these terrorists, schooled in embitterment at what they perceive has happened to their people at the hands of America, are convinced that they are dying in battle for Islam and for justice, something the Qur'an approves of, though it excludes the killing of the innocent and of collateral damage. The bombers' fervent hope of a blessed hereafter may only be a pipe dream, condemned by some of the most senior figures in Islam, but it is still encouraged by those who manipulate the current misery of the Middle East for their own political ends. Heaven, as ever, is shaped by current necessities and obsessions.

Where, then, does such obvious exploitation and sub-jectivity leave any purer notion of heaven? And where, I ask myself, does it leave my mother now? In a heaven of my own making? The collective experience of faith and death offers an inadequate answer to this most diffi-cult of questions. Our age may regard such an answer with contempt, but that is a harsh and futile judgement for, however inadequate, it allows me to create some-thing to help me cope with my grief and sense of loss. Why wouldn't we want to be up there with Beatrice and Dante? For me, it is a most entrancing vision. Where will I be when my number is up? To follow my own logic, not in a heaven of my own making but, rather, in one conjured up by those I have left behind who will, I assume, grieve for me. Selfishly, I want my own heaven for me, but the only way to get that, to take my argument to its conclusion, is to search for transcendence now. As a result, I may end up a better person in this life, but my post-mortem fate will still remain a mystery.

It all remains patently unsatisfactory. There have been moments during this journey when the act of retracing the stepping stones in heaven's development has inevi-tably left me cold and cynical. The idea of paradise has, undoubtedly, been exploited by the major faith systems as a means of capturing and holding the allegiance of their members. A bandage for our wounds, but nothing that even anticipates the hope of a cure.

Heaven, paradise, djanna, whatever one chooses to call it, has been debased by religious authorities into a set of entry criteria that so distort any spiritual values with their rigidity and idealism that they lead to absurd situations. For example, there were the two English Sunday school teachers, no doubt well-meaning women who had listened attentively to what was said in the pulpit, who, in a much reported incident in 1998, told the children in their care that the then much-mourned Diana, Princess of Wales, had gone to hell. In a narrow sense they were right: in the Ten Commandments, Christian teaching condemns adultery, and, because of the nature of Diana's death in a car crash, she had had no time to repent, and could therefore be presumed to have gone to her grave damned. However, following the rule book in this way manages to make the afterlife seem so unappealing as to be redundant.

It is a depressing picture and at times I have wondered why I have faith at all. In my wanderings, I have come close to jacking it all in, leaving the Catholic Church of my birth, and instead taking what suddenly seems the more comforting course of atheism and the very different challenge of anticipating oblivion. I could, simply, get on with enjoying what years I have left. Religion, seen during such dark passages, is all about pandering to the desire for immortality and feeding off what has been, is and will remain an unfathomable mystery, servicing the ever-changing expectations of the audience. Seen in such a light it has little appeal.

Cynics say that there are four standard reasons why religion exists at all. First, that religion provides us with explanations of life, the universe and the inexplicable; second, that it offers comfort and reassurance in a hostile world; third, that it makes for social order, promoting morality and social cohesion; and fourth, that it satisfies the innate superstition and stupidity of humankind. On all counts, heaven could be used in court to support the case for the prosecution.

If one were to add a couple of alternatives, the picture is less clear. Religion may exist because there is a God or, less prosaically, some form of divine or supernatural purpose to our existence. Or, as the anthropologist Pascal Boyer wrote in *Religion Explained*, religion may be the result of the way our brain works. Both trains of thought are part, as I have discovered on my travels, of the story of heaven. They lie behind some of the travellers' tales that I have included in this book, accounts from people who have had no truck with a 'jam-tomorrow' school of thought. To take the argument one stage further, the after-life archetype, as Carl Jung would deem it, predates organised religion and its manipulations. It has a source which is more profound than church politics and marketing. And so I remain in the pews and – just – in the fold. This world, as Emily Dickinson wrote, 'is not conclusion . . . narcotics cannot still the tooth that nibbles at the soul'.

If I have not yet reached a dead end on my journey, a point at which I have decided to turn round and give it all up, then neither have I reached my destination in any decisive way. I have struggled and failed in Cookham parish church and elsewhere for a moment of transcendence, a moment when I felt the spirit of the one I have lost was close to me, a moment when I knew, in spiritualist terms, where she was and that she was waiting for me, or even, in plain questions of belief, when I was absolutely and utterly convinced there was a God.

As I unpack my suitcases, however, I see that there has been enough in what I have observed and in what I have discovered that leaves me room (though not perhaps those who have travelled with me) for that eternal question mark. Given that humankind has spent millions of years battling to find an answer to what, if anything, happens after death, then, with hindsight, it was impossibly arrogant for me to imagine that I might have found anything approaching an answer that would work for anyone other than myself. We should all find our own answers, however flawed and provisional. Religious institutions can help us in our task, but we have to be aware of their long-standing efforts to control our imaginations in this and other matters. If I have formed any definite conclusion, it is that merely avoiding the imperative to consider death and beyond is somehow opting out of being fully human.

The whole concept of an answer, however, exposes the problem of the modern mind: we are trapped in a mindset that seeks answers, positive or negative, as a way of understanding ourselves. We are uneasy with question marks. We imagine that we are so much cleverer than past ages, that their wisdom can be surpassed by our own, passed through the filter of science and logic and reason.

The results are misleading and dispiriting. Since the eighteenth century at least, religion has stopped sailing its own ship and has changed course, almost without knowing it, towards the rational and logical. Believing in something has become synonymous with proving it. The difference between faith and belief has been blurred. Faith alone is no longer good enough; a mainstream logic has arisen. One can't prove that God/the Devil/heaven/hell exist, and so therefore one must bid them farewell – or relegate them to a miserly old age as symbols in advertisements and films. But then we can't quite be so callous or self-sacrificing, so we keep them in a cupboard, hoping that one day they might be fixed up, dusted down, and useful again.

A much more significant contribution, however, would be to reestablish a sense of the power of myth, to reverse the modern process that Saul Bellow has called 'a housecleaning of belief'. This might just return us to a context within which to contemplate heaven as more than a mere fairy story, cooked up to deal with the fear of dying. Religion and its narratives were once intimately bound up with myth. Myths were clues to the spiritual potentialities of human life, the way we expressed and gave form to our transcendent longings, our ultimate concerns. And they can be again. Myths are never true or false, they can only be living or dead. Since we can still put their appeal in modern terms, they therefore must be living. Myths in this modern sense are archetypal dreams which deal with great human problems. In Christianity, the myth of original sin, perhaps the most resonant of all, still gives us the narrative of the fall, the birth of humankind, of sex, of betrayal and of death. Indeed, from archaeological evidence, the earliest evidence of anything like mythological thinking is associated with graves. From death arose another myth – that of heaven as compensation. Darwin and other scientists can certainly challenge the literal truth of it all, but they cannot take away its resonance, the promise of fulfilment, the human at odds with his or her world, and the opaque window that it offers on to the most profound mystery of all. The myth is not there to answer, but to illuminate. Death is not a full stop, exclamation mark, nor, in our own times, a discreet footnote. It is simply the punctuation in the narrative, a question mark that leads on to what we cannot yet read.

It has become too easy to dismiss myths. 'Who needs all these Greek gods and stuff?' is a common response to any attempt to explain their ongoing worth. Yet, as

Joseph Campbell (1904–87), author, teacher at Sarah Lawrence College, and America's leading expert on comparative mythology until his death in 1987, was fond of remarking; 'The remnants of all that stuff line the walls of our interior system of belief, like shards of broken pottery in an archaeological site.' For Campbell, mythology was an interior road map of existence, drawn by people who had travelled it. His definition extends easily to heaven for it has been created by this existence, however much its most vocal proponents today claim that it has been revealed from on high.

What, then, does a mythological approach to heaven tell me about my mother's death and indeed my own? It tells me that others have been there, that I am one of many, that behind the embroidery of ages, the foolishness, the flights of fancy and the manipulation, there may be a truth, and that beyond the wish there may be something impossible in the midst of life to grasp or even imagine. We can only play and replay over and over again the different forms of the myth, acknowledging them with all their shortcomings for what they are, and drawing whatever sustenance we can.

SOURCE NOTES

All scriptural quotes in the text are from the New Jerusalem Bible. Quotes from the Qur'an are from Muhammad Asad's *The Message of the Qur'an* (Gibralter, 1980). Several books have influenced my thought throughout all twenty-one chapters and therefore it seems appropriate to list them at the start of the Source Notes rather than repeat them under each chapter heading. They are:

Karen Armstrong, *A History of God: The 4000-year Quest of Judaism, Christianity and Islam* (Heinemann, London and New York, 1993)

Jeffrey Burton Russell, *A History of Heaven: The Singing Silence* (New Jersey, 1997)

Colleen McDannell and Bernhard Lang, *Heaven: A History* (Connecticut, 1988)

Carol and Philip Zaleski, *The Book of Heaven: An Anthology of Writings from Ancient to Modern Times* (Oxford, 2000)

Introduction

Pope John Paul II, General Audience text in *l'Osservatore Romano* (23 July 1999)

Bill and Judy Guggenheim (eds), *Hello from Heaven* (New York and London, 1996)

Hal Lindsey, *The Late Great Planet Earth* (New York, 1970)

Jonathan Dollimore, *Death, Desire and Loss in Western Culture* (London, 1998)

Jim Crace, *Being Dead* (London, 2000)

Chapter One

James Charlesworth (ed.), *The Old Testament Pseudepigrapha*
(New York, 1983)
G. M. A. Grube (trans.), *Five Dialogues: Plato* (London, 1990)
Bertrand Russell, *A History of Western Philosophy* (London, 1946)
Peter Stanford, *The Devil: A Biography* (London and New York,
1996)

Traveller's Tales 1

Ben Rogers, *A. J. Ayer: A Life* (London, 1999)

Chapter Two

Patrick Olivelle (trans.), *Upanishads* (Oxford, 1998)
Karen Armstrong, *Buddah* (London and New York, 2001)
Geddes MacGregor, *Images of Afterlife: Beliefs from Antiquity to
Modern Times* (New York, 1992)
Luis Gomez, *Land of Bliss: The Paradise of the Buddha of
Measureless Light* (Honolulu, 1996)
Jane Hope and Borin Van Loon, *Buddha for Beginners*
(Cambridge, 1994)
Edward Conze (trans.), *Buddhist Scriptures* (London, 1959)
Miriam van Scott, *Encyclopedia of Heaven* (New York, 1998)

Chapter Three

A. N. Wilson, *Paul: The Mind of the Apostle* (London, 1997)
E. P. Sanders, *Paul* (Oxford, 1991)
G. R. Beasley-Murray, *The Book of Revelation* (London, 1974)
Franz Moschner, *The Kingdom of Heaven in Parables* (London, 1960)
Simon Ulrich, *Heaven in the Christian Tradition* (New York, 1958)

Chapter Four

Ancient Christian Writers Series, Vol. 6 (New Jersey, 1957)
Andrew Louth (ed.), *Eusebius's History of the Church* (London,
1965)
J. Armitage Robinson (trans.), *The Passion of Saint Perpetua*
(Cambridge, 1891)
Paul Johnson, *A History of Christianity* (London and New York,
1976)
Elizabeth Abbott, *A History of Celibacy* (Cambridge, 2001)
Henry Chadwick (trans.), *The Confessions: Saint Augustine*
(Oxford, 1991)

Garry Wills, *Saint Augustine* (Weidenfeld, 1999)

Robert Enno (ed.), *Saint Augustine's Letters* (London 1989)

Alan Bertstein, *The Formation of Hell: Death and Retribution in the Ancient and Early Christian Worlds* (New York, 1993)

David Chidester, *Christianity: A Global History* (London, 2000)

Tobias Churton, *The Gnostics* (London, 1987)

Henri Crouzel, *Origen: The Life and Thought of the First Great Theologian* (San Francisco, 1989 and London, 1998)

Robert Hughes, *Heaven and Hell in Western Art* (New York, 1968)

Chapter Five

A. Jeffery (trans.), *Muhammad and His Religion* (New Jersey, 1958)

A. Arberry (trans.), *Islam: The Koran Interpreted* (London, 1955)

Armstrong, Karen, *The Battle for God: Fundamentalism in Judaism, Christianity and Islam* (London and New York, 2000)

Armstrong, Karen, *Islam: A Short History* (London and New York, 2000)

F. E. Peters, *Muhammad and the Origins of Islam* (New York, 1994)

Muhammad Asad (trans.), *The Message of the Qur'an* (Gibralter, 1980)

Chapter Six

D. H. Farmer (ed.), *Bede's Ecclesiastical History of the English People* (London, 1990)

Colm Luibheid (trans.), *Pseudo Dionysius: The Complete Works* (Paulist Press – www.paulistpress.com – New Jersey, 1987)

Jean Carnandet (ed.), *Acta Sanctorum* (Paris, 1886)

Anthony Meisel and M. L. del Mastro (trans.), *The Rule of Saint Benedict* (London, 1975)

Peter Stanford, *The Devil: A Biography* (London and New York, 1996)

Alix de Saint-André, *The Good Angel Guide* (Paris, 1998 and London, 1999)

Andrew Louth, *Denys the Areopagite* (London, 1989)

Chapter Seven

Kenneth Clark, *Civilisation: A Personal View* (London, 1969)

William Golding, *The Spire* (London, 1964)

Chapter Eight

David Chidester, *Christianity: A Global History* (London, 2000)
Alan Press, *Anthology of Troubadour Lyrics* (Edinburgh, 1981)
Bruce Hozeski (trans.), *Hildegard of Bingen's The Book of the Rewards of Life* (London, 1964)
Fiona Maddocks, *Hildegard of Bingen: The Woman of Her Age* (London, 2001)
Jacques Le Goff, *The Birth of Purgatory* (Chicago, 1984)
Herman Pleij, *Dreaming of Cockaigne* (Columbia, 2001)
Stephen Greenblatt, *Hamlet in Purgatory* (Princeton, 2001)
Keith Thomas, *Religion and the Decline of Magic* (London, 1971)
Priscilla H. Barnum (ed.) *Dives and Pauper* (Early English Text Society, 1976 and 1980)
Norman Cohn, *Europe's Inner Demons* (London, 1975)
Anthony Kenny, *Aquinas* (Oxford, 1984)
Timothy McDermott (ed.)*Thomas Aquinas's Summa Theologiae* (London, 1991)
Bernard McGinn, *The Foundtions of Mysticism* (New York, 1991)
G. Mollat, *The Popes at Avignon* (London, 1963)
Ulrike Wiethaus (ed.), *Maps of Flesh and Light: The Religious Experience of Medieval Women Mystics* (New York, 1993)

Chapter Nine

Jonathan B. Reiss, *Luca Signorelli: The San Brizio Chapel, Orvieto* (New York, 1995)

Chapter Ten

C. H. Sisson (trans.), *Dante's Divine Comedy* (OUP, Oxford, 1980)
Hein Schulze Altcappenberg, *Sandro Botticelli: Picture Cycle for Dante's Divine Comedy* (London, 2001)
Armstrong, Karen, *The Battle for God: Fundamentalism in Judaism, Christianity and Islam* (London and New York, 2000)
George Holmes, *Dante* (Oxford, 1980)
Rachel Jacoff (ed.), *The Cambridge Companion to Dante* (Cambridge, 1993)

Chapter Eleven

Richard Marius, *Martin Luther: The Christian Between God and Death* (Boston, 1999)
J. K. Reid (ed.), *Calvin's Theological Treatises* (London, 2000)

Allison E. Peers (ed.), *Teresa of Avila: Complete Works* (London, 1946)

N. H. Keeble (ed.), *The Pilgrim's Progress: John Bunyan* (Oxford, 1984)

Peter Ackroyd, *The Life of Thomas More* (New York, 1998 and London, 1999)

Shirley du Boulay, *Teresa of Avila* (London, 1991)

V. H. H. Green *Luther and the Reformation* (London, 1964)

Christopher Ricks (ed.), *John Milton's Paradise Lost* (London, 1968)

Marina Warner, *Alone of All Her Sex* (London, 1976)

Chapter Twelve

Franz Hartmann, *Jacob Boehme* (London, 1891)

George Dole (ed.), *Emmanuel Swedenborg's Heaven and Hell* (New York, 1979)

Chapter Thirteen

Peter Ackroyd, *Blake* (London, 1995)

David Chidester, *Christianity: A Global History* (London, 2000)

Peter Gay, *The Tender Passion: Charles Kingsley and Fanny Grenfell* (Oxford, 1986)

Geoffrey Keynes, *The Letters of William Blake* (Oxford, 1980)

Elizabeth Stuart Phelps, *The Gates Ajar* (Boston, 1964)

Mark Twain, *Extract From Captain Stromfield's Visit to Heaven* (Oxford, 1996)

Bernard De Voto (ed.), *Mark Twain in Eruption* (New York, 1940)

Chapter Fourteen

Ruth Brandon, *The Spiritualists* (London, 1983)

Sheridan, Gilley, *Newman and His Age* (London, 1990)

Colin Wilson, *Afterlife* (London, 1985)

Chapter Sixteen

Ronald Hayman, *A Life of Jung* (London, 1999)

Richard and Clara Winston (trans.), *CG Jung's Memories, Dreams and Reflections* (London, 1990)

Chapter Seventeen

Richard Fox, *Reinhold Niebuhr: A Biography* (New York, 1985)

David Katz and Richard Popkin, *Messianic Revolution: Radical*

Religious Politics to the End of the Second Millennium (New York, 1999)

David McLellan, *Simone Weil: Utopian Pessimist* (London, 1989)

Francine du Plessix Gray, *Simon Weil* (London and New York, 2001)

Paul Tillich, *The Courage to Be* (Connecticut, 1952)

Chapter Eighteen

Elizabeth Kübler-Ross, *Death: The Final Stage of Growth* (New York, 1975)

Raymond Moody, *Life After Life* (New York, 1975)

Raymond Moody, *Reflections on Life After Life* (New York, 1977)

P. M. H. Atwater, *Beyond the Light* (New York, 1994)

James Lewis (ed.), *Encyclopaedia of Afterlife Beliefs and Phenomena* (Detroit, 1995)

Bill and Judy Guggenheim, *Hello from Heaven* (New York, 1976 London, 1996)

Susan Greenfield, *The Human Brain* (London, 2000)

Judith Chisholm, *Voices from Paradise: How the Dead Speak to Us* (Jon Carpenter Pub, 2000)

Chapter Nineteen

Julian Barnes, *History of the World in 10½ Chapters* (London, 1989)

Philip Pullman, *The Amber Spyglass* (London, 2001)

Roger Lancelyn Green and Walter Hooper, *C. S. Lewis: A Biography* (London, 1974)

Chapter Twenty

Adrian Glew (ed.), *Stanley Spencer's Letters and Writings* (London, 2001)

Timothy Hyman and Patrick Wright (eds), *Stanley Spencer* (London, 2001)

Chapter Twenty-One

Joseph Campbell, *The Power of Myth* (New York, 1991)

Pascal Boyer, *Religion Explained* (London, 1988)

INDEX